THE LAWYER'S GUIDE TO Palm Powered™ Handhelds

Margaret Spencer Dixon

ABA LAW PRACTICE MANAGEMENT SECTION
MARKETING • MANAGEMENT • TECHNOLOGY • FINANCE

Commitment to Quality: The Law Practice Management Section is committed to quality in our publications. Our authors are experienced practitioners in their fields. Prior to publication, the contents of all our books are rigorously reviewed by experts to ensure the highest quality product and presentation. Because we are committed to serving our readers' needs, we welcome your feedback on how we can improve future editions of this book. We invite you to fill out and return the comment card at the back of this book.

Cover design by Jim Colao.

Printed in the United States of America.

Library of Congress Cataloging-in-Publication Data

The Lawyer's Guide to Palm Powered™ Handhelds. Margaret Spencer Dixon: Library of Congress Cataloging-in-Publication Data is on file.

ISBN 1-59031-360-7

08 07 06 05 04   5 4 3 2 1

Discounts are available for books ordered in bulk. Special consideration is given to state bars, CLE programs, and other bar-related organizations. Inquire at Book Publishing, American Bar Association, 750 N. Lake Shore Drive, Chicago, Illinois 60611.

Contents

Acknowledgments

My first "thank you" rightly goes to my client Valerie Fitch, who in 2000 told me in no uncertain terms that I really had to include a discussion of PDAs in my time management seminar. Without her unsubtle but effective encouragement, I would never have made that initial terrifying leap from a paper organizer to a PDA.

Many thanks to the PDA-using lawyers and legal professionals who generously took the time to describe their experiences to me: Anne Albright, Wendy Berliner, Scott Borison, Will Buchanan, Brett Burnley, Bruce Dorner, Ron Feinman, Robert Fleming, MaryEllen Flynn, Sally Garr, Tim Gibbons, John Haller, Vedia Jones-Richardson, June Hsiao Liebert, Chet Lustgarten, Garrett Maass, Vince Marbibi, Dan Markham, Catherine McCabe, Gerald Privin, David Ransin, William Reaves, Lowell Schoenfeld, Bill Schwab, Bryan Sims, Louise Spencer, Christopher Stovall, Domingo Such, Reid Trautz, Christopher vanRoden, Bob Walker, and Howard Wolf-Rodda. Erika Mobley, Chad Roberts, and Steve Tyler also provided helpful information. I would also like to thank all the lawyers and legal professionals who have attended my seminars and shared with me their stories about how their PDAs have improved their personal and professional lives.

My heartfelt appreciation goes to those who so generously shared their expertise in the "Other Voices" part of this book: Bob Ambrogi, Larry Bodine, Dennis Kennedy, Ross Kodner, Joe Kornowski, Bob McNeill, Doug Rosenoff, and Alan Steinberg.

My grateful appreciation goes to Jeff Flax, Greg Siskind, and Dennis Kennedy (again), whose feedback and advice on the various versions of this book were crucial in shaping it into its final form. I am also grateful to Neal Cox, Tim Johnson, and others at the ABA who worked on various stages of this book's publication.

Special thanks to my wonderful editor, Beverly Loder, who with persistence and professionalism shepherded this book through its various and very different versions, throughout a time frame far longer than either of us anticipated. Bev, thank you so much for your patience and understanding through all the happy but time-consuming changes in my life that occurred during the course of this project. (When we started working together on this book in mid-2001, I was a single, childless, D.C. renter; I am now putting the finishing touches on the manuscript in late 2003 as a married Maryland mom with a mortgage.)

Finally, very special thanks to my daughter, Beth, for providing me with a unique and unavoidable internal deadline for completing the final revision of this book, and to my husband, John, for listening to me think aloud, reading my rough drafts, offering insightful feedback, and providing moral support far beyond the call of duty as I proceeded through the two-and-a-half-year gestation period for this book.

About the Author

Margaret Spencer Dixon is a consultant specializing in time management and stress management seminars for lawyers and legal professionals. She came to the field of organization and time management by way of a career in law, during which she practiced in the litigation and energy groups of Shaw Pittman in Washington, D.C. She received her undergraduate degree, cum laude, in economics from Princeton University in 1982, and received her law degree from Stanford Law School in 1985. After law school she clerked for Judge Cecil F. Poole of the United States Court of Appeals for the Ninth Circuit in San Francisco.

Ms. Spencer Dixon left the practice of law in 1992 to found Spencer Consulting, and since then has been giving speeches, writing articles, consulting, and conducting seminars on many aspects of time management and related subjects such as procrastination, stress management, how to run effective meetings, and techniques for getting the most out of a Palm Powered™ handheld. She has presented seminars for numerous law firms, CLE providers, government agencies, corporate law departments, Harvard Law School, and organizations such as the Women's Bar Association, the National Law Firm Marketing Association, and the District of Columbia Bar. Her writings include articles entitled, "Yes, You Can Learn to Keep Your Desk Clutter-Free," "Time Management Habits: How to Develop Good Ones and Kick Bad Ones," and "Overcoming Procrastination: How to Get Things Done Despite Yourself." She has been chair of the Time Management Interest Group of the American Bar Association Law Practice Management Section, and authored the chapter on time management in the ABA book *Living with the Law: Strategies to Avoid Burnout and Create Balance.* She recorded the audiotape programs "Organize Your Time and Manage Your Paperwork," and "The Palm™ Approach to So Little Time, So Much Paper" for the ABA Center for CLE. Her written materials for her seminar "Making Meetings Work" were selected as The Best of ACLEA (the Association for Continuing Legal Education) in 2001, and her written materials for her time management seminar "So Little Time, So Much Paper" were selected as The Best of ACLEA in 2003.

Ms. Spencer Dixon is based in the Washington, D.C., area, and can be reached at 301-949-2214 or at MegSpencerDixon@aol.com.

Introduction

Who Should Read This Book

If you have observed colleagues wax enthusiastic about their Palm Powered™ handhelds, you may be wondering: should I get one? What can it do for me that a paper organizer can't? How can it help me be more efficient and effective in my legal practice? Or you may have just purchased a handheld—or received one as a gift—and are looking for a simple way to learn how to use it. Or you may have been using your handheld for a while and want to learn how to do more with it, including how to find and add software programs to help you in your work. You may wonder what else you should know in order to make your handheld as useful as possible. This book answers these questions and more.

This book will be helpful for four categories of lawyers and legal professionals: (1) those who are thinking of getting a handheld, but are not yet convinced that the benefits of purchasing and learning to use one outweigh the costs in money, time, and effort; (2) those who already have a handheld and want to learn how to use it; (3) those who know how to use one or more of the main applications and want to learn how to do even more with their handhelds; and (4) beginning, intermediate, and experienced handheld users who want to learn more about law-related applications and how to use their handhelds to the fullest in both their legal practice and their lives outside the office.

This book assumes no prior knowledge of handhelds, and is written with the non-"techie" in mind.

Suggestions for Using This Book

To get the most out of this book in the least amount of time:

1. If you haven't yet decided whether to get a handheld, read Part 1 to learn what a handheld can do and how it can improve your life, and Part 2 to learn how lawyers are using handhelds to be more efficient and effective in their professional and personal lives.
2. If you already know you want to get a handheld, read appendix A to help you decide which handheld to get.
3. If you already have your handheld but have yet to begin using it, focus first on Chapters 8 through 10, which cover the nuts and bolts of using a Palm Powered™ handheld.
4. If you already have your handheld but are using only one or two of the main applications on a very basic level, go to Chapters 11 through 14, and read the chapter on whichever application(s) you are already using. Once you have mastered one main application, read the chapters on the other three applications. (You will find that once you know how to use one of the four main applications, learning to use the other three is much easier.)
5. If you are already familiar with the four main Palm OS® applications, read Chapters 15 and 16, which show you how to customize your handheld's built-in applications in order to maximize their usefulness for you. Proceed to Chapters 17 through 20 to learn about installing add-on programs to make your handheld even more versatile and useful for you.
6. Even if you are already thoroughly familiar with the four main Palm OS® applications and have already customized your handheld with add-on programs, you will find timesaving techniques and useful tips throughout this book, so skim each chapter to find ideas that appeal to you.

Currency and Comprehensiveness

As we have all come to learn in recent years, the rate of change in technology—especially computers (and handhelds are indeed computers, albeit small ones) and Internet-disseminated items such as computer programs—means that any book on the subject must do what Burgess Allison described as "counterbalance the conflicting interests of currency vs. longevity."[1] As Mr. Allison advised Jerry Lawson when the latter was writing *The Complete Internet Handbook for Lawyers:*

> Anything you put in the book that changes frequently will be likely to make the book go "out of date" very quickly. That will give it a short shelf

> life and will require rapid updates. But if the only things you cover are things that don't change frequently . . . then you're probably leaving out the most important stuff. The trick is to balance the two interests. (And it's not easy.)[2]

I've tried to balance these conflicting interests by focusing on basic ideas and techniques that can be used with any model handheld running any version of the Palm operating system, and by providing ideas for helping readers use the Internet to locate available handhelds and software themselves.

This book is not intended to be the comprehensive work on how lawyers can use Palm Powered™ handhelds; any such volume would be nothing short of encyclopedic (and would be out of date as soon as it was published). Rather, it is intended to provide lawyers and legal professionals with an understanding of the basic functions and possible uses of Palm Powered™ handhelds, in order to inspire them to actually get one of these marvelous tools and use it to its maximum potential.

A Note About Terminology

I use the terms Palm, PDA, and handheld interchangeably throughout this book. Unless the context clearly indicates otherwise, all three terms are short for such unwieldy phrases as "Palm Powered™ handheld device," "Palm Powered™ personal digital assistant," and even "Palm Powered™ cell phone."

Notes

1. Jerry Lawson, *The Complete Internet Handbook for Lawyers* (ABA Law Practice Management Section, 1999), xxi.
2. Ibid.

Part

I

Why PDAs Matter to Lawyers

What is a Palm Powered™ PDA?

1

§ 1.1 What Is a PDA?

PDA is an acronym for *personal digital assistant.* In current parlance, a PDA is a computer small enough to hold in your hand, and that serves one or more of the following functions: personal organizer, cell phone, Internet browser, e-mail receiver and sender, and basic computer. A primary characteristic distinguishing the PDA from desktop, laptop, and notebook computers is a function of its size: since a PDA is too small to incorporate a reasonably sized keyboard, data is inserted into a PDA primarily by using a stylus (a small, pen-shaped metal or plastic stick) to tap or write on the PDA's touch-sensitive screen.

PDAs are also referred to as pocket computers, palmtops, handheld computers, connected organizers, or simply handhelds.

A Palm Powered™ PDA is a PDA running the operating system developed by the Palm Corporation. An operating system, often abbreviated as OS, is the software a computer uses in order to create an environment in which other software programs (such as a word processing program or a calendar program) are run. For example, Microsoft Windows is a popular operating system for personal computers.

Palm Powered™ PDAs include not only those PDAs actually manufactured by Palm (such as the original PalmPilot), but also any PDA that uses the Palm operating system (Palm OS®), which

Palm licenses to various other PDA manufacturers, including Handspring (whose Visors and Treos products run the Palm operating system), Sony (whose Palm Powered™ Cliés have earned kudos for their superior screen clarity), IBM (whose WorkPads are clones of various models produced by Palm), FranklinCovey, Nokia, and Qualcomm.

In order to understand the full significance of Palm Powered™ PDAs, and to explain the reasons underlying the convoluted nomenclature, a brief history of PDAs is in order.

§ 1.2 A Brief History of PDAs

In the early 1980s, paper organizers such as those produced by Day-Timer, FranklinCovey, and Filofax were the latest in personal organization. Organized lawyers and countless other professionals wrote in, relied upon, and carried around their preferred organizer bound in cardboard, plastic, or leather as determined by the individual's taste and financial resources.

The PDA was born in the well-heralded year of 1984 when a British technology company, Psion, launched its first device. Although the Psion was only slightly larger than a pack of cigarettes, it weighed almost half a pound, relied on cartridges for data storage, and focused on specialized applications more than on the standard organizer functions (calendar, contact list, task list, and notes). Nonetheless, by the early 1990s, Psion had produced half a million PDAs.

Other technology companies such as Apple, Hewlett-Packard, Motorola, Sharp, and Sony took note of Psion's success, and began to develop their own PDAs. They believed that consumers would soon come to appreciate one of the major advantages of PDAs over paper organizers: synchronization, which is the ability to interexchange or "sync" information between the PDA and a desktop (or laptop) computer. This eliminates duplication of effort, since any information or change in information inserted in one device would also appear in the other after synchronization. Synchronization also reduces the need to input information directly in the PDA.

A major problem that faced the developers of these early PDAs was the issue of data input. Since PDAs are too small to include anything other than a miniscule keyboard, PDA developers sought to come up with some other way to input data with reasonable speed, accuracy, and convenience. One of the first-attempted solutions to this problem was the handwriting recognition software incorporated in the Newton MessagePad, which Apple Computing launched in 1993.

At about the size of a mini legal pad, and weighing in at almost a pound, Newton was portable but not pocketable. Its solution to the handwriting recognition problem also left something to be desired. Simply stated, Newton's handwriting recognition system attempted to learn the user's handwriting, based on interactive testing of the user's normal handwriting. The more a user used this system, the better the system became at recognizing what the user meant. However, even at its best, Newton's interpretation of a user's handwriting was not accurate enough to win consumer confidence. Garry Trudeau infamously summarized the criticism on this point with a satire of Newton's linguistic misinterpretations in his *Doonesbury* comic strip, all but striking Newton's death knell in popular culture.

In 1996, Palm Computing (then owned by US Robotics) introduced its PDA, the PalmPilot, which was the first PDA to run the fast, simple, and stable Palm operating system, as well as the first PDA specifically designed actually to fit into a shirt pocket. Its designer, Silicon Valley entrepreneur Jeff Hawkins, has written, "When I designed the original Pilot in 1995, the goal was to create a great tool that was small, simple to use, synchronizable with your PC, and inexpensive."[1] Legend has it that while he was developing the PalmPilot, Hawkins cut out a block of wood basically the same dimensions as the eventual product, and carried it around in his shirt pocket in order to see how comfortable and convenient it was. And in fact, the PalmPilot was small (4.7 inches tall, 3.1 inches wide, and 0.6 inches thick), light (less than 6 ounces), and incorporated simple, elegant software that was easy to learn and easy to use.

PDAs took a giant step forward with the Palm operating system's ingenious solution to the handwriting recognition problem. The PalmPilot incorporated a system whereby the PDA did not have to learn the user's handwriting; rather, the user had to learn a handwriting that the PDA already knew. Called Graffiti, this handwriting is basically a version of the capital block letter alphabet we all learned as children. Graffiti has only two rules, both of which are easy to master. First, each character consists of only one stroke, so that once you put stylus to screen, the entire character is drawn without lifting the stylus. Second, the character must be drawn from a specific starting point. For example, the letter *i* is a vertical line drawn from top to bottom. There are only a few exceptions to these rules.

The Graffiti system solved the problem of having the PDA distinguish between the numeral "1" and the capital letter "I" by having one place on the touch-sensitive screen on which to write letters, and another place to write numbers. Graffiti also solved the problem of distinguishing between the lower-case letter "l" and the upper-case letter "I" by having upper-case letters preceded by a simple character (a line drawn from bottom to top). This illustrates the importance of starting the character at the correct place, since Graffiti recognizes a line drawn from top to bottom as the lower-case letter "i." Graffiti also incorporated several memory aides, similar to cheat sheets, that are easily accessible within the PDA itself.

Palm also simplified the synchronization process with the development of the HotSync function, which required the user only to insert the PDA in a cradle (which on some models also serves as a recharging device), and press one button in order to initiate and complete the synchronization function. Palm PDAs can be synchronized with either the Palm Desktop, a personal information manager (PIM) program that is included on the CD-ROM that comes with every Palm Powered™ PDA, or with another PIM such as Microsoft Outlook. The software allowing this synchronization also comes with the accompanying CD-ROM, and is installed in a simple, user-friendly process. As personal computers became more common, PDAs were increasingly intended by developers (and understood by users) to be companions rather than competitors to personal computers.

Palm was eventually forced to drop the "Pilot" from the name of its products after the Pilot Pen company sued for trademark infringement. The loss of this one clear-cut noun—PalmPilot—to describe the product is one of the reasons for the confusingly similar synonyms used to describe Palm Powered™ PDAs. Palm itself officially refers to its PDAs as handhelds or connected organizers, while users commonly refer to their Palm Powered™ PDAs as simply Palms.

Also in 1996, Microsoft announced its plans to produce its own PDA, originally named the Palm PC. This time Palm Computing was the plaintiff in the resulting trademark suit, and Microsoft eventually agreed to describe its PDAs as "palm-sized PCs." Microsoft's palm-sized PCs do not run the Palm operating system, but instead use a competing operating system originally called Windows CE (which was—unhappily for Microsoft, but probably inevitably—referred to as WinCE), but which later evolved into two variants: Pocket PC and Handheld PC. The PDAs that compete head-to-head with Palm Powered™ PDAs run the Pocket PC operating system, while Handheld PC is the operating system for slightly larger portable computers that are more competitive with notebooks and laptops.

The Pocket PC operating system is tightly integrated with the Windows environment, and looks and acts very much like a smaller version of the Windows operating system used on full-sized PCs. It has the hourglass icon to indicate waiting time while the system slowly carries out a task. (The Palm operating system is so fast it has no need for an analogous icon.) Early Pocket PCs did have the option of color screens, but compared with the Palm Powered™ PDAs, they were larger and more expensive, their operating systems were slower, and they used up their batteries more quickly.

Palm also distinguished itself from Microsoft by aggressively courting the software-developer community. Palm happily shared technical information with other software developers so that these so-called third-party developers could create software that would run well on PDAs using the Palm operating system. In 2002, Palm formed PalmSource, Inc., a wholly owned subsidiary of Palm, specifically to support and encourage the innovation and development of these third-party software programs. PalmSource now boasts of over 275,000 registered software developers,[2] and over 19,000 software programs[3] that can be added on to PDAs running the Palm operating system.

A major player of note in the Palm Powered™ PDA marketplace is Handspring, a company created by none other than Jeff Hawkins himself, along with his partner Donna Dubinski, both of whom left Palm Computing just after 3Com acquired it in 1997. Handspring has focused on bringing the Palm OS to new kinds of reasonably priced devices with greater expansion capabilities than the PDAs produced by Palm; according to its Web site, the company's daily mantra is, "Keep it small, simple, affordable and connected." Handspring's solution to the nomenclature problem is to call its basic PDAs simply organizers, while those that come integrated with a cell phone are called, more futuristically, communicators.

In October 2003, Palm acquired Handspring, and combined the two companies to form palmOne, Inc. At the same time, PalmSource was spun off to become an independent company.

Another variant of handheld technology is the BlackBerry wireless handheld device, which was first announced in 1999. Produced by the Canadian company Research in Motion (RIM), Blackberries (as the product came to be known) differed from the then-existing Palm Powered™ PDAs and Pocket PCs in two major respects: (1) the primary function of a Blackberry was to send and receive wireless e-mail in real time, and (2) data was inserted using not a stylus, but a built-in thumb-operated QWERTY keyboard.

Over time, models of both Palm Powered™ PDAs and Pocket PCs have developed to the point where, for most of the standard functions, there is no obvious technological advantage to one over the other. Pocket PCs have gotten smaller; Palm Powered™ PDAs are available in color; and, thanks to Palm's aggressive outreach to third-party software developers, there are Palm-OS add-on programs that allow you do such things as edit, create, and download Word documents, and input data using non-Graffiti characters closer to your own handwriting. There are even third-party hardware options such as full-sized, portable, folding keyboards, as well as smaller snap-on devices with thumb-keyboards like those popularized by Blackberries. Palm Powered™ PDAs (especially those produced by Handspring) are available with a variety of expansion options that allow you to turn the PDA into a cell phone, GPS system, MP3 player, and digital camera. Many PDAs incorporate convergence, or the integration of two distinct technologies—the PDA and the cell phone—into the same small device. The two latest technological advances so far are Wi-Fi, which allows wireless access to the Internet when the PDA is within range of a wireless local area network (WLAN), such as those available at an increasing number of homes, offices, and so-called Internet cafés; and Bluetooth, which allows PDAs to connect wirelessly with nearby Bluetooth-enables devices such as computers, printers, and cell phones.

By 2002, the battle for dominance in the PDA operating system race between the Palm OS and Pocket PC had the latter as the underdog. According to one study, 83 percent of the PDAs in the United States run the Palm operating system.[4] The Palm OS had a worldwide market share in 2001 of 52.8 percent, compared with Pocket PC's 21 percent.[5] As with the competition in the early 1900s between Henry Ford's gasoline-powered internal combustion engine and the Stanley steam engine, and the race in the early 1990s between Microsoft Windows and the Apple Macintosh operating systems, only time will reveal whether the Palm OS or the Pocket PC operating system will emerge as the *de facto* standard of the PDA industry. It is interesting to observe that for both cars and computers, it is the relative affordability during the crucial time period rather than the inherent superiority of the technology that determined the winner. Model Ts cost less than Stanley steamers, and computers running Windows were cheaper than the Apple Macintosh. This observation bodes well for the Palm operating system, which runs on devices that are generally priced lower than their Pocket PC counterparts. Why should the economics of PDAs be any different than that of cars and computers?

§ 1.3 The Future of PDAs

Here are some thoughts about how PDAs, and lawyers' use of them, may evolve over time. All of these concepts are, if not already extant, within the realm of technological possibility.

Eventually, virtually all legal reference material—including federal and state statutes, case law, and regulations—should be available for download in a PDA-compatible format. A wide variety of professional reading (including law reviews; topic-specific newsletters and magazines; and national, state, and local legal journals and newspapers) should also be available and updated upon synchronization, through a delivery system such as AvantGo.

Eventually, a wide variety of information should be available for download in a PDA-compatible format at professional association meetings, conferences, and continuing legal education (CLE) programs. This information should include all information that is currently distributed in paper form, such as the conference schedule, description of programs, biographical information of the speakers, attendance list, handout materials, and promotional materials. They may be able to be downloaded from the Web site describing the conference, as well as available by beaming at the conference itself. The schedule information should be in such a format that a participant can select the programs he or she wants to attend, so that the title, date, time, and location would automatically appear in the calendar function of the user's PDA.

Eventually, people should be able to use PDA programs such as eWallet to purchase items by credit card or debit card, which would benefit lawyers when on business trips, purchasing office supplies, paying for walk-in registration at a conference or seminar, purchasing back-of-the-room products, and taking clients out for meals.

Eventually, PDAs should be able to make digital audio recordings that can be e-mailed wirelessly, thus providing an alternative (and possibly more convenient) method of transmitting an oral message than calling a person and leaving a voicemail message.

Eventually, you should not need an actual physical external keyboard in order to type information into your PDA, and will use instead a virtual keyboard and mouse consisting of an optical image projected onto any flat surface.[6]

Eventually, PDAs should be capable of connecting wirelessly and reliably, through the Bluetooth technology,[7] with other components such as laptop and desktop computers, printers, telephones, and cell phones to create a personal area network (PAN), which is a miniversion of a local area network (LAN). This means that a cradle would no longer be needed to synchronize data between the PDA and a user's main computer, and that a lawyer could print out any item on his or her PDA by beaming the information to a Bluetooth-enabled printer (even at another person's office). Moreover, this provides some of the benefits of convergence without some of the disadvantages: if you can dial your cell phone by tapping a telephone number in your PDA, and the PDA then transmits this number wirelessly to your telephone or cell phone, you have achieved much of the convenience of a combination cell phone and PDA, but without the disadvantages of increased bulk, the need for an earpiece, and the awkwardness of holding your PDA up to your ear.[8] Other useful applications of this technology include wirelessly connecting a PDA to an LCD projector so you could present a PowerPoint program without lugging around a laptop computer, wirelessly sending photos from a digital camera to a PDA, and wirelessly connecting your cell phone PDA to an earpiece.

Notes

1. David Pogue, *PalmPilot: The Ultimate Guide,* 2nd ed., (O'Reilly, 1999).
2. **http://www.palmsource.com/developers** (accessed October 12, 2003)
3. **http://applications.palmsource.com/Software/index.asp** (accessed October 12, 2003)
4. *Palmtop User Magazine* 1 (July 2002): 8.
5. IDC's April 2002 report, "Sync or Swim: Worldwide Smart Handheld Devices Forecast and Analysis, 2002-2006," cited at **http://www.rnpalm.com/palm_TCO.htm**
6. See **http://www.vkb.co.il**
7. See **http://www.technogadgets.com/TG31902palm.html**
8. See **http://www.beamdial.com**

What a PDA Can Do that a Paper Organizer Cannot

2

§ 2.1 Why Users of Paper Organizers Should Consider Switching to a PDA

Many lawyers are perfectly satisfied with their Day-Timers, Franklin Planners, Filofaxes, or other paper organizers. They have honed their use of these tools over years of practice, and have developed techniques that make their organizers a crucial part of their legal practice. Why should a lawyer give up such a stalwart paper companion for a PDA? This chapter explains why.

The advantages of a PDA over a paper organizer fall into two basic categories. The first category consists of differences in efficiency, which are those differences that can somehow be replicated with a paper organizer, albeit at varying costs in terms of time and convenience. For example, you could certainly attach a mini book light to allow you to read your paper organizer in the dark, but that would be somewhat less convenient than simply turning on the backlight that is built into every Palm Powered® PDA (see Section 2.7). Another example of this kind of efficiency advantage is the automatic Find function, which allows you to locate specific information anywhere within your PDA in seconds (see Section 2.8). With a paper organizer, you can eventually find what you're looking for, but it may take minutes, depending on how organized your organizer is, and how much information it contains.

The second category consists of qualitative differences in the PDA that you cannot replicate at all using a paper organizer. For example, there is nothing you can do to a paper organizer that will make it unreadable should it fall into the wrong hands. By contrast, you can set up your PDA so that it is once you turn it off, it cannot be turned back on except by inserting the proper password (see Section 2.4). For lawyers, this security concern is paramount. Another qualitative advantage of the PDA over the paper organizer is a function of the facts that (1) you can download information from the Internet and install it on your PDA, and (2) your PDA is a fully functioning computer. Thus you can download and use software such as the interactive personal navigation program Vindigo (see Section 2.15), which will give you specific directions to thousands of restaurants, stores, movies, and museums from any location in any one of dozens of major cities in the United States. Even the most detailed paper map cannot provide this depth of customized information. In short, a PDA is not simply an electronic version of a paper organizer (although many lawyers use them as such), but is a tool with far greater potential.

Besides benefiting from the things a PDA can do that a paper organizer cannot, diehard users of paper organizers stand to gain the most from making the switch to a PDA, since they have already developed the habit of using their organizers on a regular basis—and even the best organizer of any kind won't do you much good if you don't use it consistently. And if you are a FranklinCovey fan, you can even get software developed specifically so that you can use your PDA in accordance with the principles of that system, including space for your prioritized daily task list, master task list, daily record of events, values, roles, mission, and goals.

§ 2.2 A PDA Can Synchronize with Your Primary Computer

A paper organizer is an island unto itself. Unless you specifically tell your secretary what is on your schedule for the day, or provide your secretary with a contact's name and telephone number, the information in your paper organizer remains available only to you.

A PDA is part of a larger system. When you synchronize your PDA with your primary computer, all the information (including any changes to that information) in the PDA's calendar, contact list, to-do list, and notes (and other programs you have installed on your PDA) appear in your primary computer, and vice versa. This can save you from the inconvenience and embarrassment that can result from maintaining two separate calendars (the one in your paper organizer and the one in your office). If your secretary adds a meeting to your schedule for the same time as another commitment you put on your PDA's calendar, that conflict is immediately apparent after synchronization, leaving you plenty of time to reschedule one of the events.

When you carry a PDA that synchronizes with your main computer, your PDA's calendar, address book, to-do list, and notes are an interconnected part of your main system. This means that when you are away from the office and want to schedule an appointment, you can pull out your PDA and do so then and there, instead of having to wait until you are back in your office so you can look at your calendar. This also means that contact information, to-do items, and notes you insert on the fly in your PDA are inserted in your office system automatically during each synchronization, so there is no need for you or your support staff to transcribe the information from one system to another. This not only saves time but eliminates the risk of transcription errors.

The synchronization function also means that you never have to rewrite any information that already exists on your computer. You simply copy and paste the information into one of your main computer's software programs that synchronizes with the PDA, and the information is inserted in your PDA the next time you sync it.

§ 2.3 Even If You Lose Your PDA, You Do Not Lose the Information in It

If you keep your entire life in your paper organizer, you necessarily assume the risk that your organizer may go missing. The more you rely on a paper organizer, the more you stand to lose should it get lost, stolen, or destroyed. Unless you use a manual backup system such as photocopying the entire organizer (which is inconvenient and time-consuming to do every day), the time, effort, and expense associated with reassembling that information, and the stress and worry arising from being uncertain that you have recaptured *all* the information in your paper organizer, can be enormous.

However, if you keep the same information in a PDA instead of a paper organizer, and the PDA gets lost, stolen, destroyed, or simply stops working for any reason, you will lose only a fraction of the information in it—just that portion you inserted since you last synchronized your PDA with your primary computer. Since synchronizing is fast and easy, it's a simple matter to get into the habit of synchronizing at least daily. Thus the worst that can happen if you lose your PDA is that you have to get a new PDA, which after synchronizing with your primary computer then contains (almost) all of the information contained in your old PDA. The ease of recreating a PDA compared with the difficulty of recreating a paper organizer is a primary reason why users of paper organizers should consider switching to a PDA.

§ 2.4 Even If You Lose Your PDA, You Can Stop Others from Reading the Information in It

A PDA is simply more secure than a paper organizer. If your paper organizer falls into the wrong hands, all of the information in it can be read. On a PDA, not only can you make some items private so those specific items will be unreadable without inserting the proper password, you can lock the entire device so that all items—except your name and contact information—is unreadable without the password.

The seeming paradox of these last two benefits—you can lose your PDA without losing anything in it, and someone can find your PDA without finding anything in it—is one of the more amazing advantages of the PDA technology.

§ 2.5 A PDA Remains Small and Light, No Matter How Much Information You Add

When you use a paper organizer, the temptation is to add extra items and pieces of paper so that it contains whatever information you might need. Too often, the result is a heavy notebook bulging with documents, sticky notes, clippings, business cards, and receipts. Not only does the result look unprofessional, but the more information you keep in a paper organizer, the harder it is to find a specific item when you need it.

A PDA, on the other hand, stays small, light, professional-looking, and convenient to carry no matter how many pages worth of information you insert. Even the equivalent in text of *War and Peace* does not add any heft, nor make it difficult to find any specific item in the PDA.

§ 2.6 A PDA Can Reduce the Amount of Paper You Handle

By its very nature, a paper organizer encourages the use of paper. A PDA, on the other hand, can reduce the amount of paper you handle, in several ways. First, instead of using your computer to print out physical copies of items you want to have on hand, such as documents, e-mail messages, articles, cases, driving directions, and your office's Disaster Recovery Plan, you can customize the synchronization function to install these items on your PDA instead. Second, if you like to print out hard copies of important items such as your calendar and contact list as backups, you'll find that having that information automatically duplicated on your PDA may reassure you sufficiently to forgo the paper backup. Third, you can download items from the Internet, including Web versions of newspapers such as the *Wall Street Journal*, the *New York Times*, and the *Washington Post*, and read them directly on your PDA. Fourth, if you are one of the many people who stick Post-it® notes throughout their paper organizers, you can put the same information in your PDA using either the memo function (for text) or one of the add-on programs that allow you to scribble or draw directly on your PDA's screen, thus transforming it into a pad of electronic sticky notes.

§ 2.7 You Can Read a PDA in the Dark

This is one of the advantages of a PDA over a paper organizer that you won't appreciate until you experience it firsthand. There are times when it is simply inconvenient, if not impossible, to turn on a light to read or write something in your paper organizer, such as when you are traveling by car or taxi at night, or when the lights at a seminar are dimmed so that you can see the PowerPoint presentation, or when you have a concern or a brainstorm in the middle of the night and don't want to disturb a bed partner. At these times, the built-in backlight becomes a convenience you'll appreciate.

And then there was the time I was traveling by rail, and the train temporarily lost power in a tunnel; I happily continued reading my PDA, the glow of the backlight dimly revealing that the other passengers had had to put down their books, magazines, and newspapers while they waited for the lights to come back on.

§ 2.8 You Can Find Information More Quickly

Many of the paper organizer systems suggest you use them to record all kinds of information, such as to-do lists, notes from telephone calls and meetings, project plans, delegated tasks, itineraries, billable hours, journal entries, meeting agendas, company manuals, your mission statement and long-term goals, business expenses, automobile mileage, frequent-flier numbers and miles earned, driving directions, time management tips, inspirational quotations, and detailed notes to document important events such as negotiations and unusual events such as automobile accidents, and, for convenience's sake, personal items such as shopping lists, birthday lists, emergency telephone numbers for your credit cards, clothing sizes, and even sensitive information such as credit, financial, and insurance information, and your spouse's Social Security number.

Unless you scrupulously maintain and use a detailed indexing system for your paper organizer—a never-ending task which takes both time and self-discipline—it can take quite a while to find specific information in your paper organizer. And the more information you keep in your paper organizer, the longer it tends to take to find any one specific item.

With a PDA, you can find any piece of information by recalling any single word contained in the item, and using the global Find function. You don't even have to remember whether you included the item as a separate memo, or as a note in your calendar or contact list. You just tap the Find button, and insert the name, word, or phrase you know is contained in the item you are searching for. In a matter of seconds, the PDA's screen is showing a list of all the items containing the name, word, or phrase. Simply tap on the item you want, and the system takes you directly to that item.

If you are looking specifically for information that you inserted in your contact list, the search is even easier. You just press the Address Book button to go directly to your contact list, and start writing the last name of the person you're looking for. Once you've written the first letter, Address Book shows you a list of all your contacts whose last name begins with that letter. Once you've written the second letter, it shows you a list of names beginning with those two letters, and so forth as you continue to input letters. You'll find that you rarely have to write more than a few letters to pull up any specific name. As soon as the name you want appears in the list, simply tap on it to go directly to that contact's information. And if you're looking for the contact's telephone number, you don't even have to tap on the name, since the list that appears as you write your contact's name also includes the contact's telephone number.[1]

In addition, there are four fields in the contact list that you can customize to whatever information suits your purposes. For example, you can create a field for client-matter numbers, so when you do a search for a specific client-matter number, the resulting list is all those contacts connected to that number.

You can also use the Find function to identify telephone numbers, which is useful if you want to identify a telephone number on your caller ID. If for billing purposes you must correlate the telephone numbers on your phone bill with the appropriate client–matter numbers, all you need to do is tap the Find button, insert the telephone number, and tap on the resulting contact, then go to the client-matter field for that contact. You can even copy and paste both the telephone number and the client-matter number into a memo, which after synchronizing appears on your primary computer for you or your secretary to copy and paste into the appropriate billing software. This eliminates errors caused by misreading or transposing numbers.

§ 2.9 You Can Revise Information Without Messy Erasures or Cross-Outs

With a paper organizer, whenever you want to change information—such as removing an event from your calendar or updating a contact's address—you either write everything in pencil so you can erase things, or cross out items you wrote in ink and write the new information in tiny letters, or keep a supply of correction fluid or adhesive labels on hand. These options are time-consuming, messy, and inconvenient.

With a PDA, you can delete an event on your calendar in just four taps, or change its date in just five. You can change its start time in just three or four taps, and its end time in four or five. The revised information shows up fresh and clean on the appropriate date, and the electronic page for the original date returns to its pristine state.

In your PDA's contact list, you can change an individual contact's information as easily as you edit text in a word-processing document, so you can update your contact list continuously, without messy erasures or full-scale rewriting when the address book becomes unreadable, as can happen with a paper version.[2]

§ 2.10 You Can Schedule Recurring Events Quickly

If you have a meeting the first Tuesday of every month, you must insert the event on all twelve of your paper organizer's monthly calendars. With your PDA, once you've inserted the first meeting, you can add as many repeats as you like in about a dozen taps, without writing the name of the event over and over. You can even delete (or change the date and time) of one of the meetings without affecting the rest of the series.

§ 2.11 You Can Set Alarms to Alert You of Upcoming Events

With a paper organizer, there is no fast and simple way to set an alarm to go off to remind you of specific events. With a PDA, it takes just four taps to set an alarm to go off five minutes before the start of an event, and just three Graffiti strokes and two more taps to change the advance time from anywhere from 0 minutes to 99 days. The ease of setting alarms attached to specific events, and setting the advance time to the specific duration appropriate for the situation, means that your PDA can help you both remember events and get to them on time. (And yes, if the PDA is turned off when the alarm is supposed to sound, the PDA turns itself on at the crucial moment.)

I have found that relying on these alarms helps me concentrate better during the workday, because I can forget about upcoming appointments and planned telephone conferences, and just focus on the work in front of me, secure in the knowledge that my PDA's alarm will alert me of the upcoming event with the appropriate lead time. Using the PDA's alarms in this manner is superior to simply setting an alarm on a watch or clock, because when the PDA's alarm goes off, I both hear the sound and see on the screen precisely which event the alarm corresponds to.

You can also use your PDA's alarm to wake you up in the morning, so you no longer need a travel clock, or even your regular alarm clock at home.

§ 2.12 You Can Share Information More Easily with a PDA

Not only is it easier to keep information more secure on a PDA than in a paper organizer, it's easier to share information as well. With a paper organizer, the only way to disseminate the items contained in it is to photocopy the pages, or tell someone the information orally. Using the infrared (IR) port built into every PDA, you can beam individual items, categories of items, and even entire programs to other PDAs. This comes in handy when you are away from your office and want to share with colleagues items such as itineraries and draft memos, and even pass notes inconspicuously during depositions.

§ 2.13 A PDA Can Help You Manage E-mail

You can configure the synchronization feature so that your e-mail is transmitted every time you synchronize your PDA with your primary computer. Your new e-mail messages are transferred to your PDA, and you can read and write answers to them using just your PDA. The next time you synchronize, your e-mail responses are transmitted back to your primary computer, and put in your e-mail out-box for transmission. The benefit of this feature is that you can use what would otherwise be downtime (waiting for a meeting to start, nondriving commute times, waiting in line at the grocery store) to read through your e-mail and thereby keep the deluge under control.

§ 2.14 You Can Download Items from the Internet

You can download items from the Internet onto your PDA to read when you are away from your office. Using the simple, free system available at AvantGo.com, you can download information from the Web versions of such publications as the *New York Times,* the *Wall Street Journal,* the *Washington Post,* the *Law Marketing Portal,* the *ABA Journal,* and more. This means you can use your PDA to keep up with your professional reading. You also have the option of perusing the newspaper while sitting in court and waiting for your case to be called, without getting reprimanded by the bailiff as you would had you unfurled the print edition. Using a PDA looks benign; no one can tell if you are checking your calendar, reading your e-mail, playing a game, or scanning the *New York Times*. (This is one situation where a SmartPhone does not work as well as a nonconvergent PDA, since pulling out a cell phone has different implications than pulling out a straightforward PDA.)

You can also customize AvantGo to download information from your favorite Web sites each time you synchronize while your primary computer is online. Therefore, you can use your PDA to stay up to date with information on Web sites of your particular interest. This is particularly handy if you find that the bulk of your downtime tends to occur when you are away from your office, and away from a full-sized computer with real-time Internet access. Your PDA probably won't replace your regular computer for Web browsing, but it's nice to have the option of grabbing items from your favorite Web sites and reading them on your PDA during odd moments throughout the day.

§ 2.15 A PDA Can Help You Find Your Way

Your PDA can tell you how to get around in major cities in the United States. The add-on program Vindigo (available at **www.vindigo.com**) is a personal navigation program that helps you locate major intersections, subway stops, restaurants, stores, services, entertainment, and more, in cities including Atlanta, Boston, Brooklyn, Chicago, Dallas, Denver, Detroit, London, Long Beach, Los Angeles, Miami, New Orleans, New York, Philadelphia, Phoenix, San Francisco, and Washington, D.C.

Before you travel, you can download selected categories of information about the specific city onto your PDA. (I keep information for my hometown, Washington, D.C., permanently on my PDA.) After synchronizing while your primary computer is online, the most up-to-date information appears on your PDA. The program includes an interactive map that you activate by selecting an intersection. The resulting map shows exactly where you are with an "X" labeled "You." You can show or hide street names by tapping on them, and you can zoom in, zoom out, and move in all four directions by tapping on the clearly marked indicators.

More than just a map, Vindigo contains constantly updated databases of restaurants, shops, and services for each city, from which you can pick and choose the information you want. If you choose to download information about restaurants, you will get not only the name, address, telephone number, and a recent review for each restaurant, but also the ability to search for restaurants within dozens of categories (including cuisines such as French, Japanese, or Thai; specialty cuisines such as kosher or vegetarian; features such as outdoor dining, private rooms, and good views; and availability for breakfast, brunch, pretheater dinners, and late-night suppers) by name, distance from your location, cost, and rating. Once you select a restaurant, Vindigo tells you how far you are from it, how to get there by subway, on foot, or by car, shows you an interactive map framing both you and the restaurant, and provides you with a form to complete after your meal rating the food and cost, whether you would recommend the place to others, and even space to compose a short review of your own. The next time you synchronize your PDA while your primary computer is online, this feedback is sent to Vindigo, which is one way the information remains current. (The feedback form even has a box to check if the restaurant has gone out of business.)

You can conduct similar searches for shops (with categories including bookstores, clothing stores, computer stores, office-supply stores, and pharmacies—all handy to have on hand in an unfamiliar town) and services (including the travel-friendly categories of airport transport services, ATMs and banks, copy services, couriers, and taxi or car services). For rest and relaxation purposes, Vindigo also has information about bars, movies, music, and museums. Each of these categories has a depth of information similar to that for restaurants. For example, you can search for a movie by its title or by genre, and for each movie, Vindigo gives you the rating, length, leading cast members, a review, show times at all the local venues—with interactive links taking you directly to the map and directions for getting to the theater—and a feedback form where you can give your own opinion of the film. In the music category, you can view by venue or date in thirty-four categories from bluegrass, cabaret, classical, and country, to rock, New Age, punk, and Rap/Hip Hop. The museum categories provide summaries of both temporary exhibits and permanent collections.

§ 2.16 A PDA Can Help You Keep Track of Time

One of the most common ways for lawyers to use paper organizers is as a place to keep notes relating to billable time. I know I am not alone in having years of my billable time handwritten on the right-hand page of a two-page-per-day paper organizer (in my case, a senior pocket-sized Day-timer). While contemporaneous note-taking can be completely accurate, it can also be time-consuming, since at the end of the day (or week, or month), someone must calculate the total times spent for each client or project. Doing this task manually, or even inputting the daily totals into the firm's computer billing system, is not only time consuming, but risks errors of transcription or math (depending on whether subtotals are calculated prior to insertion in the computerized system).

Using a timekeeping program that you've added onto your PDA solves several problems. The risk of math errors is reduced, because the program automatically calculates billable hour totals for projects or clients over any specified time period. Errors of transcription are avoided, since most programs can generate time reports that can be synchronized back to the primary computer, from which the totals can be copied and pasted into the firm's timekeeping systems. Even better, an increasing number of popular timekeeping programs such as Abacus, DTE, PCLaw, and Time Matters have companion programs for Palm Powered™ PDAs, so that during synchronization, the information is transferred directly to the firm's main timekeeping computer system.

Moreover, using a PDA's timekeeping system is faster than keeping track of time on paper. Most timekeeping programs allow you to create lists of clients and projects, so you can identify them simply by tapping on a list. In addition, the programs have automatic timers, so that you merely tap on the timer when you begin a task, and the timer continues (even when the PDA is off) until you tap on it again, or tap on the timer for another project. Most timekeeping programs also allow you to attach notes to time records, so you can describe the work involved. When used in conjunction with Graffiti's ShortCut system, you need never insert more than a few characters to describe the work completed. Not only is it faster for a lawyer to keep track of time in this manner, it is more accurate, with no need for a secretary or assistant to do anything except possibly copy and paste the summarized information into the firm's system.

§ 2.17 You Can Use a PDA to Read and Edit Word-Processed Documents

There are a variety of programs you can add onto your PDA that allow you to transfer Microsoft Word documents to your PDA. With these programs—Quickword, WordSmith, and WordToGo are popular examples—you can either transfer a Word document you have created on your primary computer to your PDA, or transfer a document created on your PDA into your primary computer's Word program. You can edit the document on your PDA just as you can on your primary computer, cutting, copying, pasting, and even spell-checking (on recent upgrades of some software), then transfer the resulting document back to your primary computer the next time you synchronize. This ability provides the following benefits:

- You can work on documents anywhere. If you use a portable keyboard attached to your PDA, you can even leave your laptop behind and work anywhere you please—thirty thousand feet in the air, at the beach, or on your front porch if you prefer the spring breezes and chirping of birds to the recirculating air and chirping of telephones at the office.
- You can share documents with others by beaming them to their PDAs, and you can receive documents by beaming. This can facilitate drafting by committee or finalizing specific language during negotiations, since you don't have to rely on secretaries, copiers, or the awkwardness of a group of people hunching over a single laptop to read the latest revision.
- You can keep on your PDA those word-processed documents you want to have on hand for reference. The utility of this option is greatly enhanced by the fact that you can use the Find function to find the document within your PDA, and to search within the document for a specific word or phrase. Such documents include not only those which you have created, or those already on your office's computer system, but also any documents that you can get into a word-processed format. Since you can scan a hard copy of any document into your system, the possibilities for using your PDA as a repository for important information are limited only by your imagination. For example, you can have with you at all times such items as litigation scheduling orders (handy during depositions and status conferences), important case precedents, and laws and regulations you refer to frequently. Other documents that you might want to install on your PDA are items that would be too cumbersome to keep in hard copy in a paper organizer, such as firm directories, manuals, and key documents (especially your Disaster Recovery Plan).

Notes

1. You can insert up to six telephone numbers for each contact, and specify for each contact which telephone number should appear in the initial list.

2. I am related to someone who actually rewrites, by hand, her entire contact list anew every year in her paper organizer. She even claims to enjoy this task. I claim to enjoy never having to do this task.

How a PDA Can Improve Your Life

3

§ 3.1 The Benefits of Using a PDA

This chapter describes the various benefits a PDA can have in your legal practice and in your life. These benefits fall into the following four broad and overlapping categories:

1. A PDA can help you be more organized (Section 3.2).
2. A PDA can help you be more efficient (Section 3.3).
3. A PDA can help you be more effective by allowing you to transform downtime into productive time, and allowing you quickly and easily to perform a useful task which, without the PDA, would be so difficult or time-consuming that you would not do it at all (Section 3.4).
4. A PDA can help you manage your time (Section 3.5).

Section 3.6 provides advice and food for thought for lawyers who are thinking about getting a PDA.[1]

It is important for non-PDA users to read this chapter with an open mind. If you do not already use a PDA, you will probably have difficulty envisioning the profound effect one can have on your work life. When any technological innovation is first introduced, it can be hard to comprehend its potential benefits, and it is natural to be tempted to discount the new gadget as an unnecessary novelty or time-wasting toy. However, once you begin to use a valuable new technology yourself, it becomes much easier to see how helpful and convenient it is, in a way that secondhand explanations fail to convey. As more individuals become adept with a new technology, the item can rapidly shift from handy convenience to practical necessity. This phenomenon has been illustrated in the introduction of technologies from the telephone to the automobile, the fax machine, the personal computer, and the cell phone—and the PDA will ultimately go through the same evolution. Ironically, therefore, it is hard to know how much you need a PDA until you actually start using one. Many PDA users, however, decide very quickly that their PDA is an invaluable tool.

A note about efficiency versus effectiveness: whether a PDA increases your efficiency or your effectiveness in a specific instance depends on whether you would perform the particular task absent the PDA. In general, you do a task only if its usefulness (in helping you to achieve your desired outcome) justifies the time it takes. For example, you are more likely to perform a time-consuming task if you perceive its benefits to have great value, and you are less likely to perform a time-consuming task if you perceive its benefits to have little value. Similarly, the faster you can perform a task of any given usefulness, the more likely you are to perform it. If a PDA helps you more quickly complete a task that you would have done without the PDA (such as looking up a telephone number), then the PDA has increased your efficiency. If you use the PDA to complete a useful task that you would not have done at all without the PDA (such as transcribe and expand your handwritten notes from a seminar or deposition), then it has increased your effectiveness.

§ 3.2 Using a PDA to Get Organized

A PDA can help you get and stay organized physically by providing a convenient place to keep track of all kinds of information. Putting information into a PDA is better than writing something down on a piece of paper, since you can keep track of one PDA more easily than you can keep track of dozens of pieces of paper, notes, sticky notes, and so on. With a PDA, you will find you no longer need many of the paper items that the PDA can replace, such as to-do lists, calendars, address books, legal pads, and printouts of e-mail, directions, and word-processed documents. Consequently, you need much less paper to stay organized. Because a PDA is so small that you can keep it with you almost all the time, you don't have to carry any paper with you, or scrounge around for paper when you want to write something down.

A PDA can also help you get and stay organized mentally, by giving you the ability to easily store and retrieve information about tasks, deadlines, memos, and notes, so you don't have to keep everything in your head. Given the complexity of the modern law practice and modern life in general, you really can't remember everything you need to know unless you write it down somewhere, and a PDA is a most convenient place.

There are four key effects of the benefits of this kind of mental organization. First, you can focus more fully on the matter at hand (whether that involves concentrating on a tough work project or relaxing during nonwork time), since you won't be distracted by trying to remember something, or worried that you might forget something. No longer do you find yourself annoyed and stressed by thoughts such as, "Oh, no, I left that phone number in the file at work," or "I forgot to check my calendar at the office," because you have your PDA with you, and can look up the information that will put your mind at ease. This also saves time for your office staff, since you no longer need to ask for administrative details such as your next appointment, or someone's address or phone number. In other words, once you start using a PDA, it functions as a sort of external brain, thus freeing up your actual brain for more creative work. Your brain can hold only so many active thoughts at one time, and it's helpful to be able to dump extraneous thoughts to another place where you won't forget them. When you have a PDA, whenever you think of something you want to do, you have the option of dumping that thought right then from your brain into the PDA, where it will remain accessible until it is time to act on it. Once you put the information into your PDA, the thought is no longer bouncing around in your brain and inhibiting your ability to focus on the matter at hand, but is in a place where you can easily find it again, and focus on it at the appropriate time.

Second, you will find that your PDA can cure forgetfulness (also known as "senior moments") by allowing you to recall information when you need it. You can set an alarm in your PDA to remind you of something at a particular time, so you don't even have to remember that you have something to remember! It will be difficult to forget things once they are written down in your PDA and have an alarm attached to them, since your PDA turns itself on to present you with the reminder at the designated time, and will not let you access anything else in your PDA until you respond to that reminder. Even if you don't attach an alarm to an item, having a single, easily searchable location for all your important information allows you to avoid the stress and frustration of searching for information scattered among files, notepads, sticky notes, business cards, and random scraps of paper. With a PDA, you can put literally any piece of information in one central depository. Anything that you've ever jotted down on a scrap of paper, a paper napkin, or the back of your hand can be inserted in your PDA, so that information is readily accessible and available to you whenever you might need it.

Third, you will never again be unable to perform a task because you don't have the necessary information with you. When the information is in your PDA, it is with you all the time, so you won't always have to plan ahead to do something, but can just go ahead and do it if you find yourself in a convenient location or situation.

Fourth, you can avoid the negative consequences (such as stress, frustration, and increased risk of malpractice) of overlooking an appointment or forgetting to do a task in a timely manner. Once you have installed all of your important information on your PDA, you will find that you can usually look to your PDA to tell you where you should be and what you should be doing.

Subsequent chapters, especially Chapters 4 and 5, contain more specifics about how to use your PDA for staying organized.

§ 3.3 Using a PDA to Be More Efficient

Many lawyers find that using a PDA increases their efficiency by helping them accomplish many basic tasks more quickly. A PDA also allows you to keep reference materials constantly at hand, in an easily accessible, searchable form. These reference materials can include cases, statutes, rules, case logs, scheduling orders, client-matter numbers—indeed, any information that is on your computer, or which you can put on your computer, including items that can be scanned to transform them into a word-processed document. The possibilities are limited only by your imagination. You will find that with a PDA, you will be able to look up a phone number, keep track of billable time, or access any reference item in seconds.

There are various reasons why a PDA allows you to complete these administrative tasks much more quickly. Once you are in the habit of using a PDA, you will find that you automatically reach for it whenever you want to look something up, rather than turning to your Rolodex® for a phone number, your calendar for a court date, your bulletin board for a random note, your to-do list for the next task, or your desktop timekeeping program to start the timer running for the new task. Once you have grabbed your PDA, every item in it can be located in just a few quick taps.

Moreover, a PDA's instant-on feature means that you can be getting things done while your computer is still booting up.[2] Even if your desktop computer is on, sometimes it's faster to use your PDA rather than going to the desktop version of another program. If you are on the phone and taking notes in the phone-notes section of your case management system, and you need to check your schedule, it may be easier to pull your PDA off its cradle and check your schedule there.

Because your PDA helps you complete administrative tasks more quickly, you have more time available for billable work. Thus your PDA helps you provide better client service (even if you are fairly on top of things to begin with) since anything that helps you reduce the amount of time you spend on administrative items (including timekeeping) ultimately leaves you more time to attend to your clients' needs. Moreover, you are able to provide better service when a client needs a telephone number, the date of your next meeting, or some other piece of substantive or administrative information available in your PDA.

You will find that your PDA makes you more efficient, particularly when you are away from your office. Lawyers always need some type of date book; with a PDA, your calendar is always with you, so you can schedule meetings and court dates on the spot, without checking with the "official" calendar in your office.

Finally, you can use the PDA to keep track of all areas of your life, so you can more efficiently juggle the demands of your professional and your personal commitments.

Chapters 4 and 5 contain more examples of how to use your PDA to more efficiently manage your calendar, contacts, to-do lists, and miscellaneous pieces of information. Chapter 6 illustrates ways to use your PDA to more efficiently accomplish out-of-the-office aspects of tasks such as note-taking, timekeeping, tracking expenses, and keeping up with e-mail.

§ 3.4 Using a PDA to Be More Effective

A PDA can help you be more effective in a variety of ways. Because your PDA allows you to keep up-to-date versions of your calendar, contact information, reference materials, and working documents with you at all times, you have the option of working productively when you are away from the office. This includes what would otherwise be downtime, such as during your commute by rail or carpool, waiting in court for your case to be called, and even standing in line at the grocery store. By filling this gap time with productive activity, you can accomplish something you might not be able to do easily (if at all) without a PDA, such as reading articles, cases, and e-mail; responding to e-mail; reviewing your to-do list and prioritizing your tasks; reviewing and editing documents; and even (if you have access to the necessary privacy) returning client calls. Much of this can even be billable work that you would not be able to do outside the office absent your PDA. (Even if you prefer not to do billable work outside the office, using your PDA to accomplish administrative tasks away from the office means that you have freed up more office time for billable work.) Lawyer Vedia Jones-Richardson refers to this function of the PDA to transform formerly unusable time into work time, and to complete tasks in places that would otherwise not be conducive to productivity, as its ability "to transcend time and place."

Your clients can benefit from this PDA-driven increase in your effectiveness in multiple ways. For example, with the proliferation of telephone numbers these days, it can be very helpful to have constant access to a contact's multiple telephone numbers (direct work number, main office number, home phone, cell phone, car phone, pager, and so on); your PDA can provide you with all of these. Because you can look up phone numbers so easily, you can shoehorn phone calls into a few stolen moments throughout your day. Anytime you think of a phone call to make, or if you are caught at court with time before your case comes up on the calendar, you can pull out your PDA and move other things along. Moreover, if any of these numbers change, you can easily update your PDA on the spot, and these changes will be inserted into your main computer system upon your next synchronization.

Because a PDA allows you to carry the basics of your practice with you at all times, you can provide better client service by addressing your clients' concerns promptly, without waiting to get back to the office. Since you can maintain up-to-date case logs and records of telephone conversations on your PDA, you have easy access to the information necessary to respond to the client's substantive questions at all times. This means that you can return a client's call promptly upon picking up his or her voicemail message, instead of making the client wait until you return to the office and can look at the case file. This is especially handy when you are out of town.

Another increase in effectiveness due to the PDA is that both you and your support staff have a current version of your schedule, and yet both you and your secretary can make changes to your schedule. If you sync your PDA regularly, and especially just before leaving and upon returning to the office, both your office calendar and your PDA version will remain up-to-date. Appointments show up on the calendar in your PDA and in your primary computer system, whether they were booked by you or your secretary, and any conflicts are apparent upon the next synchronization. This kind of automatic continuity and efficient, reliable communication saves time and effort for both you and your office staff. You are more effective because both you and your support staff know what your schedule is—and your clients benefit from this as well.

Another way a PDA can help you increase your effectiveness is that you can insert information in ways that allow you to search quickly for specific categories of information. For example, if you are planning a business trip to a particular city, you can conduct a search for contacts or prospects in that city to help determine whether you can use your time in that city more productively by piggybacking additional meetings. Another option involves inserting contacts or events in consistent descriptive terms so that you can use your PDA to do a quick search for, say, all the expert witnesses you've ever worked with, all the meetings you've ever had with a particular client, or anything else that you might find handy.

Finally, a PDA allows you to effectively and reliably process your thoughts the first time they occur to you. For example, you might be sitting in the courtroom waiting for your case to be called, and hearing someone else's argument makes you think of a novel idea for a case of yours, so you just jot it down in your PDA. The immediacy of this transmittal and preservation of information means that you have freed yourself up to concentrate on the matter at hand, rather than being distracted by trying to remember your brainstorm. Once the idea is in your PDA, you can access it at a time when it is more productive to do something about it. Using your PDA in this way can keep your mind clear of distracting thoughts and administrative details (such as things to tell your support staff), while simultaneously preserving them accurately so you can act on them at the appropriate time in the future.

Chapters 4 and 5 further detail how lawyers use their PDAs to maintain their effectiveness by managing their schedules, lists of things to do, and other kinds of notes, memos, lists, and reminders. Chapter 6 illustrates how your PDA can help you be more effective in tracking your billable time, and how to work more effectively when your PDA allows easy access to items such as working documents, reference materials, professional reading, travel information, Excel spreadsheets, and even special calculators, password generators, and cameras.

§ 3.5 Using a PDA to Manage Your Time

A PDA helps you manage your time because it gives you immediate, constant, and interactive access to your basic time management data: your calendar and your to-do list. The PDA is small enough so that you can keep it with you all the time, so you can review this information whenever a question occurs to you, you can add tasks to your to-do list the moment you think of them, and you can check off a task as soon as you complete it. (You will find that with a PDA, you can even check and revise your to-do list surreptitiously at times and in situations where you would not be able to read through a traditional to-do list, such as in meetings or at conferences.) In contrast, if your time management system consists only of software on your desktop computer, or is contained in a bulky paper notebook or laptop computer, inevitably there are times when you are away from the system. Consequently, there is a time lag between when a task occurs to you and when you can add it to your system.

The possibility that you might forget the item before you return to the system weakens the effectiveness of the overall time management approach, and is a flaw that is removed by including a PDA as part of your computerized system.

The To Do List program is one of the four main applications native to every Palm Powered™ PDA, so many lawyers manage their time by reviewing and revising their task lists on the PDA even before they arrive at the office. A PDA allows you to focus on and plan your day ahead of time, and in a more interactive way than a paper to-do list permits, since you can easily add, delete, revise, and reprioritize items as you read through your list, and the end result is just as tidy as the initial list. With a PDA, you never again have to take the time to rewrite your entire to-do list.

Chapter 5 contains further examples of how lawyers use the Palm OS To Do List to manage their time, and Chapter 6 discusses other ways to use PDAs for time management tasks such as timekeeping.

§ 3.6 If You Are Thinking of Getting a PDA

If you are thinking of getting a PDA, but are not yet convinced that it is worth the money, time, and effort, here are some points to consider.

- **Make sure you know what you want to do with the PDA, at least initially.** Ask yourself what specific goals you want to achieve, or what problem you are trying to solve by using a PDA. Everyone wants to become more efficient, productive, and profitable, so frame your objective in more detail. Are you trying to become more organized in terms of keeping track of to-do lists and miscellaneous bits of information? Do you want to get your calendar organized? Are you trying to free up some time for rainmaking? Would you like to be able to do a quick search for all the expert witnesses you've ever worked with? Or are you simply looking to be able to get your hands on a phone number quickly when you need it? A PDA is certainly an extremely valuable tool that can help you achieve these goals. Even if it's used just as a glorified Rolodex®, a PDA can save you enough time and frustration to justify its various startup costs.
- **Consider a PDA as part of your emergency preparedness system.** Realize that a PDA is not a stand-alone tool, but part of a series of tools. Now that almost all lawyers have their own computers, using a PDA just to synchronize your calendar and contacts means you have an immediately accessible, automatic backup for that information. As lawyer Lowell Schoenfeld relates, "There was a lightning strike near

my office recently, and all the computers were out for a while, but I had all my information in my hands." Another way to look at it is this: if you lose your Day-Timer or paper planner and there's no backup, you're out of luck, and have to re-create all of that information somehow. But if you lose your PDA, you still have that information in your regular computer.

- **How much is your time worth?** The monetary cost of a basic PDA is now so low (under $100) that you can quite easily justify trying out a PDA. To do the math: if your out-of-pocket cost is $100, your billing rate is as low as $100 an hour, and your start-up time is as high as ten hours, that's $1,100. If your PDA ends up saving you only ten minutes (or $16.67) a day by making you more efficient, or allowing you to capture that much more billable time, it takes only sixty-six working days ($1,100 divided by $16.67) to recoup that $1,100. If you're cost-conscious, you can usually get a better price for a particular model by waiting until it is no longer at the cutting edge, or by purchasing the unit on sale or through a Web site such as eBay. Moreover, when you are ready to move up the technology ladder, you can recoup part of the cost of the PDA by reselling it on eBay or trading it in for a more advanced unit (be sure to save all the packaging, handbooks, and accoutrements that came with your first model), although many lawyers are so sold on the PDA that they give their old models to a spouse, legal assistant, or offspring to get them started too.
- **You should invest some time to learn how to use your PDA.** It's not hard to learn to use, but there is a learning curve. Sit down with it over a weekend and play with it. There is a basic tutorial built into the Welcome application,[3] plus each program has its own built-in tips marked with the letter "i" (for information). Once you have learned the few basics, the Palm OS is simple enough so you can figure out how to use all the standard programs within a few hours, even if you're not a "techie." The handbook that comes with each unit (and is available online at **www.palm.com**) covers the basics clearly and concisely, and is worth at least skimming through. Chapters 8 through 14 also provide a good introduction. If you don't want to take the time to teach yourself, find someone who can show you how to use it.
- **Are you already using a case management or contact management software program?** Is it one of the many that are compatible with a PDA? Especially if you're already in the habit of using such contact software, even a simple one such as Microsoft Outlook, you're really missing out on a lot by not having a PDA, and it is very easy to add that portable step.

- **Would you like to begin using a simple contact management software program?** If you're not already using contact management software, the Palm Desktop software is a good way to start, and once it's on your computer, it's easy to get into the habit of using it. It's a simple matter to install the Palm software right from the start, and to learn to sync it.
- **Do you spend a lot of time away from the office?** Would you like to have access to your most important business information during that time? You can accomplish this by adding a PDA to those basic items you keep with you most of the time (such as your wallet, keys, and cell phone) in a pocket, purse, or briefcase. If you never leave your desk you don't need a PDA, but if you do, and want to be able to do things elsewhere, you have to think about the best way of taking information with you.
- **Using a PDA at even a basic level makes you appear more organized and competent.** This can help to impress clients and intimidate opponents.
- **If you're still undecided, at least give yourself a testing period so you can make an informed decision.** Even if you're already fairly well organized, and cannot identify a specific goal to achieve with a PDA other than to become more efficient, effective, productive, and profitable, consider this: of the hundreds of lawyers with whom I have spoken, not one has regretted starting to use a PDA.[4] In fact, these reactions are typical: "I rely on [my PDA] so much that when I accidentally cracked the screen, and Palm's customer service gave me the choice of replacing it with a new unit in a few weeks for free, or a reconditioned unit the next day for $100, I chose the second option. I didn't want to be without it for that long" (Lowell Schoenfeld). "If I had it to do over, I would have gotten a Palm earlier than I did. I'd highly recommend it to any lawyer, or doctor, for that matter. I know I'm responsible for having people get a Palm, and then getting one for everyone in the office" (Garrett Maass).

My advice is to get a PDA and at least experiment with it for a month, and if at the end of that time you find that it isn't a worthwhile tool, you can always stop using it, secure in the knowledge that your decision about whether to use a PDA is now based on your actual experience rather than guesswork. My hunch is that you will keep your PDA, and find many more uses for it than you ever imagined. Because a Palm Powered™ PDA is so flexible, and there are so many useful add-on software programs for the Palm OS (and more are being developed constantly), you may end up using your PDA for purposes you could never have envisioned in advance.[5]

Notes

1. This section addresses the question of whether to get a PDA at all, not which specific model to get. To answer this very subjective question for yourself, consider the information in Appendix A, "Palm Powered™ PDAs: A Comparison of Models" as well as the Palm-OS-versus-Pocket-PC debate in Part 3, "Other Voices" (Larry Bodine's contribution, my reply, and his rejoinder).

2. I just timed how long it takes my IBM ThinkPad to boot up: two minutes exactly. If you turn on your computer only once a day, at 220 working days per year, that represents a total of 440 minutes, or 7 hours and 20 minutes, of potentially wasted time.

3. See Chapter 9 for more information about the introductory tutorial, as well as other getting-started guidelines.

4. Some have regretted the particular brand or model, but not the PDA concept in general. These individuals have invariably put their early bad experiences to good use in choosing another PDA that didn't have the elements they disliked about the first.

5. Chapter 6 gives you many ideas about how to use a PDA as more than an electronic calendar and organizer.

Part

II

Real-Life Experiences: How Lawyers Use PDAs

4

Date Book and Address Book: The PDA Applications Lawyers Use Most

§ 4.1 Introduction

All lawyers need to keep a calendar and contact list as part of their practice management system. While PDAs are capable of serving functions far beyond those of electronic date book and contact list, many lawyers choose to use them primarily as such. This chapter illustrates how even this limited use of a PDA provides enormous benefits.

The descriptions below were gathered during one-on-one phone interviews with lawyers who use Palm Powered™ PDAs, and are meant to inspire you to try their techniques, and to adapt them to meet your own needs.

A major overarching advantage of using a PDA to manage your calendar and contact list is immediacy; the convenience of having your entire calendar and contact list constantly available is practically indescribable. Once you get used to having thousands of contact names and phone numbers in your pocket or purse at all times, you will wonder how you ever got along without it. Trial lawyer David Ransin of Springfield, Missouri, describes it well: "I'm a solo with a 100 percent contingent practice, so my practice is on my mind 24-7. Using the [Palm Powered™]

Visor has allowed me a peace of mind and comfort level due to the fact that I have immediate access to information even when I'm away from the office. I remember one time six years ago; I was trying to call in to my office to access the computerized office calendar system, but the dial-up connection was so slow. Now everything's right there in my shirt pocket, and I no longer need dial-up access. If I'm wondering what's on my schedule for Monday morning, even if it's ten on a Saturday night, all I have to do is press the calendar button, and, boom, there it is. I think knowing that my schedule is being properly managed has even affected my bottom line, since I can be an overall better and more confident lawyer, with no anxiety about, 'Oh my gosh, have I forgotten something?' The PDA helps me walk out of the office knowing I have everything I might need in terms of my case management system right there, so I can sleep at night knowing that everything's going to be well in the morning."

§ 4.2 The Benefits of Using a PDA to Manage Your Calendar

- **A PDA's convenience and immediacy breed good habits of calendar usage.** Because a PDA is so compact, it is easy and ergonomic to carry with you all the time. When your calendar is right at hand, you are more likely to enter items as soon as you learn of them. This means your calendar is more accurate, since you avoid the risks associated with having to wait until you are back at the office, such as misremembering the date, time, or location of the event, or even forgetting to insert the event altogether. Once you know you can always make a calendar entry immediately, it is easy to get into the habit of doing so consistently. Your calendar is comprehensive and complete, so you can use it with confidence. It will soon become a habit to check your PDA calendar regularly—many lawyers like to do this first thing in the morning, or even last thing the day before—to see what is on your schedule.
- **You don't run out of space in a PDA's calendar.** While a small paper calendar can provide much of the convenience described above, a PDA can hold literally thousands of times the amount of information that even someone with tiny handwriting could possibly fit in a pocket-sized paper calendar. With a portable paper calendar, you are basically limited to writing in the small space designated for each day. In contrast, even the smallest PDA has room for you to insert literally hundreds of appointments in a single day, and to find and view them easily by scrolling down the electronic page or using the Palm OS built-in search function.

- **You can put a lot of helpful information in each calendar entry.** Not only is there room to schedule many events in a single day, there is room to include several pages of additional information for each event (by attaching an electronic note to the calendar entry). Such notes can include things like background information for the event, driving directions, meeting agendas, what floor the main reception desk is on, what courtroom a hearing will be held in, and anything else you might need to make the event go more smoothly. Moreover, if this information is available on your computer (in the form of a Web page or Word document), you can insert this information efficiently by copying and pasting it onto your desktop calendar, then synchronizing your PDA with the desktop computer. A most efficient variation of this technique occurs when someone sends you e-mail about an upcoming event, and you simply copy the entire e-mail into an electronic note attached to the event in your calendar.
- **A PDA's comprehensiveness facilitates juggling multiple responsibilities.** The best calendars are those that are comprehensive enough to include all of your personal and professional commitments. With a PDA, there is ample room to include everything: work appointments and deadlines, family commitments and soccer games, doctor appointments and exercise sessions. While the PDA cannot give you more time in each day, it can help you organize and allocate your time so you can be confident you are focusing on the appropriate priority at the proper time.
- **A PDA allows you to schedule events without checking with the "official" calendar back at the office.** Because your PDA calendar is synchronized with your desktop calendar, the PDA version is essentially the same as your desktop calendar, just on another electronic platform.[1] This means you can rely on your PDA to tell you with a high level of certainty whether you can commit to an event on a particular date and time.[2] This is especially important when scheduling official events such as court appearances. Clients will appreciate your ability to schedule meetings efficiently yourself, instead of having to call your office first, or—even worse—being told you'll have your secretary call them to schedule the meeting. And if you ever run into clients who say, "Oh, yes, I've been meaning to call you—I need to talk to you about something," you can pull out your PDA and schedule an appointment right then, instead of waiting for them to call you later.
- **A PDA allows your support staff to schedule events for you.** Since the synchronization function works both ways, your staff can also schedule events for you on the desktop version of your calendar program without having to check with you first. Any conflicts between events that either of you have scheduled since the last synchronization are im-

mediately apparent, since the HotSync program points them out. It's usually a simple matter to straighten out such conflicts provided you catch them promptly. Using a network of this sort is much faster than manually reconciling two handwritten calendars, and your support staff will appreciate being relieved of that tedious duty.

- **You can locate entries electronically.** You can find any event in your PDA calendar quickly and easily, since you can search for an entry electronically rather than by visually scanning the entries on multiple pages of a paper calendar. Bryan Sims, an Illinois litigator, uses this function frequently "to locate when we're in court next, or to find the last few times we've been in court, while all the other lawyers are looking through their files." This feature is also handy when completing reimbursement forms or time sheets, since you can easily see where you were traveling or what you were doing on a particular day.
- **Using a PDA instills client confidence.** Maryland litigator MaryEllen Flynn observes, "Clients love it when their lawyer is tech-savvy—it gives them a sense of confidence when you use the Find feature to answer them when they ask, 'When do we go to court?'" As one Boston associate (who wishes to remain anonymous) relates: "Clients are impressed when I pull out my PDA—they'll say, 'Oh, she's organized.' I used to carry around a big notebook with papers coming out of it and stickies all over it. It kept me organized, but didn't *look* organized. We're in the age of technology now, and it impresses clients to see that I'm right there with technology. Once I went to a meeting with a partner, and when it was time to schedule the next meeting he whipped out an old ratty calendar. I pulled out my Palm and with two points of the stylus I was done."
- **You have the option of setting an alarm for each calendar entry.** This feature allows you to customize an alarm to go off anywhere from ninety-nine days before a deadline or event, up to the moment the event is set to begin. This means you can set the alarm to go off in enough time to allow you to prepare for and travel to the event, whether it's a meeting in the office next door or a CLE conference next month. If a client asks you to call at a particular time, you can insert the call as an event in your calendar, and set an alarm to go off a few minutes before the client expects your call. Howard Wolf-Rodda, a lawyer in Washington, D.C., uses his PDA calendar as a comprehensive tickler system for time-sensitive deadlines and reminders: "I've found it's made it much less stressful to keep track of deadlines. As a litigator, I need to keep track of scheduling orders and cutoffs for discovery, and I have my tickle system built right into the calendar system. Let's say I have a discovery cutoff of August 1. I'll set that up as a set of recurring events in my calendar so that I'm reminded of the deadline six times:

ninety days before, then at sixty days, thirty days, three weeks, two weeks, and finally one week before the deadline. Tracking litigation has become so much more pain-free. The Palm is much better than a paper calendar or a thousand sticky notes, since you have to remember to check the calendar, while the Palm beeps at me, and I can't do anything else on it without tapping on the reminder. I can't ignore it. Even if I'm not there when the alarm goes off, the reminder will pop back up when you turn it on, and you can't do anything else until you tap it." MaryEllen Flynn uses the alarm feature to help her relax when she's away from the office: "I'll set an alarm so that when I go out to lunch, I can forget about everything and just relax and enjoy myself, and the beep reminds me when I have fifteen minutes to get back to the office."

- **It's easy to make changes to a PDA calendar**. All it takes is a few taps of your stylus to change the date, time, or length of an event, or even to delete it completely. This is especially handy when a case settles. As Howard Wolf-Rodda explains, "I used to have this Day-Timer book that I'd write everything down in. I'd have deadlines and reminders at three dozen different places, and if a case settled, I had to go through and erase all those entries. Now, I can do that in just a few taps." Lawyer Ron Feinman of Lynchburg, Virginia, takes advantage of this benefit to balance his various commitments: "The Palm does give you the opportunity to schedule your whole life. I'd been doing that with pen and paper for years, but the Palm is even more convenient because it's so easy to spread my commitments out over the week. I schedule some things on Monday, some on Tuesday, and spread them out through the week. The Palm calendar's daily, weekly, and monthly views even allow me to schedule tasks throughout the month, and also to reschedule things very easily. I couldn't really do that in my handwritten calendar book."

§ 4.3 The Benefits of Using a PDA to Manage Your Contact List

Many of the benefits of using a PDA to manage your contact list are similar to the benefits of using a PDA to manage your calendar.

- **A PDA provides convenience and immediacy.** Having quick access to all of your contacts' multiple telephone numbers saves you a lot of time in various ways. Once you have mastered the basics of the program, it takes literally only two or three seconds to look up most numbers, since all you have to do is tap on the button that opens the contact list, then write the first few letters of the contact's last name. This can drastically reduce the amount of time you spend searching for telephone numbers. This time can really add up, because too many people fail to leave their telephone number on their voice-mail messages (because, after all, they know you have their numbers) but if you can't access it easily, locating a number can add an annoying, potentially time-consuming extra step to the otherwise simple process of returning a phone call. Especially when you are away from your office, having telephone numbers at hand means you can return the call right away without calling your office first to get the number; if that is your current standard procedure, a PDA cuts by half the number of telephone calls you must make—plus you can call your clients back without delay. Finally, every time you call the office to get a telephone number, it takes up staff time that's not being otherwise productive. And that's assuming you are trying to return the call during office hours, rather than during the evening or weekend when your staff is unlikely to be available, and when it's even more likely the client call is an emergency situation requiring a prompt response.

- **A PDA gives you consistency and ease of use.** Because your PDA phone directory is with you all the time, it's easy to get into the habit of inserting a new person's contact information as soon as you get it. This means both your PDA phone directory, and the directory on the computer with which you synchronize your PDA, is comprehensive and current. This in turn encourages you to use the PDA even more often, and the resulting snowball effect helps you develop and maintain the habit of using the phone directory consistently. Howard Wolf-Rodda describes this phenomenon: "I use the phone directory constantly. Before, I kept an alphabetical phone list in my Day-Timer, but that didn't really work. Now I keep them all my contacts in the Palm. Every time I stumble across someone new in a case, they get an address entry. I tend to be much more disciplined about putting contacts in my Palm than I was about putting them in my Day-Timer, because it's much easier. Before the Palm, there just wasn't this consistency. Contacts were either on the firm's system, or I'd have to go find the file to find the note that I wrote when I had a conversation with the person and jotted down his phone number. It was a real scrounging effort. I was much more disorganized at keeping track of contacts. This makes it so much easier to be organized. Even just this piece of the Palm has changed my life because calling people up is much less stressful."
- **You can put a lot of helpful information in each contact entry.** Unlike a paper telephone directory, there is plenty of room to include a lot of background information about each contact. It can be very helpful to keep notes about how you met a person, the various contacts you have had with him or her over the years, and even such memory

joggers as a birthday and the names of a spouse and children. If the contact is a client, you can keep a case log attached to the contact information, including such items as what you did during the case, any conversations with opposing counsel, and the specifics of settlement negotiations. If you're on the road, these notes help you update clients about the status of their cases. All of this information becomes a gigantic database of information, which you can put to good use in your marketing efforts, and use to keep in touch with all of your existing clients on a regular basis.

- **A PDA's comprehensiveness facilitates juggling multiple responsibilities.** At first it may seem odd to maintain a contact list that includes professional colleagues in the same place as your personal contacts such as friends, plumbers, and baby-sitters, but integrating this information into one system can be a big help in balancing the many disparate responsibilities in your life. The Palm OS allows you to create up to fifteen categories in most programs, including Address Book, so you can organize your contacts simply into business and personal, or subdivide them into even more descriptive categories. For example, in balancing her responsibilities as a wife, mother, and managing partner for litigation at her law firm, MaryEllen Flynn has found it useful to separate her contacts as follows: "The business categories include regular business contacts, including clients, vendors, Montgomery County courts, District of Columbia courts, litigation experts, and something I call Solo and Small Firm, since I work with that section of the Maryland Bar Association. On the personal side, I have categories for each of my children, which includes their friends and activities, vendors in my personal life, and, finally, a category for food, which includes restaurants and take-out places." It's also useful to create a category for each professional association you belong to, so you can read through that category and review the relevant contact notes to refresh your memory about other members' names and background information before each meeting or conference; your colleagues will be flattered that you remembered so much about them, and will credit you with an excellent memory.
- **You can locate contacts electronically.** Even though you can categorize your contacts in a PDA, it's not really necessary to do so, since you can always locate a contact by searching for any word you have inserted in a contact record or the associated notes. This means you can include descriptors such as "expert witness," "mediator," or "printer," and conduct an electronic search for those terms. This yields a list of all contacts whose records contain that term, and tapping on the contact's name in that list takes you directly to that contact's record.

- **It's simple to make changes to a PDA contact list.** With the PDA, you can edit out the old information and add in the new information quickly and tidily, and the changes are uploaded to your desktop program the next time you synchronize your PDA. As government lawyer Catherine McCabe says, "Compared to the Franklin Planner, the address book is more efficient because it's easy to make changes. In my Franklin Planner address book, I'd cross the old things out and squoosh the new things in."
- **A PDA provides extra efficiency through convergence with a cell phone.** If you get a PDA such as the SmartPhone, which merges the PDA with a cell phone, you can place telephone calls even more quickly because you can automatically dial any number in your contact list just by tapping on it. These devices usually also include a caller ID feature that allows you to capture the number from which a call is made, and export that number into a contact's record for future reference. Both of these features are especially handy if you use your driving time to catch up on your telephone calls.
- **Ease of sharing information with other PDA users.** If you want to share any information in your phone list with another Palm Powered™ PDA user, you can beam the entire contact record to your colleague's PDA. This process takes just a few seconds, and is more accurate than having your colleague copy down all the information by hand. Palm Powered™ PDAs even allow you to beam your own contact information to another Palm PDA by pressing a single button for two seconds. When you distribute your information in this manner, it shows up in your clients' and prospects' PDAs within seconds, with 100 percent accuracy. You can even attach several pages of information to this electronic business card, such as your bio and areas of expertise, so you can use this technique as part of your overall marketing strategy.
- **Synchronizing your PDA with your desktop computer provides an automatic, up-to-date backup of all your contact information.** Having a duplicate of all this information avoids the headaches of reconstructing your telephone list from scratch in the event either platform crashes, or is lost, stolen, or destroyed.

Notes

1. An added benefit of this duplication is that some malpractice insurance carriers may consider your PDA as one of its required backup systems.

2. If you want to be able to rely on your PDA calendar with complete certainty, you must forfeit the option of allowing your support staff to schedule items on the desktop version of your calendar while you are away from the office.

5

To Do List and Memo Pad: Keeping Track of Ideas, Information, and Things to Do

§ 5.1 Introduction

All lawyers should maintain a prioritized task list as a key part of their practice management system. In fact, failure to make and follow such a list is a malpractice warning signal as identified by Nancy Byerly Jones, past executive director and management counsel for the North Carolina State Bar's Executive Lawyers' Management Assistance Program.[1] Almost as important as tracking tasks is the ability to efficiently capture, store, and retrieve those random and not-so-random thoughts, ideas, and plans that seem to occur most often when you are in the worst position for acting on them. This chapter describes the benefits of using the To Do List and Memo Pad functions built into every Palm Powered™ PDA in order to manage tasks and keep track of information.

As in Chapter 4, the descriptions below were provided to me during one-on-one telephone interviews with lawyers who use Palm Powered™ PDAs, and are intended to illustrate the benefits of using a PDA in order to inspire you to adopt similar techniques, and adapt them for your own use in ways that work best for you.

§ 5.2 The Benefits of Using the Palm OS® To Do List

The Palm OS To Do program can help you get organized, especially when used as an adjunct to a desktop to-do list such as Microsoft Outlook or the To Do function in the Palm Desktop. You can capture and record your tasks and plans as they occur to you, and then synchronize the changes to the desktop system. Having your entire to-do list on your PDA and with you at all times allows you to review your list as often as you like, and to act on items whenever you find a convenient moment, without having to find and juggle paper to-do lists or carry a heavy notebook required by a comprehensive, paper-based to-do system.

Here are a variety of ways in which the Palm OS To Do List program can help you manage your task list:

- **You can easily categorize your tasks.** The Palm OS To Do List program allows you to create up to fifteen categories into which to put your tasks. It is a simple matter to create new categories and to shift tasks from one category to another, so the PDA offers greater flexibility than a paper to-do list. You can easily shift between viewing a single category of tasks, and viewing all your tasks together at one time. This means that you can get an overview of your entire to-do list, and a more targeted view of just those tasks related to a particular case or project. Howard Wolf-Rodda says, "For me, the to-do list is of equal importance with the calendar function. I put all my work tasks on the to-do list. I use the categories function to break my tasks first by my areas of practice—government contracts, bankruptcy, other litigation—and for major cases I'm working on at any given time. Usually there are only two or three cases so big they merit their own category. For minor cases, I categorize tasks by the partners with whom I work. Plus I have a category for specific tasks I'm doing for specific clients. I also have a generic 'other' category. I usually look at all the tasks together, then I look at tasks by category in order to review the to-do list for individual cases."
- **You can easily keep track of deadlines.** The Palm OS To Do List gives you the option of setting a specific due date for a task, or leaving this field empty. You also have the option of making tasks appear in order of their due date, with overdue items appearing at the head of the list, highlighted with exclamation points. It's simple to change a due date, so that if one task slips behind schedule you can easily set more realistic deadlines for subsequent tasks in the same project. You can manage your projects very effectively by keeping your tasks sorted by

date, and frequently scanning down through your list to remind yourself of tasks that aren't due just yet.

- **You can plan your day at your convenience.** Catherine McCabe describes an excellent and frequently used method for using a PDA to-do list to plan in an efficient and orderly manner: "When I want to get an overview of my task list each day, first I'll go through each category separately—I have ten categories in my to-do list—and adjust the due dates and priorities as needed.[2] Then I'll go back and look at all the tasks for the day, and cross-compare the priorities for items in different categories. For example, when I compare priorities and due dates within a single category, I'll be thinking, 'This client needs these five things done,' and when I go back to the 'All' view to cross-compare items in different categories, I'll be thinking, 'My client might want this done, but court needs this tomorrow.' I generally do that on the Palm, not on my desktop computer, because my quiet time is riding the Metro to work or sitting in a boring meeting. While it is easier to see more things at one time on the computer, I just don't have the necessary quiet time when I'm at my desk."
- **You can attach a lot of information to each task.** Just as in the Palm OS calendar and contact list programs, the Palm OS To Do List allows you to attach an electronic note (consisting of up to several pages of text) to each task entry. This means you can describe the task briefly in the actual to-do list, and use the space in the attached note for details, substeps, background information, or things to discuss with colleagues in connection with the task. You can create this note by copying and pasting the contents of a Word document, e-mail, or Web site into your desktop computer's to-do list and then synchronizing, or you can create it from scratch to your preferences and specifications, either on your desktop or on your PDA. You can follow the example of North Carolina lawyer Vedia Jones-Richardson, who uses the notes option to "store a project history, which is basically a running status sheet or log of activities for that project. I'll start each entry with the date, then follow it with a record of what I did, or what I delegated, or what I was thinking about, or what activity or task should take place next in that case. Since I have this log for each project always with me, if I run across a piece of mail that's relevant to the project, or think about what I want to do in the case, I'll pull up the to-do item for that matter, and the log's always right there. It's easy to refer to it and to add things as I think of them."
- **You can use To Do List to facilitate timekeeping.** Once you have checked off a task as complete, the Palm OS automatically replaces

the task's due date with the date you marked the task as completed.[3] This comes in handy when describing your work for timekeeping purposes, because you can determine the day you completed a particular task, and you can easily locate all the tasks you checked off as completed on a given day.

§ 5.3 The Benefits of Using the Palm OS® Memo Pad

Using your PDA as an electronic memo pad means that you no longer have to look for slips of paper or grope for a pen when you want to jot down a quick note. More importantly, you will be able to find any existing note quickly whenever you need it. Here are the primary benefits of using your PDA as a memo pad:

- **You won't have to deal with lots of random pieces of paper**. Because you can keep your PDA with you at all times, you can develop the habit of jotting information down in its memo pad rather than on whatever random piece of paper happens to be at hand. This means that all of this information is located in one place, so you know where to go to look for it. When all of your notes are centrally located in your PDA, you won't have to spend time scrounging around in your office, looking for the legal pad, sticky note, used envelope, or paper napkin that you grabbed to scribble what has now become valuable information. You will even find at times that your PDA can replace an entire physical file for various administrative or miscellaneous projects.
- **You can find your information when you need it.** Replacing scraps of paper with an orderly list of memos is a huge timesaver, and a crucial part of your overall organizational system. The Palm OS offers you a variety of ways to organize your memos. You can either leave your memos listed in the order in which you created them or sort your memos alphabetically. In addition, you can filter memos into up to fifteen categories of your own creation, and you can use the electronic search feature to locate an item if you remember even a single word contained in the item.
- **You can easily transform a document on your desktop into a PDA memo.** You can create a memo by copying and pasting any text from e-mail, a Word document, or Web site to your desktop memo pad (which you then HotSync onto your PDA). Once it's in your PDA, you can easily review it later at your convenience, even when you are away from your office. Vedia Jones-Richardson relates, "I'm on a number of

different community boards, and I get lots of information via e-mail about different work committees. I'll keep memos on my PDA for each of the committees I'm on. Plus I have a memo with a list of all those committees, so I can pull it up and read it off to people who want me to do even more."

- **You can easily transform a Palm OS memo into a word-processed document.** The stepping-stone process works both ways: the cursory notes in your PDA's Memo Pad can often be used as a rough first draft for a more formal memo or document. Should you find it necessary to write a report, memorandum, or send an e-mail message based on information in your memo pad, you can copy and paste the information from the desktop version of your memo pad into the appropriate word-processing or e-mail program. Catherine McCabe uses this technique often, and calls it "so easy to do, really wonderful, and a huge time-saver."
- **You can easily share memos with other Palm PDA users.** You can beam entire memos from one PDA to another in seconds, so you can use Memo Pad as a high-tech way of passing notes and sharing documents. Ron Feinman has used Memo Pad to beam brief messages to people in meetings, as well as comments to and from co-counsel in a mediation, so they could silently share their reactions to the other side's negotiating position. Once, when neither he nor his co-counsel had immediate access to a full-sized computer, the co-counsel put his proposed opening statement into a series of memos, and beamed it to him in order to get his comments.
- **Finally, and most importantly, you can use Memo Pad for all different kinds of information.** Unlike the Palm OS programs for calendaring, contact lists, and task lists, the memo pad is designed for an infinite variety of types of information. With Memo Pad, you can quickly, easily, and conveniently record, store, and retrieve *all* kinds of text-based information to help you keep both your professional and personal lives running smoothly. You will find it so easy to record and retrieve information with your PDA that you will start keeping track of things you otherwise wouldn't, which means you can become even more organized, efficient, and effective. The options are limitless. Here are a few real-world examples:
  - David Ransin, a lawyer in Springfield, Missouri, uses Memo Pad to store information in categories ranging from "business, office remodel, notes from a traumatic brain injury case, the upcoming ATLA conference in Atlanta (which includes information about people I visited during my last trip to that city, along with their ad-

dresses and the corresponding directions)." On the personal side, he also maintains Memo Pad categories for "home repair, farm, general personal items, and investments."

- Maryland lawyer Christopher vanRoden reports, "I'm a guardian for a woman, and I use my Palm to keep track of bank account numbers, which bills need to be paid, and the due dates for those bills. We're making some physical improvements at the office, and whenever I talk with contractors, I take notes on my Palm, so what they said, their cost estimates, and all the information I need is at my fingertips, so I don't have to pull a hard file. I also keep memos for information about upgrading our phone systems, client information, things to look for in particular cases, and recurring tasks for clients. I have a memo for e-mail settings, since I have a bunch of e-mail addresses both for home and office, and I need all the details of all the settings in a central location in case something shuts down and I have to set it up again."
- Scott Borison, a law office administrator and the self-described "techno-person" at a law firm in Portland, Oregon, keeps memos on outstanding computer issues, along with "all the assorted log-in names one accumulates on the Internet. I also keep everyone's password so I can log in to any computer in the office whenever I need to do a software update."
- Catherine McCabe says, "Since I'm the deputy chief of a section [in the Department of Justice] I have a category in my Memo Pad called Management Issues. I have separate categories for the different regions of the country that I cover, and categories for a few special litigation cases I oversee. Within each category I have things like delegated tasks, issues, meetings notes, and draft memos I want to circulate. When I have to know who the people are in the regional offices, I make a memo consisting of a list of people's names so I can remind myself before I get there who the major players are."
- MaryEllen Flynn maintains memos for "all the plans we have for next year so when I meet with partners and staff I have all the necessary information right there; a memo entitled Office Manager which lists things I want to discuss; notes for our next lawyer meeting, notes for our next staff meeting, and a memo of ideas related to the Solo and Small Firm Forum of the Maryland State Bar Association, of which I'm an active member."
- Chicago lawyer Domingo Such says, "I use the memo function for things like goals for my practice, year-end planning, and inspirational things that are nice to have easy access to."
- Boston lawyer Wendy Berliner keeps "random things in my notepad, like contact information for my parents when they travel; in-

formation for an event I ran for my alumni association, for which I kept a memo with contact numbers and the attendee list; and information for a meeting I was running, and I had to keep track of who was coming and whom I had to remind. I recently purchased a condo, and kept memos for everything about it—information about the mortgage company, the real estate broker, and the home inspector."

- Vedia Jones-Richardson uses "the memo function for plans for things I'd like to do, such as gardening, including such things as plants I like and descriptions about environmental needs which I'll just drag from the Web. I have a category entitled Money, which is where I'll keep notes about investments, and good mutual funds. Generally this information comes to me in an e-mail, or I find it bobbing on the Internet, so I copy and paste it into a memo to keep it handy. On the personal side, I have three kids, a husband, and a father-in-law to consider when planning meals, so I keep notes on what works for everyone. I'll also keep information so I can go shopping for things for the home, so if I want something to go in a particular place, I'll measure the space first and put that information in my Visor, then I'll measure how wide a cabinet is before I buy it so I don't get something that won't fit in the space. I'll jot down ideas for moving things around in the house and in the garden. I also keep a very handy ongoing packing list, which I add to whenever I think of something. There are sections of the list for different packing situations, such as trips to the beach, trips with the kids, et cetera. I keep lists of books for my kids, so when I'm in the library I know what authors are good for kids in their age group."
- Reid Trautz, practice management advisor with the District of Columbia Bar, uses his Memo Pad for "all my little notes of things to remember that you don't need very often but when you do, it's really frustrating not to be able to find the slip of paper it's written on."

In addition to the memo ideas already mentioned, the individuals I interviewed also used their Palm OS Memo Pad for the following kinds of information:[4]

Practice Related Information

- Bar numbers
- Business development ideas
- Driving directions (frequently copied and pasted from e-mail or MapQuest)
- Federal tax ID number
- Frequent-flier miles

- Frequent-flier numbers
- Instructions for using cell phones (such as how to set up call waiting or call forwarding)
- Instructions for using computer programs
- Itineraries, flight information, and other travel information for specific trips
- Log-in names and passwords for specific Web sites
- Log-in names and passwords for Westlaw and Lexis, and their help line telephone numbers
- Monthly summary of billable time
- Quotations
- Real estate information for office space
- Software license numbers
- Specifications for modems the firm is thinking of buying
- Technical tips for how to use computer programs
- Tips on time management
- Web sites

Personal, Household, Family Information

- Book descriptions from Amazon.com
- Books to read (in general)
- Books to read (for upcoming book-club meetings)
- Charitable donations for the year
- Checking account numbers
- Honeydew list (as in "Honey, would you please do these chores?")
- How to barbeque a turkey
- Jokes
- Notes "for the novel I'm thinking of writing"
- Notes for events (meetings, weddings, memorial services)
- Real estate information for home purchase
- Things to get "at different stores I go to regularly"
- Things "to fit on my boat"
- Travel ideas "and information about different places I'd like to go to"
- Travel plans for specific trips
- Vehicle information

Notes

1. Checklist of malpractice warning signals distributed as part of a program entitled "Reducing the Risk: Enhancing the Bottom Line," presented by the National Academy of Law, Ethics, and Management in Las Vegas, Nevada; reprinted in the Bar Association of the District of Columbia Monthly Newsletter, Volume 1, Issue 4 (April 1996).
2. The Palm OS To Do List allows you to assign one of five priorities to each task.

3. In the Palm To Do List, just checking off a task as completed does not delete the task from the program; you must either delete the individual task, or use the menu command to delete all To Do items marked as completed. This distinction is easy to overlook, because you can arrange to have a task disappear from the screen the moment it is checked off as completed, by setting up a view that includes only pending tasks. When you change the view to pull up completed tasks, the date in the Due Date column is the date the task was checked off as completed. See Section 13.2 for a description of the viewing options in To Do List.

4. See also Chapter 14 for more ideas.

Other Uses of a PDA

6

§ 6.1 Introduction

This chapter is intended to provide the non-PDA user, as well as those who use no more than the four main applications discussed in Chapters 4 and 5, with a glimpse of other ways to use PDAs to be more efficient and effective at work, to assist in balancing work and home responsibilities, and even to indulge in some well-earned rest and relaxation.

As in the preceding two chapters, these ideas are illustrative and inspirational rather than comprehensive, and are intended to assist you in generating your own ideas of how to use your PDA. Chapters 15 through 20 contain further ideas.

§ 6.2 Note-Taking Without a Laptop

Until recently, the laptop computer was clearly the mobile technology of choice for word processing away from the office. However, now there are a wide variety of portable keyboards for PDAs, and so the PDA-keyboard combination comprises a smaller, lighter, more convenient alternative for most out-of-office word-processing situations, particularly note-taking. Even the two-page limitation on items in the built-in Palm Memo Pad function is no longer an inconvenience given the variety of add-on software allowing you effectively to put Word documents on your PDA.

Here are some specific out-of-office note-taking situations where you will find it very convenient to use a PDA and portable keyboard instead of a laptop:

- **For off-site document reviews and legal research.** Cataloging documents by hand can be tedious, time-consuming, and result in notes that are difficult to decipher back at the office. Taking notes on your PDA saves you time during the actual document review (if, like many lawyers, you can type much faster than you can write by hand), and you will return to the office with a nice neat typed list of documents. Even if your typed notes are sketchy, once you return to the office you can sync your PDA with your desktop computer, and transfer your notes to a Word document and clean them up in that format, which usually has more editing tools (such as the find-and-replace feature) than the PDA. Thus you save time back at the office, because you cut out the process of dictating a memo from your handwritten notes. Even better, the final product is more accurate, since it is easier to input exactly what the documents say when you are typing rather than writing by hand. The same principles apply when taking notes in the course of legal research.
- **When defending depositions**. Tennessee lawyer Tim Gibbons describes his technique for note-taking while defending depositions: "I'll take voluminous notes, including my own thoughts about strategy, such as where I think the other side is going in the case, things we should do, and areas we should follow up on. I put those editorial comments in boldface to make them stand out. After HotSyncing the notes to my main computer, I'll go back and cull out those comments, and use them as the basis for a memo about where I think we should go in the case."
- **At professional conferences and CLE programs**. How often have you actually transcribed your handwritten conference notes after returning to your office? If you are like most lawyers, your answer will be somewhere between "rarely" and "never." If you take notes on your PDA in the first place, there is no need to transcribe them, and after performing a HotSync, you can easily store them in the appropriate computer file for ease of future reference.
- **When you want to take notes discreetly**. Using a PDA (without a keyboard) to take notes means no one will be certain whether you are taking notes, or just updating your calendar. This can be handy when you want to be unobtrusive, such as at a town meeting or Congressional hearing.

- **When you don't want to risk intimidating someone by using a laptop**. Believe it or not, some people perceive a laptop computer to be something of a barrier to the free flow of communication, and so object to lawyers using a laptop to take notes. In contrast, it is much easier for the old-fashioned CEO or timid interviewee to overlook (or look over) a PDA. Amazingly, people who might object to your taking notes on a laptop may have no problem with your using a PDA instead.
- **When you don't want to deal with the inconvenience of a laptop**. Note-taking with a PDA instead of a laptop means you have less extra weight to lug around, no need to worry about battery time or finding a power outlet, no dealing with boot-up time, and no concern about people tripping over extension cords and sending your expensive laptop crashing to the floor.
- **When you are not certain you will need to take notes**. A PDA and portable keyboard are both small and light, and so are convenient to bring along even when you are not sure you will be taking notes. As Howard Wolf-Rodda relates, "The first time I took notes with my Visor and a folding keyboard, I was in another lawyer's office during a conference call with a judge. I pulled out my keyboard and plopped it down on my colleague's desk. It was great—at first he laughed at my nerdhood, but then he was impressed when he saw how thorough my notes were." You never know when a meeting or interview will evolve to the point where you want to take notes, but if you keep your PDA and portable keyboard in your briefcase at all times, it's available whenever you need it.

§ 6.3 Working on Documents Outside the Office

The combination of the PDA, the portable keyboard, and the ability to install a Palm OS version of Microsoft Word on your PDA means you have the opportunity to create, read, edit, and format documents when you are away from the office, without using a laptop. When you sync your PDA with your primary computer, all the changes are updated on both platforms. If your job offers the flexibility and you want the change of scene, you can leave the office and set up your PDA and keyboard in a coffeehouse, restaurant, your home office, or anywhere else. Howard Wolf-Rodda remembers one time, "just a regular workday that I worked at home, which I'll do on some days when I can't be interrupted. It was a beautiful, calm spring day, the birds were whistling, and my porch was a much more pleasant work environment than the office." Other lawyers have exercised this option while sitting in the back of courtrooms, while traveling by rail or air, and even on vacations (not a pleasant thought, but unfortunately a realistic one).

Even if you prefer not to work on important projects outside the office, you can use your PDA and keyboard to work on nonbillable memos and letters, thus freeing up more office time to dedicate to billable work.

Personally, I have found a PDA with a portable keyboard to be massively more convenient than a laptop for working on documents while traveling. The batteries in my laptop last no more than two hours at best, so it is impractical to use without consistent, convenient access to a power supply. In contrast, the long-lasting batteries in my Palm Vx have essentially eliminated the need for concern about power supply. When I travel, I plug in my PDA overnight using the travel recharging cord, which plugs into a standard wall socket. (This replaces the constant recharging during normal day-to-day use, when the PDA is sitting in the cradle next to my desktop computer.) Even this overnight recharging is unnecessary on short trips. Even with no recharging, a full week of heavy PDA use every day (demonstrating how to use the Palm PDA in full days' worth of consulting sessions with half-a-dozen lawyers a day) left my Palm Vx with an acceptable 20 percent of its battery power. When I upgraded to a Palm m515, which is more power-hungry due to its color screen, I find that even the m515 lasts a full travel day without needing a recharge.

A PDA and a portable keyboard are much more convenient than a laptop in other ways as well. For example, I am writing these words at about sixteen thousand feet, aboard a flight twenty minutes from Dulles Airport. I have always been reluctant to pull out my laptop while flying, not only because I didn't want to risk draining the battery, but because I was worried about having a beverage spill into the keyboard, or having the computer slip off the airline's flimsy plastic pull-down tray. To make matters worse, the time required to start up and shut down the Windows operating system made it inconvenient and awkward to repeatedly stow and pull out the computer in response to the food and drink service, and to seatmates' needs for access to the aisle. In contrast, it takes less than fifteen seconds (I just timed it) to unfold a portable keyboard, attach the PDA, and start typing, which is fast enough to set it up and take it down as often as circumstances require. The PDA and keyboard are small and light enough to fit comfortably and securely on the plastic pull-down tray, and both are small enough to fit into a purse or pocket, so you can get to them without awkwardly removing your briefcase from an overhead luggage bin or underneath the seat in front of you. It's also easier to go through airline security with a PDA than with a laptop, because you don't have to pull out the PDA and put it through the security scanner in a separate plastic container. Since a PDA is so much smaller than a laptop, it's much less noticeable to prospective thieves. Finally, the consequences of losing a PDA are much less than the consequences of losing a laptop, since a PDA is cheaper to replace, and it is easy to install all the information from your lost PDA onto a new device.[1]

§ 6.4 Timekeeping

There are a variety of ways in which a PDA can help you track billable time conveniently and accurately. Without exception, every lawyer I've spoken with who uses a PDA to keep track of billable time has felt he or she has been able to capture more billable time as a result.

First of all, you can use your PDA to record your activities as they occur. When you keep track of time contemporaneously, your descriptions tend to be more specific, and your time totals more accurate, since you don't have to rely on your memory for keeping track of this important information. With a PDA, your timekeeping procedures can remain the same whether you are in the office, on the road, in court, in the law library, or at home, and this consistency will help you develop and maintain the excellent habit of contemporaneous timekeeping. Without this consistency, it is all too easy to lose track of billable time, particularly when you are away from your office and your primary timekeeping system. With a PDA, you can maintain your timekeeping procedure even if you're at a courthouse and find you have some free time until your case will be called, and you spend that time looking for that deed, divorce, or pleading you have been meaning to locate. As solo practitioner Bob Walker says, "I work outside Washington, D.C., so whenever I have to come into the District I try to do more than one thing at a time. It really helps to note what I worked on at the time I worked on it, since you tend to forget things by the time you're back at the office. There's no more guesswork involved, either—I just start the timer just as I do at the office."

Using your PDA to keep track of your billable time is efficient because it reduces or eliminates duplication of effort. If you normally keep track of time by hand, when it comes time to enter your time into your office's timekeeping system, either you or your secretary must go through your handwritten notes and translate them into a format compatible with the timekeeping system. However, if you have been keeping track of time on your PDA from the outset, your timekeeping notes are already in an electronic form, and already on your office's main computer system (assuming you synchronize your PDA with your office's computer system). Therefore, neither you nor your staff need spend any time transcribing your timekeeping notes, but can copy and paste the information directly into your firm's official timekeeping program. This is not only more efficient, but more accurate, since the risk of transcription errors is eliminated. Even if there are errors or typos in your initial notes, it is easier to catch and correct these on your primary computer system, which is more likely to have an automatic spell-checker. Leaving these corrections to your secretary or administrative assistant not only saves you time, but in the process allows your support staff to learn what you're working on, which helps them to feel like a part of the team.

Another subtle benefit of contemporaneous timekeeping is that when you record your time while the activity is occurring—such as taking notes directly in your timekeeping program while you are talking on the telephone with your client—the time you spend on timekeeping is itself billable. If you wait until the activity is over, the time you spend recording the activity becomes unbillable administrative time.

There are many simple add-on timekeeping programs available, complete with timers and summary functions.[2] Using such a program on your PDA can help you capture more billable time, because it takes just a tap or two to start and stop the timer, so you can efficiently record even short bursts of activity (which too often many lawyers fail to record at all), since you won't have to add up your time manually, and even those three- or six-minute time periods add up over the course of the day or week.

A timer is also helpful if you have many clients and many different matters, since it is extremely time-consuming to write down every short task or phone call on a per-client basis and then enter it into your computer. With the PDA, you can capture every moment of billable time in just a few seconds. In addition, if your clients call you at home, you can pull out your PDA and start the timer, and not have to worry about writing down the time on a scratch pad.

You can even get Palm OS versions of various popular desktop or network timekeeping programs, so the information is transferred to your desktop program automatically and seamlessly upon HotSyncing.[3] This is the ultimate in efficiency, so it pays to research whether a Palm OS version of your organization's official timekeeping system exists, or can be created by a programmer hired specifically for that purpose.

Even if you don't want to install an add-on program designed specifically for timekeeping, there are various ways to use the built-in functions of the PDA to track billable time. Some lawyers just open up Memo Pad and jot down the client name, the case name, the amount of time spent, and a short description of what they did. Even if they don't sync that information to their firm's official timekeeping program, when they prepare their time reports they don't have to worry about remembering all of that information, or hunt for random slips of paper; they know exactly where they recorded all of these specifics. Some lawyers make even this rudimentary note-taking more efficient by using Graffiti ShortCuts[4] for client names, case names, client-matter numbers, and commonly used descriptors for billable work. You can also use the Palm OS built-in time-stamp Graffiti shortcut for entering the exact start and end times of a task without having to consult a clock. When it's time to calculate your billable time, all the necessary raw data will have been preserved, and so calculating your time totals is all that remains to be done.

Another efficient way to keep track of billable time using one of the built-in Palm OS functions is to insert your billable activities in the calendar program, and record a description of the work performed during that time period as a note attached to the event. If you sync your PDA with your office system, your secretary has access to your calendar, which becomes your time record as each day passes. Your secretary can calculate time totals and copy and paste your descriptions of work performed from your calendar into your firm's timekeeping system. Another benefit of this system is that you don't have to relinquish your physical calendar to your secretary, since there is an electronic copy of it on your firm's computer system.

If you don't have to keep track of your billable time per se, but have to account for the number of hours you work anyway (as required for some government and corporate lawyers), it's a simple matter to keep a running list of your daily and cumulative hours in a memo on your PDA, perhaps creating a new memo every month.

§ 6.5 Keeping Documents Handy

One of the many useful functions a PDA can perform is to give you to constant, convenient, and interactive access to documents, texts, and reference materials you have HotSynced onto your PDA. These items can include Word documents you or others have created, items you copy and paste from other documents such as e-mail or Internet Web pages, and documents others have specifically formatted to work well on the Palm operating system. Many lawyers have installed and used a wide variety of federal and state laws and rules such as rules of civil procedure; criminal codes; case law relevant to a specific court appearance; the federal patent, trademark, and copyright statutes; the Internal Revenue Code, and many, many more. Most PDA add-on document programs allow you to insert bookmarks at any particular point in the text, and many lawyers find it convenient to bookmark sections of the rules or laws, then use the Palm OS Find function to search within that section for exactly the part they want. With reference materials conveniently accessible and searchable on your PDA, you don't need to lug around a lot of books and papers when you want access to them away from your office, whether you are appearing in court or just working at home.

Here are some inspirational, real-world examples and war stories:

- Washington, D.C., litigation associate Will Buchanan recalls an instance during a deposition when none of the other lawyers could recall the precise wording of the relevant Federal Rule of Civil Procedure. "Everyone else was on the record fumbling around, saying 'I think it says thus and so,' and when it was my turn, I quoted Rule 30(b)(6) of the Federal Rules of Civil Procedure verbatim. Everyone looked amazed that I'd memorized that rule, or so they thought. Only after we were off the record did I 'fess up and admit that I'd read the rule out of my Palm, where I'd downloaded the entire FRCP. Then everyone laughed and wanted to see my Palm and read the rule, but if you just read the written record of the deposition, it looks really great."
- Georgia lawyer Christopher Stovall uses "Wordsmith from Blue Nomad, which is great for syncing with Word documents. Every few months our office manager will create a new office directory in a Word document, and I'll just sync it up to my Visor. Since I have all that information with me, I can call people on weekends if something urgent comes up. The directory has our office's internal phone numbers, so I don't have to place any calls through our receptionist, and I can reach people in the office even if the receptionist isn't there."

  Christopher also likes Wordsmith "because it's so good at retaining Word's rich text format, such as italics and underlining. I use it as a quick-and-dirty companion to AvantGo, in that if I see an interesting article on a Web site, I'll save it as a Word document, then I'll open it in Word, click on Wordsmith, HotSync, and, presto chango, I have a handheld version of the Web page. I'll admit, this procedure isn't very good for very graphic-intensive items, but most of the time it's better than having five to ten pages of printout. When I'm going to be out of town or on vacation, I'll load up my Visor with reading material. I'll pick two or three long articles that I've already saved on my desktop and HotSync them to the Visor. This way I can read a lot of Web content offline. For reading purposes, this technique is almost as good as having a PDA with wireless access to the Internet, and it's a lot more cost effective, since I'm not paying $30 or $40 a month for wireless access, plus I don't have to buy a modem."
- Howard Wolf-Rodda says, "I have my secretary scan in scheduling orders in all my cases, so if I have a question I can just look right at the document on my Palm using Documents To Go. If I'm at a deposition or status conference I just pop it right up. Non-Palm users think I'm a geek but it's totally handy. Other Palm users are just impressed—I could even beam it to them."

- Georgia lawyer Gerald Privin reports, "The Georgia Association of Criminal Defense Lawyers has a Web site, **www.gacdl.org**, where you can download recent case law. That gives you the freedom in the courtroom to read if you have downtime. I enlarge the font so it's easy to read. In fact, you can download the entire bench book that judges get when they attend their own continuing education programs. That came in handy recently in court. A few weeks ago we had a motions calendar, and since I'd been reading these cases I was aware of a recent case that was on point for the motion I was arguing. I cited the case, saying to the judge, 'which I'm sure you recall from the judges' seminar.' The judge just smiled at me and said, 'Motion granted.'"

  Gerald has also downloaded "Crimes and Punishment" from **www.gacdl.org**, which contains all the schedules of crimes with their various punishments. "So instead of carrying around Title 16 of the Georgia Code, I have all that information on my Palm. If a client asks if the maximum punishment for a crime is fifteen years, I can use bookmarks or the global search function to look it up and tell him, 'No, it's twenty-five.'"
- Ohio lawyer John Haller relates, "I downloaded the Federal Rules of Civil Procedure onto my Palm Vx, which came in really handy one time. I was in a conference in the judge's chambers in federal bankruptcy court in Pennsylvania and no one could find a copy of the FRCP—apparently the judge's clerk had taken his copy someplace. Opposing counsel said, 'Mr. Haller can't do this,' and I said, 'It's right there in the rules,' which I had on my Palm. I showed it to the judge, and he said, 'Look at that, Mr. Plaintiff's Attorney, he can do it.' A little later another issue came up, and again I said, 'It's in the rules,' and the judge didn't even check this time. He just said, 'I believe you.' Basically, I had instant credibility, since I had the only copy of the rules. The other attorney was very frustrated."

§ 6.6 E-mail and Internet Access

Many lawyers use their PDAs to read and reply to e-mail. With Palm cell phone combinations,[5] or wireless Palm Powered™ PDAs such as the Palm VII, the Palm i705, and the Tungsten, or any Palm model to which you have attached an external modem, you can access the Internet, and retrieve, read, and reply to e-mail on line in real time. Even with nonwireless models without a modem, you can configure the Mail program (which comes with every Palm Powered™ PDA) to HotSync any unread e-mail from your main computer's e-mail in-box to your PDA. You can read and write replies to your e-mail on the PDA, then HotSync your replies back to your main computer's e-mail program, from which they are sent out over the Internet. Many lawyers have found even this offline e-mail capability to be extremely useful.

Here are a variety of benefits you can derive from your PDA's e-mail and Internet access capability:

- **Managing e-mail overload**. It seems as if the number of e-mails each of us receives grows daily. In order to keep up with this constant influx, it can be very helpful to use your PDA at least to skim through your e-mails to determine which ones are worth reading in depth. Whether you have HotSynced the contents of your e-mail in-box onto your PDA, or your PDA has the capability to receive e-mails directly, having your e-mails on your PDA means you can read through them at times and places that would otherwise be nonproductive. Even if you prefer to sort your e-mail initially on your desktop computer, if you leave the low-level e-mail in your desktop's e-mail in-box for syncing onto your PDA, you can review these lower-priority e-mails during what would otherwise be downtime away from the office, which frees up office time for more valuable work. The extra benefit of being able to receive e-mail on your PDA wirelessly is that it allows you, as New York lawyer Chet Lustgarten puts it, "to be efficient because I can get on my e-mail anywhere, and I'm away from my desk a lot of the time. Even when I'm away from a computer, in a restaurant, in Starbucks, I can still reach my e-mail. All the world is my office. The concept of being connected everywhere is immensely powerful."
- **Sending e-mail away from the office**. Of course, being able to read e-mail is only half the equation; with a PDA, you can initiate and respond to e-mail as well. If your access is offline, your e-mail won't be sent until the next time you HotSync, but that is still more efficient than reading printouts of your e-mail. If you prefer wireless access you can avoid even that time delay. Although at this stage of technological development the connection speed on a PDA tends to be more cumbersome than on a desktop, it is still, as Ron Feinman has discovered, "very useful to be able to send the occasional e-mail wirelessly. The connection speed is slow, but it's very doable for those times when you really need to get or send something." Arizona lawyer Robert Fleming says, "I can take care of e-mail while waiting for a case in court. I can e-mail the office saying I just realized I needed something here." While he doesn't use his Palm e-mail program on a regular basis, New Hampshire lawyer and technology consultant Bruce Dorner finds it useful to "send myself an e-mail for any follow-up tasks I have to do once I'm back in the office, because it helps to have a visual reminder

show up my big computer." Of course, you can also send e-mail to your support staff, so you don't have to wait until you return to the office to let your staff know whenever you think of something you would like them to do. David Ransin has found this technique helps him fight his tendency toward procrastination, "which is the bane of every lawyer I know. With the Palm I can process a thought the first time it occurs to me. If I have a thought at ten o'clock at night about something I want my staff to do, I'll write out an e-mail right away, and then I can forget about it. For example, I use a priority call system to guard my time, and my secretary screens all my calls, and only the people on the priority call list get through to me. That list is constantly changing, and I use the Palm e-mail to let my secretary know who's on the list and who's off at any given moment."

- **Keeping up with professional reading**. There is a wide and ever-growing variety of legal publications available as e-newsletters, or on the Internet, so you can download this content onto your PDA to read at your convenience. One easy way to accomplish this is to set your AvantGo channels[6] to automatically download your preferred publications.
- **Internet access in a pinch**. You can also surf the Web on your PDA with programs like Eudora Web or AOLWebClip.[7] While Web pages are slower to load and less visually detailed than on a desktop computer, it is very handy to have this backup access to the Web. Bryan Sims tells of the time "when my computer at home died, and I had to search for tech support on Microsoft's Web site. I plugged a modem into my Visor's springboard expansion slot, and went to the Web site on the Visor. I was able to get my home computer up and running again, and didn't have to wait until I got back to the office to start working again." Another time off-site Internet access can be invaluable is when you need to do some quick legal research. Gerald Privin likes being able to "access a Web service I subscribe to that allows attorneys to e-mail specific questions, say, 'What's the effect of a second DUI on a driver's license?' and by the next day four different attorneys will have answered you. I also used Westlaw Wireless, which was the next best thing to sliced bread, but very expensive. But it was great because you got the answer right there, and then you could e-mail the citation to your office."
- **Virus protection**. Christopher Stovall describes how he uses the Palm's e-mail function for virus protection: "If I get a suspicious e-mail on my desktop computer, I'll sync it to my Visor and open it there. You can usually identify the fingerprint of a possible virus: either it's gibberish or poor English or has a weird attachment. Virtually all the time our network antivirus software will catch it, but every now and then

I'll get a suspicious e-mail. I've heard nothing about Palm viruses for about a year and a half, so I assume most e-mail viruses are designed to take down a Windows machine rather than exploiting anything in the Palm operating system. Even if my assumption is wrong, it's better to have a crashed Visor than a crashed desktop, because you can always do a hard reset, HotSync, and start over."[8]

§ 6.7 Networking

You can use a PDA to facilitate both technological and human forms of networking.

- **Your PDA can be a low-tech way to connect with your secretary**. The HotSync function can be used connect a PDA-using lawyer with his desktop-using secretary. Bruce Dorner tells of a solo personal-injury lawyer who asked for his help in automating his practice.[9] The lawyer had never used a computer, and had no interest in learning how to do so, or even learning how to type. His secretary had the only computer in the office. The lawyer followed Bruce's advice to purchase a Palm Powered™ PDA and have his secretary install the Palm Desktop software on her computer. This solved the lawyer's primary problem of inefficient coordination of his schedule between himself and his secretary. It was a revelation, Bruce told me, that a Palm appeared to be the best way to connect the lawyer with his secretary. As Bruce put it, "Whenever this attorney arrives at his office, his secretary will grab his necktie and hold it until he gives her his Palm. Once it's synced, she'll let go of his necktie and give him back his Palm. She'll do the same thing after lunch, and again before going home. She used to have to flip through page after page in her version of his diary, manually updating any changes he'd made in his paper calendar."[10] From this experience Bruce concluded, "For a solo office this may be all that's needed to keep an attorney and secretary from tripping over each other with missed appointments or unrecorded critical dates. . . . [W]hile most people look at the [Palm] solely as an accessory to a computer, it can also be used as an alternative to learning to use a computer. This is particularly useful for those middle-aged lawyers who never learned to type and have been left in the dust of the computer revolution. They want to know how they can compete, and this offers a way for them to enter the computer age."[11]
- **Your PDA can be the link between your home and office computers**. The HotSync function can also be used as a low-tech way to network two computers. Bryan Sims describes how he uses his Visor as a way

to link his office and home computers. "I HotSync my Visor with both computers. At the office, I try to HotSync first thing whenever I get to the office, then again before I leave at the end of the day. Once I get home, I sync the Visor with my home computer. So I have three complete copies of everything. Since the backups are at different locations, a catastrophe either at home or at the office would destroy only one backup." Moreover, this facilitates working at home, since any changes you make in any documents synced onto a PDA used in this manner will travel with you to be synced onto your office computer.

- **Your PDA can assist you in your person-to-person networking**. PDAs can be used to facilitate networking in the nontechnical sense as well. You can use your PDA to beam your own contact record—your electronic business card, if you will—to other Palm PDA users. Robert Fleming relates, "The other day I was at a meeting and realized I didn't have any business cards, so we beamed each other our cards." Bruce Dorner has found that "it's really nice to exchange electronic business cards with other people who have Palms—you just tap a few times, and I've got your card, you've got mine, with no scanning necessary. I would caution Palm users not to keep personal information in a note attached to their own entry in their Palm address book. A lot of people put down things like the codes to their home security systems, their Social Security number, and their bank account numbers. I got a lot of nifty stuff that way." In addition, keeping memory-jogging notes in your contacts' Address Book entries can enhance your networking efforts, as illustrated by this lawyer (who wishes to remain anonymous): "I was in at a meeting yesterday, and three people I didn't recognize came up to me. I snuck up to my SmartPhone and reminded myself where I met them—it was great. Nobody realized I was looking up their contact information, because I was just tapping on my SmartPhone."

§ 6.8 Travel

The portability of a PDA makes it a handy companion on the road, both for excursions around town and for longer trips. Here are some ways to get the most from your PDA when traveling.

- **Using your PDA to manage your itinerary**. Even without a specific add-on itinerary program, a basic PDA is wonderful for organizing travel information. You can insert airline flights as events in your calendar,[12] and attach notes for details such as confirmation numbers and seat assignments. If your travel arrangements are made by e-mail, you can simply copy and paste the e-mail into your desktop calendar software as an attached note, and HotSync it to your PDA. Hotel information can also be inserted as an event on the appropriate day (again, with confirmation numbers and specifics like checkout time contained in an attached note), or, if you stay frequently at a particular hotel, you might want to enter the hotel as a separate contact record. It is easy to share your travel information from your PDA: you can either beam the events directly to another PDA, or e-mail a detailed version of your calendar. Bruce Dorner recounts the benefits of these techniques: "When I receive an e-mail from the airline with the flight schedule, or a confirmation from the hotel, I'll copy and paste it into a note attached to the corresponding event in Date Book, so everything's right in there, and I don't have to go digging through my briefcase to find things. Also, in case my secretary wants to get in touch with me, she has access to the HotSynced copy of my calendar, so she has all the flight information and contact data for the hotel. I'll e-mail all that to my wife. The Palm gives me the ability to have all the information myself, and to share it, all without using any paper." If your PDA has wireless capability, you can access the Internet to get updated flight information instead of having to call the airline's 800 number and wade through its cumbersome voicemail options.

There are also add-on programs, such as Gulliver, which are specifically designed to help you manage your itinerary, and come preinstalled with the toll-free numbers for airlines, hotel chains, and car rental agencies. If you travel very frequently, it can be easier to use such a program, since the programs usually allow you to insert information quickly by tapping a pull-down menu of preinstalled options.

- **Handy travel information**. There are many add-on programs containing information helpful for travelers. For example, the program Worldphone has the international toll-free access numbers for telephone carriers such as MCI and Sprint, and the program WorldMate has international telephone area codes. You can also download any number of maps and guides for countries, cities, and public transportation systems around the globe; and install your choice of bilingual or multilingual translating dictionaries. The popular Web-clipping program AvantGo can provide you with up-to-date weather forecasts.
- **Handy travel devices**. There are also many add-on interactive programs containing functions designed for travelers. You can choose among dozens of different travel clocks. WorldMate contains conversions calculators for currency and clothing sizes, as well as a clock you can set for six different time zones. Even the popular freeware program BigClock works well for traveling, because you can set it to show

two different time zones simultaneously. Some wireless PDAs, such as the Kyocera SmartPhone, automatically update the time to correspond to whatever time zone you're in. You can also attach a global positioning system to certain models of PDAs. Finally, there are a plethora of add-ons for those who travel by car, such as programs to calculate and track your auto mileage and service needs.

- **Customized directions.** You can install the Palm OS version of the popular program MapQuest (which provides step-by-step, customized driving directions between specific locations, including residential addresses) to download information from the Internet either directly (with a wireless PDA) or by HotSyncing your PDA with a computer that is online. If you do a lot of driving, the wireless version is most helpful, since if you get lost you can obtain updated directions from your actual location to your intended destination. MapQuest is also good for documenting mileage for tax deduction purposes.

  The personal navigation program Vindigo (described in detail in Section 2.15) helps you locate restaurants, entertainment, stores, and services (such as banks, ATM's, parking lots, and public restrooms) in dozens of major cities by providing interactive maps as well as directions for walking, driving, or using public transportation. Howard Wolf-Rodda uses Vindigo "if I'm looking for a place to entertain a client, I'll search for good restaurants near the client's site. Vindigo includes restaurant reviews, so I can say to the client, 'Oh, this got a good review, what do you think?'"
- **Travel journal**. And of course, you can always use the PDA's Memo Pad (and, ideally, a portable keyboard) for recording the highlights of your trip.

§ 6.9 Tracking Expenses

One of the built-in but lesser-used programs on the Palm OS is the Expense program. While not as versatile as the many add-on expense tracking programs,[13] it can be a valuable part of your office organizational system. If you keep your PDA with you at all times, the Expense program is a convenient place to record business expenses (including auto mileage) quickly on the spot, including background information such as form of payment, vendor, location, and other individuals present at business meals. You can also attach a lengthy note to each expense entry, so you can include a client-matter number and other specifics. As always, the constant presence of your PDA means you can develop the habit of inserting all of your expense information immediately, so your expense reports are complete and accurate. Even small items such as the legal pads you buy at Office Depot or Wal-Mart, and taxicab fare[14] for short jaunts, are likely to end up in your PDA. After synchronizing your PDA with your desktop computer, you or your secretary can print out expense reports in Microsoft Excel format, and copy and paste the information into the firm's official expense reporting program.

Bryan Sims has written,[15] "[A]lthough it may be hard to believe, my Visor saves me money. It does this with its expense tracking program. As a litigator, I average four mornings a week in court. Because I practice in the Chicago suburbs, I must drive to and from various courthouses, pay tolls to get to and from court, and pay parking fees, whether meters or in a garage. Any time that I incur an expense such as this, I immediately record it in my Visor. At the end of the month, and after a quick synch, I have a spreadsheet that totals my mileage and other expenses for the month. Thus, by spending a few seconds recording the charges when they are incurred, and less than two minutes generating the final spreadsheet, I have accurately recorded and reported all of my expenses. I know other attorneys who spend up to an hour at the end of every month trying to calculate their reimbursable expenses. Not only is that hour at the end of the month wasted time, but there is no doubt in my mind that those attorneys forget expenses for which they are entitled to reimbursement. By using the simple program included with my Visor, I waste none of my time that I could use working, and I know that I am submitting an accurate expense report."

§ 6.10 Miscellaneous Work-Related Uses of a PDA

Here is an illustrative sampling of various other uses for your Palm Powered™ PDA:

- **Electronic sticky notes.** There are several add-on programs, such as Diddlebug and BugMe, designed to function as the electronic equivalent of a pad of sticky notes. (Later Palm OS models also come with a similar but less powerful program, NotePad.[16]) The outstanding benefit of these programs is that you can attach a customized alarm to each note. While it is easy to overlook a paper sticky note that ends up as one of dozens mounted on the rim of your computer monitor, you cannot ignore the electronic version, since a note pops up on your PDA's screen at the designated time even if the PDA is off or you are using another application. Christopher Stovall is a typical Diddlebug user: "I like it for jotting things down when I'm in a hurry and don't have two hands free to do Graffiti. I'll set an alarm if it's something I need to remember. I use it for both business and personal stuff, things like a phone number or a time entry I want to remember to put in the system when I get back to the office. Or I'll be reading something and see a case mentioned and jot it down in Diddlebug. I use it basically instead of the Memo function." Reid Trautz uses Diddlebug when "a quick thought comes to me and I want to get it down fast, or if I'm listening to the radio and they mention a Web site I want to check out, it goes in Diddlebug first. I usually open my Palm with that program, and generally have about five or six things that pop up at me."

Bruce Dorner uses SimpleSketch, which like Diddlebug allows you to sketch directly on the Palm's screen. "I'll use it if I need to do a sketch of an intersection where an accident happened, or if I need to draw a diagram of where people were standing when an incident occurred. For example, in a slip-and-fall case, I'll sketch out where the counter was, where the piece of lettuce was on the floor. Or I'll just use it when I'm having a bad Graffiti day, and find it easier to just write on the screen than deal with Graffiti."

- **Camera.** Certain Palm Powered™ PDAs allow you to attach various pieces of hardware add-on devices. Gerald Privin tells this story about using his PDA with an attached camera: "I was in another county on a case once, and while I was there I realized I was near the scene of another case I was handling—a criminal case in which I had to show my client was wrongfully stopped by the police, who claimed that my client had made an illegal left turn. When I finished with the first case, I made a side trip to the location where the police stopped my client. I keep a camera module for my Visor in my briefcase at all times, which is no problem since it's so light and small. I attached the camera to my Visor using the springboard attachment slot, and used the Visor to take pictures of the scene. When I got back to my office, I printed the pictures out on my computer's color printer. At the hearing on our motion to suppress, I was able to ask to the police officer, 'Is that what the street looked like?' Our motion was granted, and I'm convinced it was because the judge saw those pictures of that location. The judge was familiar with that area, and knew that everyone turned at that particular location, which is basically a dirt path. The picture really was worth a thousand words. And another time I was driving somewhere with a client, and at a red light the car in front of us rolled backwards into us, so while the two drivers were arguing I took out my Visor and the camera attachment and took pictures. It was helpful to show it to the insurance company, and ultimately my client was held not responsible. Another reason I like the camera module is that you can take pictures unobtrusively because it doesn't look like you're holding a camera."

- **Clocks and timers.** There are many uses for the various clocks and timers you can install on your PDA. Gerald Privin uses BigClock as his regular alarm clock. "It goes off every morning at 6:45 a.m.—you can hear it from across the room. The screen on my Visor Prism is so bright, I've used it as a nightlight, and even as a flashlight." Bruce Dorner also uses BigClock in court: "If the judge gives me fifteen minutes I'll time it on BigClock. That way I don't have to keep looking at my wristwatch." Whenever Minnesota lawyer Don Aldrich stands up in court, he limits himself "to twenty minutes. Studies have shown this is the attention span of the average juror. I load up BigClock with its huge timer, and have the Palm lying open on the podium. I like to move around a lot, and I can see the time from quite some distance without anyone knowing what I am doing."[17] On a personal note, I use BigClock frequently as well. If I'm working on a crucial document, I'll set the count-down timer to go off at least every thirty minutes to remind me to save and back up the document. I also use the count-timer as an antiprocrastination device.[18]
- **Oral argument.** PDAs can assist you in court in ways other than keeping track of time. David Ransin "argued a motion off my Visor. I took Graffiti notes on what opposing counsel said, and just argued from that. The judge was looking at me funny. I had no paper there at all." Gerald Privin has also argued bench motions from his PDA, but for tactical reasons refrains from doing so in front of juries. "Once I tried to do a *voir dire* with all the questions on my Palm, but I don't do that any more. Juries think you're a wise guy trying to dazzle them. But judges don't care how the information is presented as long as it is correct." Don Aldrich uses outlining software on his Palm III to prepare for oral argument.
- **Excel spreadsheet.** Just as you can install add-on programs that sync seamlessly with your desktop Microsoft Word documents, so can you install programs that sync with your desktop's Microsoft Excel spreadsheet. (I have actually found the PDA versions of Excel easier to learn to use than the desktop versions.) Gerald Privin uses a PDA version of Excel to manage "some commercial accounts that I'm doing collections for. I have spreadsheets showing how the judgment is accruing interest, how the garnishment has affected the amount, and how the money is to be distributed—how much goes to the client, and how much to the attorney. You can do all that on Excel spreadsheet, which I keep it on my Prism as well as my desktop. When clients see it on the Prism, they get a kick out of it—the device is so tiny, yet you have a spreadsheet on it. They'll ask me to fax or e-mail it to them, and of course I do." Garrett Maass syncs his Excel spreadsheets with his Kyocera SmartPhone using Quicksheet, "which does everything Excel

does. I use it for managing the grading in the classes I teach in criminal law and paralegal skills at the College in Legal Arts in Portland."

- **Date counters.** There are various small add-on programs that serve the limited but useful function of calculating the number of days between dates, or projecting what date is a certain number of days from another date. Christopher Stovall says about the freeware program Dates!: "It's a small program but I use it all the time to calculate response deadlines for discovery, at least to double-check my own calculation if I've done it in my head." Bruce Dorner also likes Dates! "I do a lot of business with ninety days for return of service. I tend to look for free tools. As a solo attorney, one of my mottoes is 'Never spend money if you can get it for free.'"
- **Financial calculators.** If the basic calculator already on your PDA is insufficient for your needs, there are a variety of powerful add-on financial calculators available for installation on a Palm Powered™ PDA. Some of these calculators are specifically designed to calculate depreciation, bond price/yield functions, mortgage payments (under both the U.S. and Canadian systems), capital growth, and rates of return. The programmable KK-12C Financial Calculator emulates the functions of the popular Hewlett-Packard handheld HP-12C Programmable Financial Calculator.[19] Florida lawyer Lowell Schoenfeld uses the calculator Parens Lite frequently, "especially the amortization program. I also created memos with the Federal Estate Tax Tables and Unified Credits, so I can sit in meetings and easily calculate someone's estate tax obligation assuming deaths in different calendar years."
- **Password generator.** Robert Fleming likes the "simple freeware program Strip, at **www.zetetic.net**, which is a secure tool for recalling important passwords. It will also generate random passwords for you, and store them automatically."
- **An escape hatch.** One lawyer shared a technique with the proviso that he remain anonymous. This PDA user would set an alarm to go off on the PDA during meetings, then use that as an excuse to leave the meeting. There is actually an add-on program specifically designed to assist you in executing this ploy: NerdAlert (**www.hottrix.com**) lets you set your handheld's sound to go off after a brief time delay, with different sound effects so you can pick one that emulates your cell phone's ring tone.

§ 6.11 Juggling Work and Home

A big part of any lawyer's life is managing work obligations in light of personal responsibilities such as community, household, and parental activities. A PDA can help lawyers manage all of these duties more effectively. As Domingo Such puts it, "When the personal is under control you can focus more on the business." The following stories illustrate ways lawyers have used their Palm Powered™ PDAs to successfully juggle the multiple areas of their lives.

- **Multitasking**. Vedia Jones-Richardson finds her Visor helps with multitasking. "I like having things handy for downtime. I can be at a soccer game reading e-mails, or if I have fifteen minutes to spare when I'm shopping, I can use that time productively since I keep my kids' and husband's clothing sizes stored in their contact record. I've been experimenting with different shopping add-ons, such as Shopper and Jshopper, which allow you to categorize things by store. I also have a running memo that consists of more long-term things I'm looking for, such as wines I like. I keep a separate list for Christmas, which is handy because sometimes I'll buy a gift and then forget about it. When I was shopping for a computer I kept a list of specs. I have a memo with the product number for the ink cartridge my printer uses. The PDA also helps when I'm assigned soccer-related tasks such as bringing snacks to the next practice session, or reminding myself when the next PTA meeting is scheduled." Catherine McCabe used her PDA "to give a speech at her sister's birthday party. I saw someone do that at a goodbye dinner for a work colleague. I find that the integration between items in my personal and work life is easier and more time efficient with the Palm than it was with the Franklin Planner."
- **Keeping track of anniversaries and gift ideas**. Reid Trautz half-jokingly says, "This Palm saved my marriage. I keep an ongoing memo called Gifts. When I get an idea for a gift, or someone gives me an idea, or my wife drops hints throughout the year, I make a note in the memo. When our anniversary, my wife's birthday, or the holidays roll around, I no longer have to go to her two days before to try to figure out what she wants. I do the same with my kids." Domingo Such also uses his Palm Powered™ cell phone to "put down things like my anniversary so I can plan ahead and can buy a gift ahead of time. It does help my marriage."
- **Major purchases**. There are a huge number of add-on programs that can help you manage the various potentially time-consuming projects of modern life. For example, Christopher Stovall "downloaded a freeware application called Loan Helper, which was useful when we went car shopping. It has fields for the trade-in amount, base price of the new car, tax rate, additional fees, down payment, interest rate, and the installment period. You fill in the data you know and the program solves it for whatever you leave blank. I also have LubeLog to keep

track of car maintenance and services. You define a vehicle and every time you get an oil change you can fill in the date and the mileage, then can scroll through and track your service records." Many lawyers (myself included) have used their PDAs to keep track of the myriad of details involved in buying or selling a house and refinancing a mortgage.

§ 6.12 Recreation

Since a well-balanced mix of work and play can help you manage stress and contribute to your health and productivity, it is appropriate to use your PDA to help you have fun. There are basically two ways to use a PDA for recreation: with the necessary software and content, a PDA facilitates real-world recreational activities such as exercising and movie-going, while other add-on programs transform the PDA into a self-contained entertainment device for activities such as reading, games, and crossword puzzles. The latter category is especially convenient when you want to be discreet, such as when you are in court waiting for your case to come up. In such circumstances, it would be inappropriate to pull out a GameBoy or a newspaper, but if you are just using your PDA (with the sound turned off), no one knows for certain that you're not just checking your calendar. Bryan Sims agrees that AvantGo and Palm games "are amazingly useful when you're sitting in court waiting for the judge to come out." Don Aldrich writes, "It is a lifesaver for those indefinite periods of waiting a working lawyer is constantly faced with. I swear, I spend half my life sitting in a courtroom or hallway waiting. There are plenty of cool time-wasters available, for cheap or free."[20]

Here are some ideas for using your PDA to help you relax and enjoy yourself.

- **Reading**. Install one of the many Palm document readers on your PDA, and you can download and read the ever-growing number of e-books available for the Palm platform. You can use AvantGo to download current, PDA-friendly editions of a wide variety of newspapers and periodicals automatically each time you HotSync (provided your desktop computer is online). Reid Trautz says, "I like that with AvantGo I can read the newspaper and other things on the go. That's how I keep up with my hometown newspaper (the *Minneapolis Star Tribune*), and the *Wall Street Journal*." Virginia lawyer Bob Walker also likes AvantGo "for CNN, the *Washington Post*, the *New York Times*, and the bankruptcy headlines." Gerald Privin used his Palm Powered™ Prism "for recreation when my family and I went on a mission trip to South America, and instead of carrying books with me, I loaded e-books on my Visor and took a lot of AAA batteries. When you read on a PDA, you can read in bed without disturbing anyone." New Hampshire lawyer Louise Spencer also touts the ability to read in bed without turning on a light as a valuable aid in maintaining marital harmony.

- **Games**. There are hundreds, if not thousands, of games available for installation on your Palm Powered™ PDA. These include versions of standard card games such as bridge, pinochle, and multiple variations of solitaire; board games such as Scrabble, chess, and backgammon; and all sorts of action, adventure, and arcade games. An unscientific sampling suggests that the simple game Bejeweled is among the most popular.[21] Don Aldrich reports, "My main passion in life is chess. Chess Recorder allows me to record or load games, with notes. Knight Pad allows me to directly download my e-mail games to the Palm to be worked on in spare moments."[22] Bruce Dorner likes Pocket Chess, and enjoys sampling trial versions of other programs "that I'll download, use for a while, then delete." Another lawyer, who for obvious reasons prefers to remain anonymous, plays the politically incorrect game DopeWars in its Palm add-on version.[23] The lawyer confides, "I keep it purposely misfiled in the 'Utilities' category so my kids won't find it when they borrow my Palm to play games on it."
- **Crossword puzzles.** There are dozens of crossword programs available from sites such as **www.palm.com** and **www.palmgear.com**. Gerald Privin, who likes to do crossword puzzles on his Visor, reports, "For a one-time fee you can subscribe to the *New York Times* crossword puzzle, and then download ten to fifteen at a time. When the puzzle's on your Palm you can have fun in the courtroom without ticking off the judge, as you would if you pulled out an actual newspaper."
- **Movie information**. If you live in one the major cities covered by the personal navigation program Vindigo, you will find it more efficient to consult your recently synced PDA than your local newspaper to determine where and when particular movies are playing. With Vindigo, you simply insert the name of the movie and the program will tell you where it is playing, so you don't have to read through all the theater listings in the newspaper to locate a particular movie. Vindigo also provides you with movie reviews and directions to the theater. Vindigo allows you to keep a customized list of movies you want to see, so you can cross-compare with your movie-going companions to determine which movies are on all of your lists. These lists remain handy for years in case you miss a movie's first run, and plan to rent the video instead.
- **Music**. There is an impressive variety of Palm add-on programs for the amateur musician. There are programs that allow you write, edit, and

actually play music on your PDA; programs that serve as metronomes, tuning forks, and ear trainers; and programs that help you learn how to read music. Music aficionados can download a dictionary of musical terms as well as database programs specifically designed to keep track of every possible parameter of a library of music records, tapes, CDs, and DVDs.

- **Aviation**. There are dozens of programs to help the amateur pilot make flight-related calculations, record data, and keep other important information close at hand. For example, there are programs containing FAA questions from the private-pilot written examination, airport directories, and logbooks (both permanent versions as well as temporary ones intended to hold data about a flight until you can enter it into your official written logbook). You can download programs to track VFR[24] trip information while flying, software that allows wireless PDAs to access up-to-the-minute information such as weather forecasts, airport delays, and RVR[25] airport data; and programs with flight-planning functions allowing you to calculate fuel flow, fuel required, rate of climb and descent, stall speed, true airspeed, calibrated airspeed, equivalent airspeed, and many other key variables. Robert Fleming, who flies a Cessna 207, uses an add-on program designed for pilots going through the preflight and postflight checklists, but "it's also good for things like shutting down the summer cabin for the winter, or getting ready to go to court."
- **Fitness**. Whether your are a lifelong exerciser or a fitness wannabe, there are numerous add-on programs you can use to plan, record, and monitor your exercise, weight, food intake, and other health-related information. There are logs designed for walkers, runners, swimmers, cyclists, and weight-lifters; many of these logs can be adapted for use with other activities as well. There are programs to help you quit smoking; track your water intake; limit your calories; record your blood pressure; and calculate your body-mass index, ideal weight, basal metabolism rate, body fat percentage, and heart rate. A meditation timer program helps you relax by playing a tone at specific intervals to alert you to breathe at the rate you desire. There are database programs with a vast store of information such as calorie counts for specific foods and activities, and cookbooks specializing in nutritious recipes.

Notes

1. See Section 2.3.
2. See Chapter 19 for more information about timekeeping programs for Palm OS.
3. See Chapter 19.
4. See Section 15.5 for a complete explanation of Graffiti ShortCuts, including time stamps.

5. One of the most intriguing recent developments has been the convergence of PDAs and cell phones. Users like having to carry only one device instead of two—since you have one less device to keep track of—and they enjoy the benefits of integrating the Palm and cell phone functions, which allows them the efficiency of such conveniences as dialing the cell phone by tapping on a person's name in Address Book, automatically exporting caller ID information to Address Book, Internet access, and fax capability. The one potential disadvantage of a combination PDA and cell phone—the inconvenience of referring to your PDA while you are holding the cell phone to your ear—is solved by using a headset or the speaker-phone feature of some models, such as the Kyocera SmartPhone.

6. See Sections 2.14 and 18.5 for discussions of AvantGo.

7. See Section 18.4 for more information about programs for Internet access using your PDA.

8. See Section 22.1 for a discussion of a hard reset, and see generally Chapter 22 for information on troubleshooting. See also Section 21.8 for a discussion of viruses that have affected the Palm operating system.

9. Bruce recounted this story both in a one-on-one telephone interview with me, and in his article "A Solution for the Technophobic Lawyer," which was originally published in *Lawyers Weekly USA* (January 25, 1999), and reprinted in NetTech's *Legal Technology Strategies Newsletter* (April 1999), **http://www.nettechinc.com/issue8.htm**

10. Telephone interview with the author.

11. "A Solution for the Technophobic Lawyer," supra.

12. You can either round departure and arrival times to the nearest five minutes (as required by the limitations of the built-in calendar program), or you can install a simple add-on utility such as Time Hack, which allows you to set start and end time to the minute.

13. Its options, which cannot be edited, apply only to business expenses.

14. On many occasions when I have worked late, I have used my PDA's backlight to calculate and record taxicab fares in the dark.

15. TechnoFeature: My Multi-Faceted Prism, TechnoLawyer Community e-mail (May 14, 2002). Originally published on pdaJD.com (**http://www.pdajd.com/vertical/features/MyMulti.xml**) on December 26, 2002.

16. The difference between newer NotePad and the original Memo Pad is that NotePad captures sketches, drawings, and handwriting, while Memo Pad allows you to insert only text via Graffiti, the on-screen keyboard, or a portable keyboard. (NotePad does not translate handwriting into electronic text.) Unlike Diddlebug and BugMe, NotePad does not allow you to attach alarms to notes.

17. Don C. Aldrich, "How One Attorney Uses a PalmPilot," NetTech Inc.'s *Legal Technology Strategies,* Issue #10 (June 1, 1999), at **www.nettechinc.com/lts.htm**

18. As I describe in my time management seminars, the technique is this: set the timer for fifteen minutes, and for just those fifteen minutes, work full-blast on the project on which you've been procrastinating. When the timer goes off, decide immediately whether to stop at that moment, or to reset the timer and work for another fifteen minutes. Invariably, those first fifteen minutes break the inertial barrier so that it's more tempting to keep going than it is to stop.

19. The KK-12C Financial Calculator is available from **www.palm.com**

20. Don C. Aldrich, "How One Attorney Uses a PalmPilot," NetTech Inc.'s *Legal Technology Strategies,* Issue #10 (June 1, 1999), at **www.nettechinc.com/lts.htm**

21. Purely in the interest of research, I decided to test this game's appeal for myself. As a result, I can personally vouch for the entertainment value, addictiveness, and time-wasting potential of Bejeweled.

22. Don C. Aldrich, "How One Attorney Uses a PalmPilot," NetTech Inc.'s *Legal Technology Strategies,* Issue #10 (June 1, 1999), at **www.nettechinc.com/lts.htm**

23. Based on a DOS game of the same name and available on a variety of Web sites (do a Google search for "DopeWars and Palm"), DopeWars is described as "intended for mature audiences only" and "is a game in which the objective is to make money through buying and selling illicit narcotics. There are eight types of drugs and six locations. At each location, five to seven drugs will be commodities. At the beginning of the game, you have a small amount of cash, an empty savings account, and a sizable debt to a loan shark. Police officers, money troubles, and market forces make this strategy game a challenge."

24. Visual flight rules.

25. Runway visual range.

Part

III

Other Voices

Other Voices

7

This section contains lists of the "Top Ten" (or five, or twelve) suggestions on various aspects of Palm usage from other experienced Palm users, all of whom are lawyers or legal professionals. It also includes a spirited debate on the relative merits of the Palm OS versus the Pocket PC operating system. Similar suggestions show up on various different lists (and in other parts of this book as well); these areas of consensus are probably worth special attention. While I don't agree with all of the guest contributors' suggestions, I found them interesting and informative, and I'm confident that you will too.

Alan J. Steinberg's Top Ten Tips for Getting the Most from Your PDA

1. Use your PDA [Alan uses a Palm m505 in the latest chapter of his life] for client identification. In my small firm, I am a rainmaker as well as the janitor. When I'm at social functions and recognize clients but cannot recall their names, I sometimes can recall where they worked. By utilizing the search feature in my PDA, I can search for all contacts that work for the XYZ Company. Hopefully, when the Palm presents me with the choices it has made using employer's name, the name association will prompt me to remember the name of the client. In the client data list, I also list names of spouse and children. You would be surprised how effective it is to walk up to

client John Jones and ask about Mrs. Susie Jones, his wife, and little Danny and little Sheila. You can see it in their eyes.

2. In my PDA, I have imported the names of all forty-two judges, clerks, and the respective telephone numbers of the circuits in which I practice. When I go to court, I can search for the appropriate division in which I have to appear and not have to walk to the main signboard for directions. In addition, the listing comes in very handy when I need to contact a judge or a clerk. In our circuits, there is a rotation of judges from various courtrooms to different courtrooms and, therefore, I have to keep this list up to date, which is not a big deal. Having it on my PDA has saved a lot of time on many occasions.
3. I have reduced certain court rules and key statutes to text files and imported them into my PDA. I find this particularly handy for my domestic work. In addition, we use a Form 14, the spreadsheet of which has been imported into my PDA for reference. In Missouri, the Form 14 is the Child Support Guide that is federally mandated and used in all states. I use the Palm-licensed eBook Reader that came with my PDA.
4. My PDA links with our office and document manager, Time Matters. By syncing two or three times a week, my PDA stays current with all of our clients and the various phone numbers and scheduling aspects that the office and document manager brings to my attention on my PC.
5. I quit bringing my laptop to seminars when I bought the PDA foldable keyboard. The keyboard is in three parts, and when it collapses, it is roughly the size of the PDA. I have no trouble in keyboarding the necessary notes into the PDA and uploading when syncing to my laptop when I return to my office. This saves a lot of wear and tear on my back.
6. Any attorney who involves himself or herself in litigation knows well that often one will be sitting around the courtroom waiting for something to happen. I have purchased novels as well as nonfiction books and carry them with me in my PDA. At present, I'm reading Jack Walsh's biography *Jack: Straight from the Gut*. See Web sites for eBook offerings, such as **www.pimpoint.com** and **www.topicsites.com**.
7. Recently, I had occasion to travel to Toronto, Canada. The exchange rate was 1.50 to 1. It's a good thing I had my currency converter with me, as it enabled me to make a quick conclusion as to what my wife was purchasing. Converters may be obtained from various Web sites, such as **www.oanda.com** and **http://pda.fastnet.it**.
8. Backup, backup, backup. I would have to say that since I am syncing with the office document and case manager, the backup necessity

has lessened somewhat from the days when my PDA was operating by itself. Nevertheless, I have an awful lot of ancillary programs loaded in my PDA to where it would be a great hassle for reinstallation rather than making simple backups. The newer PDAs have backup cards that fit in an expansion slot. It is so simple, why not do it all the time? Consider a program called Backup Buddy. I've been using this program for many years, and it is one of the best bargains available.

9. Syncing my PDA takes about ten minutes. If I want to install a single program, I have an ancillary product called Install Buddy. (I am not subject to any relationship with Alexander Hinds Company that distributes any of the Buddy programs.) Install Buddy will simply install a program or a file without the necessity of syncing to our office document and case manager. You might consider a stand-alone install program. It takes just a few seconds. While the standard PDA HotSync programs will do what Install Buddy does, Install Buddy does it in seconds and without modification of standard presets.
10. Sometimes I wonder whether I should carry my PDA with me, particularly on the weekends. Invariably, the day that I forget to carry my PDA, or decide "it just ain't worth it today" is the day I find that I really need it. Bottom line—carry your PDA with you at all times.

Attorney **Alan J. Steinberg** has written a variety of articles on technology for lawyers, including "How the Palm Pilot will Change Your Life and Save You Money," "How the Palm Pilot Can Synchronize with your Docket Manager," and "How I Carry My Palm Pilot With Me All the Time." His detailed bio can be found at **www.steinberglaw.com/Alan.htm**, and his articles at **www.steinberglaw.com/AlanArticles.htm**.

Bob Ambrogi's Top Ten Law-Related Web Sites

Handhelds using the Palm operating system are power tools for the mobile lawyer. Thanks to the Palm, a lawyer need never be away from essential reference texts, key office documents, or important software applications.

But like any power tool, Palms are of limited use without the add-ons and how-to manuals that let users tailor them to specific tasks. If the Palm is a power tool, then the Web is its supply store.

Here is where Palm-using lawyers will find the software, documents, user guides and legal texts that take the Palm from techno-toy to law-practice essential. If you think Palms are just about calendars and contacts, the Web will prove you wrong.

Where on the Web do you find these applications? What follows are my picks of the Top Ten Web sites for Palm-using lawyers.

1. JurisPDA, **www.JurisPDA.com**
   Surprisingly few sites devote themselves exclusively to lawyers' use of the Palm. Of the handful that do, this is the best. Created for lawyers and law students by two professors and a librarian at New York Law School, the site aims to answer the question, "How can I use my handheld to be more effective and efficient?" It does this through its two main sections, one an inventory of useful software for lawyers and the other a collection of legal reference materials that you can download to a Palm, including the Constitution, the Federal Rules of Evidence and assorted Supreme Court cases. Elsewhere, the site provides tips on buying and getting started with a handheld, offers a Palm glossary, and lists links to other useful sites.
2. MemoWare, **www.memoware.com**
   Several sites let you download legal texts and documents to read on your Palm, but the best of them, weighing selection and ease of use, is MemoWare. From its front page, follow the "Law & Government" link to find hundreds of law-related documents, almost all of them offered free. Documents include practical tools, such as the Federal Criminal History Calculator and the Federal Sentencing Guidelines Lookup; various state and federal laws and regulations; selected court rules; historical documents, including landmark decisions from the Supreme Court; and items of current interest. All documents are labeled with date, format, creator, and file size to guide you in selecting.
3. DataViz, **www.dataviz.com**
   DataViz makes one of the handiest products out there for Palm-using lawyers. Called Documents To Go, it lets you use Word, Excel, and PowerPoint files on your handheld, as well as synchronize and view e-mail attachments, PDF files, pictures and charts. This means you can take Office files with you when you are on the road, retaining formatting and metadata,[1] and also create new files that you can later synchronize with your PC. Most Palm and Sony handhelds now come bundled with this software, but if you do not already have it, it is well worth the low price.
4. Palm Computing Resources for Lawyers,
   http://www.nettechinc.com/palm.htm
   A legal-technology consulting firm, NetTech, maintains this collection of links to Web resources for lawyers using Palms. The page could use an update; some links are dead. Nevertheless, it remains

useful as a starting point for finding legal and general resources and software for the Palm.

5. pdaJD, **www.pdajd.com**
   Ostensibly a site for lawyers, pdaJD manages to come across as surprisingly generic. In actuality, it is one of a series of "pda vertical" sites, each targeted at a specific profession: lawyers, doctors, financial professionals, realtors, and educators. Each draws content from the others, meaning that the "Articles" section, for example, is as likely to have a piece written by an MD as by a JD. That said, you can find some useful articles here—some actually written by or for lawyers—along with features such as a legal industry discussion board.
6. Palm Digital Media, **www.peanutpress.com**
   Known for years as Peanut Press before it was purchased by a subsidiary of Palm Inc., Palm Digital Media offers a selection of legal texts, among many other topics, that you can download and read on your Palm. Titles range from the practical to the educational to the entertaining. They include the Federalist Papers and the Texas Rules of Evidence alongside *Ladies and Gentlemen of the Jury: The Greatest Closing Arguments in Modern Law.* These texts are not free, but not expensive either. The Constitution costs $3.00; a legal dictionary is $12.75.
7. AvantGo, **avantgo.com**
   With so much of the information lawyers want being on the Web, AvantGo is an essential tool for the Palm. This free service allows you to download virtually any Web content to your Palm, whether or not you have a modem. On your way to a hearing, for example, you could go to a court's Web site and download its local rules, then store a map and driving directions. Even better, AvantGo offers exclusive news and information channels designed for the Palm. No modem is necessary. Select the sites you want, and when you sync your Palm with your computer, the Web pages are downloaded or updated, available for browsing offline. Of course, if your Palm has a modem, you can connect directly to the Internet and use AvantGo to browse any Web site.
8. MapQuest, **www.mapquest.com**
   Ten minutes before trial, and you can't find the courthouse! If you have a wireless handheld, not a problem. Just go to MapQuest and download the driving directions. But even those without wireless access can get driving directions on their Palm, simply by planning ahead. Go to MapQuest, get the map or driving directions you need, then click on the button, "Download Map to PDA." (If you haven't al-

ready, you will first need to install AvantGo.) Another map site, MapBlast, **www.mapblast.com**, offers a similar service.

9. Vindigo, **www.vindigo.com**
   Deposition completed, you emerge to an unfamiliar Manhattan street corner hungry and craving Indian food. With Vindigo, enter your address into your Palm, and up come the closest Indian restaurants. Check their reviews and ratings, then get detailed walking directions and maps to the one you select. After dinner, find local movie listings, the best nightspots, places to shop, or the nearest ATM. Vindigo covers an ever-expanding list of U.S. cities, and whether you are a visitor to the city or a resident, you will find this "personal navigator" indispensable. Long available for free, Vindigo now costs $24.95 a year. A similar service, still free, is Jungleport, **www.jungleport.com**.
10. PalmGear, **www.palmgear.com**
    For keeping up generally with the latest applications, utilities, games, or whatever for your Palm, PalmGear is a good choice. Besides downloads, the site offers news updates, tips, and more for Palm users.

Robert J. Ambrogi, a lawyer and journalist, is the author of *The Essential Guide to the Best (and Worst) Legal Sites on the Web*, and founder of the first Internet newsletter for lawyers, *legal.online*. Since 1993, he has written a syndicated monthly column about the Web, and he also writes the monthly "Web Watch" column for *Law Technology News*. When not writing about the Web, Ambrogi is vice president of editorial services for Jaffe Associates, **www.jaffeassociates.com**, and was formerly editorial director of the *National Law Journal*, director of the American Lawyer Media News Service, and coeditor of *Lawyers Weekly USA*. He can be reached at **rambrogi@legaline.com**.

Dennis M. Kennedy's Ten Tips for Users of Palm Powered™ Handheld Devices[2]

While handheld devices, the Palm computing devices in particular, give you an excellent "out of the box" experience, both their utility and your enjoyment can be greatly increased by taking advantage of a few simple tricks and techniques. I have used a Palm device for several years now and have collected the following ten favorite tips that I routinely share with handheld users.

1. Visit **pdaJD.com** regularly. **PdaJD.com** (**www.pdajd.com**) is a type of Web site known as a vertical portal, or vortal. That simply means that it is an excellent collection of resources on a specific topic for a specific audience. In the case of **pdaJD.com**, the topic is personal digital assistants and the audience is the legal profession. It is a one-stop

shop for lawyers and others to find information, articles, resources, and links to other helpful Web sites, all in one convenient place. New articles and content are added on a regular basis. The focus is on the practicing lawyer and this makes **pdaJD.com** much more useful to legal professionals than the standard Palm or PDA resource sites.

2. Get an outliner. Handheld devices can be extremely useful for putting together ideas and planning projects. A highly useful category of software products for lawyers includes outliners and other organizational programs. There are several excellent outliners for Palm devices in particular. My personal favorite is called BrainForest (**www.ultrasoft.com**), which has a lot of useful features and a helpful "leaf and branch" metaphor for organizing information and outlines. These outliner programs can help you plan articles and presentations, manage projects, and build sophisticated to-do lists, as well as store useful information in an outline format. BrainForest, in fact, is the one program on my Palm device that I use most often.
3. The Scotch tape trick. With good reason, Palm device users often worry about scratches and other wear and tear on the screen, especially in the area where Graffiti characters are entered by writing on the screen with a stylus. A very inexpensive and useful trick is to place a piece of Scotch Magic Tape (the kind commonly used to wrap presents) over the portion of the Palm screen where Graffiti characters are entered. This simple technique has two excellent benefits. First, it protects that portion of the screen from scratches by adding an inexpensive transparent protection. Second, the texture of the magic tape provides a better tactile experience (it's a better writing feel) and makes it a bit easier to write Graffiti characters.
4. Replace standard programs aggressively. Whether it is the calendar, to-do list, notes, address book, or calculator, third-party software providers have provided better versions of each of the standard programs found on Palm and other devices. These standard program replacements are inexpensive (usually $15 to $20) and add the features that you may think are "missing" from the standard programs supplied on your handheld device. Often these programs provide enhanced functionality and improve usability. For example, an enhanced calendar program may provide a variety of useful views, such as weekly calendar views, that are not available in the standard calendar program.
5. Look for software answers to all your wishes. There are now more than nineteen thousand programs that have been written for Palm devices. These programs have an amazing scope and variety, and run the range from the general to the highly specific. A trip to a Web site like **Palmgear.com** (**www.palmgear.com**) will often reveal a variety

of useful, often free, programs that will accomplish specific tasks or provide a specific functionality that you might be looking for. These days, in nearly every case, if you wish there were a certain type of Palm program, someone has already written it.

6. Buy a Palm book. While the operation of handheld devices, especially the Palm computing devices, is often intuitive and straightforward, every Palm user should think about buying a standard user guide such as David Pogue's *Palm Pilot: The Ultimate Guide* (Second Edition). Pogue's book explains all of the Palm basics and provides hundreds of tips, software recommendations, and other useful help. Pogue's book, in particular, comes with a CD that contains a large number of trial programs, free programs, and shareware to help you get started using your Palm computing device. There are other, more current books (Pogue's second edition has become a bit dated), so check out other books that are available and find a book to help you learn more about effectively using your Palm device.
7. Subscribe to *Handheld Computing Magazine*'s e-mail newsletter. To keep up to date with current developments, especially on Palm computing devices, *Handheld Computing Magazine*'s e-mail newsletter is an excellent resource. This free e-mail newsletter comes to you on a weekly basis in a PDF format, with a short feature article and short reviews, news, and links to useful sites and new software. This newsletter is a great way to keep up to date with current developments, learn about new product announcements, and to find new and useful software. Information about subscribing to the weekly newsletter and the print version of the magazine can be found at **www.hhcmag.com**, an essential resource.
8. Sync addresses to handheld only. One of the most highly downloaded Palm programs is a program called UnDupe, which allows you to eliminate duplicate entries in your Palm address book. The reason this program is so popular is that it is very easy to accidentally duplicate all the entries in your address book when syncing data between your Palm and your desktop. Your choice is either to spend a significant amount of time deleting the duplicate entries or using a program such as UnDupe. My approach is to treat my Outlook address book as the gold-standard, permanent address book, and to take no risks with it. You can either sync down to your handheld, sync up to your desktop, or sync in a way that tries to reconcile the addresses. It is the reconciliation that leads to the duplication. I recommend that you only sync down to your Palm or other handheld device. The only disadvantage of this approach is that if you collect an address from somebody while you are out of the office, you have to enter that address by hand rather than syncing up from your Palm device. I think that is

a small price to pay to eliminate the danger of overwriting your desktop address book or duplicating all of its entries.

9. Match your style. The people who have the best results with a handheld device have spent some time thinking about how they will use it, how they will carry it, and the situations in which it will help them. Any PDA's greatest utility will be realized when it is used and carried by you on a regular basis. As a result, it can be seen as a kind of accessory to your clothing and other items that you carry. Although people sometimes chuckle about this, it can be a very difficult decision deciding what case to use for your Palm computing device. A friend of mine once spent a large amount of time and a lot of effort trying to find a brown carrying case for a Palm device to wear with his brown suit. The choice of a handheld device should be in part based on how it fits into your professional image.
10. Give up the paper. If you try to hang on to your Day-Timer, notebook, or other ways of keeping information, your transition to and use of a handheld device will be a little shaky and will proceed in a bumpy manner. The better approach is to commit to using the Palm and make an effort to use it for everything from the beginning. Throw away or hide your existing calendars and other paper. By committing to the handheld, you greatly increase your likelihood of a successful experience.

Conclusion: Handheld computing devices offer a lot of potential for assisting you to manage information, especially when you are outside of the office. In order for them to be most useful to you, you need to increase the likelihood for success and to increase their usability and usefulness for you. By taking advantage of these ten tips and techniques, you can improve your handheld experience, help organize yourself, and make yourself more productive.

Dennis M. Kennedy is an attorney, legal technology and Internet expert, author, and speaker based in St. Louis, Missouri. He can be reached at **dmk@denniskennedy.com**.

Doug Rosenoff's Twelve Reasons for Going with a Wireless PDA

1. A wireless PDA keeps you current. There is no other tool or technology available that will keep you more up to date and in touch than a wireless PDA.
2. A wireless PDA gives you space. With a wireless PDA, you can access e-mail and the Web in courtrooms, client sites, at home, in the air-

port, and elsewhere. Taxi cabs, trains, buses, and airports all become minioffices.

3. A wireless PDA saves you time: why spend minutes unpacking the laptop, finding a phone, booting up, logging in, and starting up the application? With the nearly instantaneous instant-on of a PDA, you can be up and running in seconds.
4. A wireless PDA allows you to give your clients outstanding service. Nothing impresses clients like near real-time responsiveness, timeliness, and accessibility when needed and appropriate.
5. A wireless PDA helps you to be more efficient. Because you aren't bound by the normal computer access rules, you can work at odd times that normally aren't productive or computer-friendly. Travel time, waiting time, and what would otherwise be downtime can now be productive time.
6. A wireless PDA gives you portability. Remember when portable computers were nicknamed "luggables"? The state of the art has become better, but even today's ultra-light laptops still weigh in at several pounds. Wireless PDAs allow you to travel light, without the bulk of the usual additional laptop infrastructure such as transformers, RJ-11 phone cords, RJ-45 Ethernet cables, jack splitters, outboard CD and floppy drives, extra batteries, and the like. Just bring your wireless PDA and a keyboard that folds down to PDA size, but gives you full-speed, full-size touch-typing capabilities.
7. Wireless PDAs are rapidly becoming productivity tools of choice among firms both large and small. Your peers are using wireless PDAs to keep in touch with their clients and colleagues. Being out of touch may mean being left behind competitively.
8. Web browsers for wireless PDAs are rapidly getting more reliable, faster, and intuitive to use. While they still don't support sites with frames, Javascript, cookies and the like, these limitations don't make them any less flexible or useful. Google and other well-designed sites remain as functional in a wireless browser as they do on a big screen. Many Web sites also have subsites specifically designed for wireless PDAs.
9. Robust and convenient tools are available for supporting attachments and faxes for wireless PDAs. Most of the current crop of built-in PDA e-mail programs don't handle PDF (Adobe Acrobat) files, Word documents, and other attachments well. However, there are a number of e-mail based services that will translate your attachment and send it back to you as an e-mail as well as send faxes directly from your wireless PDA.
10. Applications specific to lawyers' needs are available now. Legal research tools for document retrieval, database searches and citator

services are available from Westlaw (**www.westlaw.com/wireless/**) and LexisOne (via **www.netalive.com**). Wireless legal directories are also available from West Legal Directory. Other tools for timekeeping and client-matter management are quickly becoming available as well: ask your favorite vendor what they have now and what they're planning to launch in the future.

11. Being outside the coverage area doesn't mean being completely out of touch. As with nonwireless PDAs, you can work asynchronously, calendaring, responding to existing e-mail, and composing new e-mails. Your responses just won't go out until you're back in coverage.
12. Factors to consider when looking into buying wireless PDAs:
    - Color (color devices drain batteries faster)
    - Battery life (see Color above)
    - Memory (more is always better)
    - Expandability (memory cards and other peripherals)
    - Operating system (compatibility with your infrastructure versus application requirements and availability)
    - Software (Personal Information Manager [PIM] functions, e-mail programs, Web browsers, attachment and fax applications, legal applications)
    - Accessory costs (outboard modem (if needed), extra chargers, sync cables or cradles, folding keyboards, cases that fit device with modem)
    - Device costs (hardware, software both for the device and your e-mail server)
    - Wireless Internet Service Provider (ISP) costs (for setup and on-going connectivity for both e-mail and Web browsers)
    - Wireless coverage and speed (minor differences depending on data network in the U.S.; big differences when you look abroad or down the road a couple of years)
    - Hardware (style, size, shape, weight, portability; integrated modem or add-on?)
    - Convergent devices (can you combine a mobile phone and PDA to simplify your life still more?)

To paraphrase John Lennon, "Life is what happens while you're away from the office." Staying connected means keeping little problems little when and while you can. But balance is critical, too. Turn your wireless PDA off before it loses its convenience value and becomes a professional ball and chain.

Doug Rosenoff is Director of Global Product Technology Strategy for Thomson Legal and Regulatory Group. He was the original designer and product manager for Wireless Westlaw and is a dyed-in-the-wool wireless PDA user. He can be reached at **doug.rosenoff@westgroup.com**.

Joe Kornowski's Ten Tips for Wirelessly Enabling Your Law Practice

As a busy professional, why should you have to waste time sitting in traffic or in a courthouse hallway waiting until you get back to the office to access a case, Web site, or document? If you have a wireless-enabled Palm PDA, consider the following ten tips to leverage your out-of-office time and get more out of your wireless PDA:

1. Talk to the Palm! With the convergence of voice and data on Palm PDAs now a practical reality, lawyers can eliminate the need to carry a separate cell phone and PDA by choosing one of the Handspring Treo communicators (**www.handspring.com**), Kyocera SmartPhones (**www.kyocera-wireless.com**), or Samsung's SPH-i300 (**www.samsung electronics.com**). These devices offer the virtues of a PDA and a full-featured cell phone, with access to the Web and e-mail, operating on GSM[3] and CDMA[4] cellular networks.
2. Legal research to go. What if you find yourself in the client's office and need to look up a code section, or you are in an arbitration hearing and opposing counsel cites a case that you don't know about? Well, if you are a Westlaw or LexisNexis subscriber, and you have a wireless Palm PDA, you may be in luck. Westlaw Wireless (**www.westlaw.com/wireless**) offers a Web-clipping application to Westlaw subscribers enabling them to find a document, KeyCite a citation, search Westlaw, and access the West Legal Directory. LexisNexis users can have new case decision information delivered via email to their wireless Palm-powered PDAs through services such as Electronic Advance Sheets case summaries (**http://www.lexis one.com**). For those interested in tracking changes to pending legislation up to the minute, twelve states now offer a way to track the status of legislative bills wirelessly (**http://www.telicon.com**).
3. Your travel concierge. The value of wireless connectivity from your Palm PDA is at its pinnacle when it comes to getting you where you want to go. A number of travel-related sites and airlines provide a Web-clipping application (PQA[5]) for Palm VII/VIIx/i705, access to an AvantGo channel, or e-mailed alerts to review itineraries, check flights, obtain flight schedule and gate information, etc. These sites include **Travelocity.com** (**www.travelocity.com**), Orbitz (**www.orbitz.com**), Sabre's VirtuallyThere (**www.virtuallythere.com**), America West, American Airlines, Continental Airlines, and United Airlines.
4. Finding your way there. Wireless driving directions from Mobile MapQuest (accessible via a Web clipping application or a Palm Web

browser like Blazer or the GoAmerica browser) or MSN Mobile offer one great advantage over desktop access. If you rely on downloaded and printed directions, and become lost, getting back on course can be a challenge. But with wireless access to the driving directions site, you simply pull over, enter the street address where you are and the destination address, and you're back on the road headed in the right direction.

5. When you absolutely, positively need to track it. When you need to know exactly when your shipped documents have reached their destination for review, signature, or filing, no matter where you are, FedEx Wireless Solutions offers a wireless clipping application for download to a Palm PDA that allows Palm users to track their shipments. UPS PDA Solutions similarly allows Palm users to locate the whereabouts of their UPS shipments, calculate shipping costs and transit times, and find the closest UPS drop-off locations. See **www.fedex.com** and **www.ups.com** for more information on these services.
6. E-mail: the killer app. E-mail is the proverbial killer app on a wireless Palm device. Great uses besides the lawyer's one-to-one communications with colleagues, office staff, and clients include notification of newly decided cases, (such as that provided by LexisNexis Electronic Advance Sheets), CNN Breaking News alerts, and notification of changes in flight schedules. E-mail applications usually come bundled with wireless services.
7. Short Message Service (SMS). The Short Message Service allows anyone with wireless service on a GSM network, like that provided through Handspring Treo devices, to send a short text message to another SMS user's cell phone (often to a non-GSM network). Unlike most wireless Palm devices that do not provide notification of new e-mail messages, SMS notifies the user through vibrate mode or audible beep when a text message has been received. During conferences or court appearances where a voice call is impractical or not allowed, this can be an effective and discreet way to receive messages.
8. Wi-Fi: broadband for PDAs. While some people still don't have broadband Internet access from their desktops, it is now possible for Palm PDA owners to access the Internet at speeds up to 11 Mbps.[6] Known as Wi-Fi, wireless LAN, or 802.11b,[7] this technology enables anyone with an 802.11b card in a PDA to connect to the Internet or a private network via a local "access point," which must be located within approximately three hundred feet of their device, if indoors. Fast synchronization of a Palm's e-mail application with the law firm's net-

work e-mail server is an obvious benefit, as well as faster access speeds for wireless legal research. Newer applications will rely on the high bandwidth connection to view video wirelessly (for example, remote viewing of videotaped depositions or other evidence, and on-line CLE). Xircom (**www.xircom.com**) makes wireless LAN modules for both Palm and Handspring PDAs.

9. Bluetooth. Allowing a PDA user to create what has become known as a personal area network, add-ins like the Red M-Blade springboard module for the Handspring Visor, and the Palm Bluetooth card for Palm m-series PDAs use very short-range (up to approximately thirty feet) wireless technology called Bluetooth to connect to a cell phone to access the Internet or print wirelessly to a Bluetooth-enabled printer.
10. AvantGo. Although the AvantGo mobile Internet service (**www.avantgo.com**) started out as a way to synchronize Web content to your PDA, the service can be accessed wirelessly and offers high-value content to lawyers, including the *State Bar of Michigan E-Journal,* which provides Michigan and federal court opinion case summaries organized by area of practice; the *ABA Journal Mobile Edition*; CCH Mobile *Tax Tracker News*; and the LawMarketing Portal.

Joe Kornowski is Sr. Director, National Product Planning, Small Law Markets, at LexisNexis, as well as a California lawyer with a passion for mobile solutions for lawyers. He also serves as an advisor to Courtroom Connect. He can be reached at **joe.kornowski@lexisnexis.com**.

Larry Bodine's Top Ten Reasons to Switch to a Pocket PC

It's time to dump your Palm handheld and buy the better technology offered by Pocket PCs. That would include getting a Compaq iPaq, like I have, or a Toshiba e series, Audiovox Maestro, NEC MobilPro, Casio E-200, or HP Jornada. Palm and its partisans at Sony and Handspring have dropped the ball and fallen behind in technology. Here are good reasons to make the switch:

1. More upgrades earlier. Pocket PCs are for tech-savvy users who appreciate the latest improvements and newest developments. If you're in no rush to have the latest features first, then Palm is the way to go. In the last two years, Palm established a reputation of coming out with less-attractive products at a slower pace.
2. Familiar software. "Software matters," as Microsoft asserts. The Pocket PC gives me the familiar "Start" icon and a pull-down menu in-

cluding my Outlook calendar, contacts, notes and tasks, in-box, and Internet Explorer built in. I can read and edit Word and Excel, check spelling, count words, open Word and Excel attachments in e-mails, plus view and edit PowerPoint presentations.

3. Faster operation. My iPaq is fast. It has a 206-MHz processor that instantly switches from one function to another and immediately loads my *New York Times, Wall Street Journal*, and LawMarketing Portal articles downloaded via AvantGo. With the Palm, the screen would go blank while loading one of these applications and made me wait before returning to life and showing my selection. New Pocket PCs are even faster and have 400-MHz Intel XScale processors.
4. More memory. I used to have a Palm VII, which had a memory that kept filing up. I had to delete applets, graphics, and documents to make room for new ones. I hated this. So I bought an iPaq with 64K of memory built in, and have never had this problem again.
5. Better screen. The black-on-green screen of the Palm was always hard to read. The iPaq color screen is wonderful. It reminds me of the days when people began changing from black-and-white TVs to color sets. The iPaq gives you 4,096 colors, which is plenty good for me. A little light sensor adjusts the picture so you can see well in an office or outdoors. You can also adjust the brightness to five different levels. Meanwhile, Palm admitted in August 2002 that its color handhelds don't display as many colors as advertised.
6. Rechargeable batteries. With the old Palm VII, I had to become a quick-change artist with the AAA batteries. I kept supplies of tiny batteries in my desk downtown, briefcase, and home office. If the batteries died in the Palm VII, I'd lose all my data. The iPaq came with a rechargeable lithium battery so I don't have to swap out dinky batteries. It lasts about a day per charge. Granted, most handhelds come with rechargeable batteries now, but my iPaq had one earlier.
7. More handy helpers. The iPaq does what it's supposed to. It keeps my appointments, stores my contact information, records my to-do lists, and gives me reminders. The calendar can be set to an "agenda" view that displays only appointments and not empty hours of the day. It can be set to delete past appointments older than two weeks to eliminate clutter. Contacts can be viewed by name or by company.
8. Non-losable stylus. The iPaq stylus clicks into its storage silo securely and pops up when I press a button to get it. This has prevented me from losing the stylus. I still have the original stylus that came with the handheld when I bought it in August 2001. Few Palm users can make this claim.

9. Auto-completion of words. The iPaq virtual or "soft" keyboard is very nice. It auto-completes words for you and remembers more words the more you use it. I liked this feature so much that I stopped using the "graffiti" or character-recognition method.
10. Lots of extras. The iPaq has Microsoft Reader, which allows you to read text and pictures and enables me to read a book on the handheld. Then there's the Media Player, which plays MP3 sound files. It's also got Microsoft Money to keep track of accounts, investments and payees.

Pocket PCs typically cost $100 more than Palm OS handhelds, but you get what you pay for. For these reasons, I renounced my Palm citizenship and went over to the other side—the Microsoft Pocket PC world. I am well pleased with my top-of-the-line Compaq iPaq. I felt like a Betamax owner switching to VHS, or a Chevy owner switching to Subaru, or a baseball fan switching to extreme skateboarding. I was leaving the herd and joining the smaller, but smarter minority. For more information see **www.pocketpc.com**.

Larry Bodine is a Chicago-area marketing and Web consultant. Larry advises law firms on marketing strategy, business development tactics, and Web projects. He is founder of the LawMarketing Listserv (**www.lawmarketing.biz**) and LawMarketing Portal (**www.lawmarketing.com**). He can be reached at 630-942-0977 and **Lbodine@LawMarketing.com**.

Meg Spencer Dixon's Rejoinder to Larry Bodine's Top Ten Reasons to Switch to a Pocket PC

1. Response to "more upgrades earlier." This point doesn't address the superiority of the Pocket PC operating system versus the Palm operating system, but apparently only Palm brand products. The Sony Clié (which runs the Palm OS) incorporates advanced improvements, as do the Handspring brand Visor and Treo.
2. Response to "familiar software." Preferring to see the "familiar 'Start' icon and pull-down menu" is a matter of individual taste. However, you can easily sync the Palm OS applications with Microsoft desktop software, including Outlook calendar, contacts, notes and tasks, using the software that comes with every Palm OS PDA. There are also add-on programs for the Palm OS that allow you to "read and edit Word and Excel, check spelling, count words, open Word and Excel attachments in e-mails, plus view and edit PowerPoint presentations." More recent PDAs come bundled with software to support

Microsoft Outlook e-mail, Word documents, Excel spreadsheets, and PowerPoint presentations.

3. Response to "faster operation." Recent Palm OS PDAs have a Dragonball processor that runs at 66 MHz. For most applications, the difference in speed would be imperceptible; for larger applications, the difference would be a matter of a few seconds, if that. Plus, the marginally faster speed makes the battery life much shorter; see point number 6 below.
4. Response to "more memory." Recent Palm OS PDAs have expansion slots that allow you to insert up to 64 MB of memory in a module the size of a postage stamp.
5. Response to "better screen." Three points:
   - "The iPaq color screen is wonderful. It reminds me of the days when people began changing from black-and-white TVs to color sets." I fully agree with the second sentence, but since there are many Palm OS PDAs with color screens, the choice is between color and grayscale, not color and Palm.
   - "The black-on-green screen of the Palm was always hard to read." This is an anecdotal statement, the truth of which is debatable. While I've heard people say that the color screen is easier to read than the grayscale, I've also heard of people who have been happy with their simple, non-battery-hungry grayscale screens. (I've been reading my grayscale screen easily for almost two years.)
   - "The iPaq gives you 4,096 colors, which is plenty good for me. . . . Meanwhile, Palm admitted in August 2002 that its color handhelds don't display as many colors as advertised." Actually, this involved only one model, the Palm m130, which Palm admitted displayed not 65,536 colors, but only (!) 58,621. (See, for example, **http://ptech.wsj.com/archive/mailbox-20020822.html**.) Even with this concession, the m130 displays over fourteen times as many colors as the iPaq, which is plenty good for me.
6. Response to "rechargeable batteries." Two points:
   - "The iPaq came with a rechargeable lithium battery so I don't have to swap out dinky batteries. It lasts about a day per charge." Most Palm OS PDAs now come with rechargeable lithium batteries, and the charge lasts far more than a day. My Palm Vx, after five days with heavy use without a recharge, usually has about 20% of its battery power left. (Color screens and triple-fast processors take their toll in battery life.)
   - "Granted, most handhelds come with rechargeable batteries now, but my iPaq had one earlier." Do we really want to take the "earlier

is better" approach? The Palm OS would come out way ahead of Pocket PC on this one.

7. Response to "more handy helpers." You can say exactly the same things about Palm OS PDAs (except that "agenda view" is called "compress day view.")
8. Response to "non-losable stylus." Three points:
   - "Non-losable stylus." Huh??? Then why do they all come with extra styli?? (Click on "What's in the box?" under "Product information" for each iPaq model at **http://www.compaq.com/products/handhelds/pocketpc**.) (Palm OS PDAs also come with multiple styli.)
   - "The iPaq stylus clicks into its storage silo securely." So do the Palm styli.
   - "I still have the original stylus that came with the handheld when I bought it in August 2001. Few Palm users can make this claim." This is an anecdotal statement that I believe is simply wrong. Although anyone could lose a stylus, I have never heard complaints about this being a problem, with any brand of PDA. In fact, I still have the original stylus that came with my Palm Vx in December 2000; my husband still has the original stylus that came with his Palm IIIc in the spring of 2001; my stepmother still has the original stylus that came with her Palm m505 in December 2001 . . . I could go on. . . .
9. Response to "auto-completion of words." The Palm add-on program WordComplete (**www.cic.com**) does the same thing, plus it lets you choose whether or not to add specific words to a custom dictionary.
10. Response to "lots of extras." Not only can Palm OS PDAs do everything mentioned in this point, they can do a lot more, since there are many more add-on programs for Palm PDAs (about nineteen thousand total, according to PalmSource [**www.palmos.com**]), plus you have the option (it may cost you, but it's possible) of hiring a software developer to write a Palm OS program to do exactly what you want it to, since Palm shares programming information with its registered developers. (Would that Bill Gates would do the same . . .)

Larry Bodine's Rebuttal to Meg Spencer Dixon's Rejoinder

1. More upgrades earlier. Good points. Let me note that Sprint just came out with the Treo device—a PDA and cell phone combo with a color screen. It's very popular with lawyers and I wanted one immediately when I saw one in operation. The operating system is Palm, so there you go.

2. Familiar software. Yeah, but it's not Windows. Only Pocket PCs run Microsoft programs in their native OS.
3. Faster operation. In PDA time, a "couple of seconds" is a couple of days. Speed matters. That's why Chevy makes Corvettes and why Compaq makes iPaq.
4. More memory. The iPaq has the memory built in, which in my view is the preferred option. I don't need to strap, plug, or attach anything to the iPaq to get acres of space to work with—it's built in.
5. Better screen. I don't disagree. But when I put the screens of the various PDAs side by side, the iPaq was the best. It only took one look.
6. Rechargeable batteries. OK, fair enough.
7. More handy helpers. Point taken. But as I recall, the Palm had an irremediable problem with duplicate records. The more often you synced it, the more duplicates would pile up. In contrast, Pocket PCs de-dupe identical records automatically.
8. Non-losable stylus. Ah, you minimize an important point here. Losing styli is a big deal. The Palm users I see are constantly tapping their screens with pens and other plastic objects, because they lost their stylus. You actually insert the iPaq stylus into a silo, and it can't be jostled loose, bounced out or lost in luggage. The iPaq stylus comes out only when its owner presses a specific button. None of the Palms I owned had that mechanism.
9. Auto-completion of words. Again, Palm has an add-on that does the job of something that is built-in with the iPaq. It's like saying, "My car will go as fast as your Corvette, so long as I add on an engine, air intake, exhaust system, suspension, and body."
10. Lots of extras. OK, you get to have the last point.

Ross Kodner's Palm Tips

1. The Urge to converge! My favorite Palm-sized tip is to simplify. I used to carry three separate gadgets everywhere I went—all strapped to my belt. Each morning, I would scour the house for my PalmPilot, my cell phone and my BlackBerry. Invariably, one of my rugrats will have dragged off one of the devices to use in their play (like the time I found my BlackBerry duct-taped to a Barbie's head—go figure). So time-precious morning minutes were wasted almost every day. And worse, some days, one of the gizmos would refuse to be found. So many a day were spent Palm-less or sans cell phone. *But not any more!* The solution has been convergence—the blending of Palm, cell phone, and wireless e-mail into a single compact device. My first foray into the genre was with the best of the second-generation converged devices,

the Kyocera QCP-6035 SmartPhone, since replaced by Kyocera's wonderful newer 7135 SmartPhone (with the lusted-for-next converged device being the Samsung i500, a 3/4-scale version of the Kyocera). (The SmartPhone was, and still is, a nearly perfect melding of a capable cell phone with a full-blown wireless Palm. Think about what would result if you tossed your Nokia cell phone and wireless-enabled Palm into a Cuisinart and pressed "puree"—a seamless mix (admittedly, with lots of unsavory plastic chunks). No more days without my Palm! Since I generally never forget my cell phone, it guarantees me that my Palm is always with me, and even better, I haven't missed my BlackBerry since it was relegated to the basement gadget graveyard. So whether it's a Kyocera SmartPhone, a Handspring/PalmOne Treo, a Samsung smart phone, or even future devices, stop the madness and get converged now!

2. **AvantGo.com**. All Palm users. Go there. Now. Trust me. AvantGo allows you to coordinate the downloading of a ton of Palm-compatible content from multiple Web sites every time you synchronize with your PC. Whether it's the *Wall Street Journal*, or CNN, or David Letterman's Top Ten list, the range of Palm-portable Net sources is mind-boggling and constantly growing. Mechanically, AvantGo couldn't be much easier to use. Go to the Web site. Follow the instructions. Select the Web sites you wish to view the content of. Then the next time you plug your Palm in to sync it, be sure your PC has a Net connection, and the latest AvantGo-coordinated Web content will download to the Palm. And the best thing about AvantGo? It's . . . *free*!
3. Laptop versus Palm: How do you decide? Far too many lawyers spend too much money on laptops they don't need. If a lawyer wants to access his or her calendar and Rolodex when away from the office—and that's it—a solid case for a laptop has not been made. Why spend $3,000 on a laptop to accomplish tasks that a $500 Palm will handle perfectly adequately? To view a calendar and a Rolodex, a Palm makes much more sense—it's "instant on," low risk if you lose it, and little to lose financially speaking. Now add one of the many portable keyboards to your Palm and you have an even more versatile combination (see the folding Stoaway keyboards available from **www.palm.com** and **www.targus.com**). You now have a minilaptop-substitute that is ready to take notes in any meeting or proceeding.
4. Essential Palm service. Vindigo gets you where you want to go! For $25 you get "ultimate" city travel guides. Information includes color maps, restaurant info and customer reviews and ratings, museum info, movie times, times and venues for local musical events and the-

ater productions, nightlife info, essential info like parking, ATMs, gas stations, airport info, and more. Why would anyone travel to one of the included cities without it? Beats me (**www.vindigo.com**).

5. Take a note please. OK, so you can't master Graffiti and you can't type, so even Palm keyboards don't help. But . . . *aha!* You can *write!* That's where Seiko Instruments InkLink comes in. This device includes a "clip" that attaches to the upper edge of an ordinary legal pad. A cable clips to the infrared port of a Palm (or even a laptop). Using the provided ballpoint pen, which has a built-in transceiver, anything you write on the legal pad is transferred to the Palm display and stored as a file. These note files can then be transferred to your PC when you sync. A fantastic way to take and store notes without having the hassle of having to scan papers—$99 and it has a portable carrying kit. Info is at **http://www.seikosmart.com/products/inklink.html**.

Ross L. Kodner is a lawyer and the founder and president of MicroLaw, a consulting company which assists lawyers and their staff in all aspects of practice automation and legal technology. His detailed bio can be found at **www.microlaw.com/team/kodner.html**.

Bob McNeill's Top Twelve Reasons a PDA Is Essential to a Modern Law Practice Management System

Sidebar:

A "law practice management system" is the sum of all systems, programs, and procedures used by a law practice to process its work and manage the business. It includes contact and case management, calendaring and docketing, workflow management, document assembly and management, file notes, e-mail, timekeeping and billing, and accounting and financial management, and so on.

Some of the most popular legal-specific practice management software programs are Time Matters, Amicus Attorney, PracticeMaster, Abacus, ProLaw, and Needles. Non-legal-specific programs include Outlook, Goldmine, and ACT!

The purpose of a computerized law practice management system is to get your work done "better, faster, and cheaper," that is, to produce higher-quality work product, in less time, at lower cost by building expertise into the system, automating routine documents and tasks, and putting most of the information used by the practice at everyone's fingertips. A PDA can provide additional leverage to such a system because of its:

1. Portability. Lawyers do not work in the office all the time. We go to court, work at home, and meet at clients' offices or nursing homes. Much of the information needed to be productive outside the office can be stored on a PDA, such as contacts, calendar, tasks, and memos. A PDA lets you take your practice information with you, without lugging a laptop computer. Time is saved by not having to call the office to obtain information that could be stored on a PDA. How many times have you called the office to find a telephone number that was in your practice management system? Being able to work "anytime, anywhere," not only means you can be more productive, it also allows you to be more responsive to your clients.
2. Single point of entry. One of the principles of a well-designed practice management system is to enter all information once and only once, and then use it elsewhere as needed. Once a client's name and address is entered into a law practice management system, it can be viewed like an index card on each person's computer so you can get rid of each staff person's paper desktop Rolodex®. The same name and address information can be used to create a retainer agreement and other standard documents. It can also be sent to the billing system to open up a new matter. Connecting your PDA to your practice management system extends these efficiencies further; like a very long hose on a vacuum cleaner, you can suck information in from places you could not reach before. With your PDA, you can enter the name and e-mail address of someone you meet at a social function so that you can add that person to your practice management systems' newsletter mailing list. Better yet, instead of inputting the name and address manually, it can be beamed into your PDA.
3. Synchronization. How do you keep all the information in the PDA current? Entering information directly into a PDA using the Palm's Graffiti is not very efficient. Built-in or add-on keyboards are better, but better yet is the ability to automatically synchronize all the information in your practice management system with the PDA. Placing the PDA in its cradle and pushing a button is all it takes to synchronize. This is much more efficient because the information is

already in your practice management system. Most legal-specific practice management systems have some type of Palm synchronization, and some have Windows CE and Pocket PC synchronization, but what exactly they synchronize varies. Some have the ability to define the scope of the synchronization so that you do not have to see the entire firm's contacts or calendars on your PDA, just your contacts or calendar.

4. Calendaring. Having an up-to-date calendar at your fingertips makes it easy to schedule and reschedule appointments, pick a new trial date, plan a vacation, and so on. Usually, this means that the office does not have an up-to-date copy of your calendar, and that someone has to reconcile your personal calendar with the main calendar at the office. It also means that before you can be sure a date is free you have to call the office to check the office calendar. Being able to synchronize the office-wide practice management system calendar with your PDA calendar with the push of a button reduces or eliminates the need to check for conflicts between the two calendars and makes you more productive. Because everyone can access everyone else's calendar (unless prevented by security restrictions), scheduling attorneys for hearings and meetings is a snap. Your clients will appreciate not having to be put on hold while the staff checks two calendars for conflicts.
5. Task management. Being able to review your to-do list on your PDA, and to add new items and change existing ones, means being able to make use of time that would otherwise be wasted. How many times have you been stuck in court or in traffic and wished you had your to-do list with you so that you could take care of simple tasks by dictating a letter or delegating tasks? How do you remember to add an item to your to-do list when you are out of the office and a great idea pops into your head? Jot it down on a piece of paper and hope it makes it back to the office? Adding, changing, and marking done to-do's on your PDA, and synchronizing the changes to your practice management system, makes you more efficient and make use of otherwise wasted time.
6. File notes. A practice management system is only as good as the information in it. When you are not sitting at your desk, how do you record information concerning a telephone call, meeting, or hearing? To create longer notes, dictating on a hand-held recorder is probably best, even though it requires time on the part of the staff to transcribe it and your time to review it, which means it may not get to the electronic "file" for a couple of days. For short notes, creating a

memo on the PDA gets the job done quicker and easier, if your PDA synchronizes memos and notes with your law practice management system software. Entering lots of text into a PDA is not its strong suit, so if you plan on entering lots of notes, check out the size of the PDA display and available methods of text entry, such as Graffiti, minikeyboard, external keyboards, and folding portable keyboards, to make sure you will be comfortable with the amount of text entry you plan to do.

7. Capturing caller ID information. If you use a combination PDA-mobile telephone, such as the Kyocera's SmartPhone or Handspring's Treo, and you have caller ID, then you can add a contact's name and telephone number to the PDA's contact list. When you synchronize the PDA with your law practice management system, the new contact will be added to the office's practice management system. With very little work, you can add new contacts to your system, so you can follow up with them, include them in your marketing efforts, etc.
8. Billing. One of the tenets of good billing practices is to record the work as close as possible to the time it is done because it is more likely to be recorded accurately. The more time that elapses between the time the work is done and the time it is recorded, the more likely it won't be recorded at all, or will be recorded incorrectly. If the time recorded is more than was actually spent, then the client is overcharged; if less, the lawyer is underpaying himself or herself. Many of the legal-specific time and billing applications have remote data entry programs that run on PDAs, with the ability to enter time and expenses on the PDA and then transfer the information to the billing system during the synchronization process. Recording work when it is fresh in your mind avoids having to recall it hours or days later when trying to enter the information into the billing system.
9. Expenses. How do you keep track of miscellaneous costs, travel mileage, and other out-of-pocket expenses? A jumble of papers kept in a shoe box until the end of the year when you dump it on your secretary's desk? Most PDAs have an application for tracking expenses as part of their standard array of programs, which can synchronize with a spreadsheet such as Microsoft Excel. Even if you do not synchronize your PDA with your billing system, tracking expenses when they are incurred makes it more likely you will track them at all.
10. Documents. In addition to being able to view static documents, such as statutes and rules of evidence, if you need to be able to review and perhaps create documents on the go, then you should investigate whether synchronizing your word-processing documents, spreadsheets, PDF files, and so on, to your PDA is the answer. There are

add-on programs that will let you load a Word or WordPerfect file onto your PDA, make changes on the PDA, and then synchronize it back to your desktop computer. The obvious limitations are the size of the PDA display and the input capabilities of the PDA.

11. E-mail. E-mail is on its way to replacing regular ("snail") mail as the most common method of communication between lawyers and their clients, other lawyers, and so on. Therefore, your practice management system has to be able to manage at least client-matter-related e-mail. How you should handle the barrage of e-mail you receive is beyond the scope of this writing. One tool, however, is to read and respond to e-mails using your PDA, either with a live Internet connection on the PDA, or by synchronizing with the e-mail application on your desktop computer that is connected to the Internet. Using your PDA to help process your e-mail gives you the option of doing so at slack times when you are not in the office and do not have regular e-mail access available.
12. Internet access. Being able to access the Internet is increasingly important for lawyers. Some PDAs have the ability to access the Internet over a wireless connection, and some Web sites can deliver content in a format that is easier for the small display of a PDA to handle. With this combination, you can perform Lexis or WestLaw legal research, or other Internet research, "anytime, anyplace," giving you more flexibility in where and when you do your work.

Robert S. McNeill is the principal of the McNeill Group, Ltd., **www.McNeillGroup.org**, which specializes in designing law practice management systems for law firms, corporate law departments, and government agencies. He has more than twenty years' experience as a practicing attorney and legal technologist, and has been intimately involved in leveraging law with technology for over a decade. Since 1990, he has regularly presented educational programs to bar associations, and has taught law practice management CLE programs over the Internet.

Notes

1. Essentially data about data, metadata describes characteristics about how specific data was compiled. For example, Microsoft Word automatically compiles such metadata as the document's author, creation date, and how many times the document was edited, which anyone can access (even from an e-mailed version of the document) by opening the "Properties" category in the "File" menu.

2. This list has been previously published as a chapter in Dennis Kennedy's online legal technology primer at **http://www.denniskennedy.com/palmten.htm**, under the title "Palm Computing for Legal Professionals: Ten Practical Tips to Enhance the Value of Your Palm Computing Device."

3. Global System for Mobile Communications, one of the leading digital cellular systems. This definition, and the others in this chapter, were derived from the more detailed, technical definitions at Webopedia (**www.pcwebopedia.com**), an online dictionary of computer and Internet technology terms.

4. Code-Division Multiple Access, a digital cellular technology.

5. Palm Query Application, a Web clipping application that allows Palm PDA users to interact wirelessly with Web content.

6. Megabits per second, a measure of data transfer speed.

7. 802.11 refers to a family of specifications developed by the Institute of Electrical and Electronics Engineers (IEEE) for wireless LAN technology. 802.11b (also referred to as 802.11 High Rate or Wi-Fi) is an extension to 802.11 that provides 11 Mbps transmission (with a fallback to 5.5, 2, and 1 Mbps).

Part IV

The Nuts and Bolts of Using a Palm Powered™ PDA

A Tour Around a PDA

8

§ 8.1 Introduction

This chapter describes the physical setup of one of the most popular Palm devices, the Palm V model (which includes the Palm V and the Palm Vx). The Palm V is very similar to the m500 series, and is substantially similar to many Palm models. The built-in software of the Palm Vx is version 3.5 of each of the twelve basic applications (except that the System software is version 3.5.0), and the technical discussions in Chapters 8 through 22 are based on these versions. (Of course, later versions can be expected to contain some new features.)

§ 8.2 A Walk Around the Device

Front: Most of the front of the device consists of a $2^{1}/_{4}$-inch-square, touch-sensitive **Liquid Crystal Display (LCD) screen**. Below that is a $^{3}/_{4}$-inch-by-$2^{1}/_{4}$-inch touch-sensitive area that includes a rectangle outlining the **Graffiti area**, on each side of which are two silk-screened buttons (also known as soft buttons). Below that are five physical (or hard) buttons, which are (from left to right) the **Date Book button**, the **Address Book button**, the hourglass-shaped **scroll button** (two separate buttons on earlier models), the **To Do List button**, and the **Memo Pad button**. Except for the scroll button, each of these physical buttons is also a power button, so you can turn the device on and go directly to one of the four main applications in one step. The green button on the front of the device is the **power/backlight button**. Holding the button down for a few seconds turns on the backlight.

Back: A recessed **reset button** is on the back of the device.

Top: The **IR port** is at the center of the top of the device. On the top left side is the **contrast button**, which triggers an on-screen contrast slider button that you adjust using your stylus or the scroll button. (Some earlier models have a physical wheel that controls the contrast.)

Bottom: There is a **serial port** at the bottom of the device, which is used primarily to connect the device to your HotSync cradle for recharging and for synchronizing data with your laptop or desktop computer.

Sides: On most models, each side of the device has a channel in which you can keep your stylus when not in use. If you're right-handed, keep the stylus on the right, and use the left-side channel for the leather flip-cover that came with the device, and vice-versa for lefties.

§ 8.3 The On-Screen Buttons

The four silk-screened buttons (also known as soft buttons) are:

- Upper left: the **Applications button**, also known as the **Home button**. Current models sport an icon of a house; older versions have a curved arrow and the word "applications." Pressing this button takes you to "home base" (formally known as the applications launcher) where you can open any application (or software) that's on your Palm.
- Lower left: the **Menu button**, which has an icon of a pull-down menu. Pressing this button makes visible the menu bar and pull-down menus at the top of the screen. This button is pretty much unnecessary, since in most applications you can accomplish the same thing by tapping the top of the screen (which saves time, since your stylus is already positioned to make the next tap). To make a pull-down menu disappear without choosing one of its options, tap elsewhere on the screen.
- Upper right: the **Calculator button**, which launches Palm's built-in calculator. This is the one soft-screen button that can be reset to launch another application (see Section 15.2).
- Lower right: the **Find button**, which allows you to search for a string of text anywhere in your Palm.

§ 8.4 The Built-In Applications

Most current Palms come with at least the following twelve applications already installed. To find these applications on your Palm, use the stylus to tap on the

Home button. (If fewer than twelve icons appear, tap on the triangle in the upper right corner of the screen, then tap on the word "All." See Figure 8-A.)

8-A:

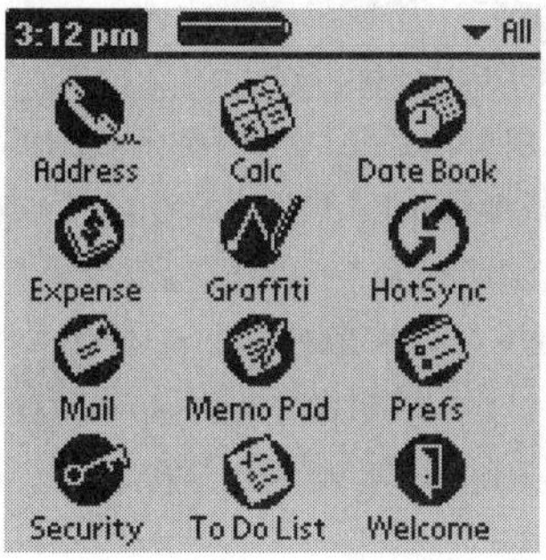

- **Address Book** keeps track of contact information such as names, phone numbers, addresses, and e-mail addresses using fourteen ready-made fields, four customizable fields, and the option to add extensive notes for each contact (ideal for driving directions, name of spouse, and so on.)
- **Calculator** is a basic, simple calculator. It's nice to have a calculator handy, plus you can copy and paste numbers to and from Calculator and other applications. (With the backlight feature, you can calculate taxi tips even in the dark.)
- **Date Book** is your calendar. Use it to schedule events, appointments, meetings, or anything you want to remember that corresponds to a specific date. You can set alarms to remind you in advance of an event, set up repeating events (such as a monthly meeting), multiday events, and even events such as work deadlines, birthdays, and anniversaries that have dates but no specific times.
- **Expense** allows you to record business expenses easily. The pick-list of available categories is not editable (unusual for Palm) and is clearly targeted to business rather than personal expenses. You also need Microsoft Excel on your laptop or desktop in order to open spreadsheets containing Expense data.
- **Graffiti** is a tutorial on Palm's handwriting recognition system. Each Graffiti character closely resembles the printed, capital version of that letter, and many of the punctuation marks are intuitively obvious. (For example, a period is a dot.)
- **HotSync** allows you to synchronize the information on your Palm with your laptop or desktop computer. Once you've installed the Palm Desktop software on your primary computer, you can HotSync by placing your Palm in its cradle and pressing the cradle's only button.

- **Mail** allows you to download and read your e-mail on your Palm, either by HotSyncing e-mail between your primary computer and your Palm, or by attaching your Palm directly to a modem.
- **Memo Pad** allows you to jot down random thoughts, lists, information, notes, and so on, and organize, categorize, and locate the information quickly (using the Find feature).
- **Prefs** (preferences) allows you to configure the format and workings of your Palm in various ways.
- **Security** allows you to mask or hide information using a password. You can also configure it so that you need the password to show anything other than the Owner screen—handy when traveling but inconvenient to deal with on an hourly basis.
- **To Do List** is used to keep track of tasks, or anything else you want to remember, that don't necessarily correspond to a specific date or time.
- **Welcome** walks you through the initial setup of your Palm, and remains permanently available to refresh your memory and reconfigure certain items.

Tapping on an icon opens (or "launches") the application.

One of the beauties of the Palm operating system is what you *won't* find. For example, there's no (perceptible) start-up time; the screen is alive the moment you press the power button or one of the four application buttons. There's no need to save anything, since whatever you input is saved automatically. You don't have to close an application, since launching another application automatically closes the previous one. Moreover, the system is relatively robust, and rarely crashes. Even then, most crashes are easily fixed with a soft reset, which is done by inserting the end of an unfolded paper clip in the recessed reset button on the back of the device. (You may already have a reset tool handy; if you're using a metal stylus, try unscrewing the top.) Finally, feel free to explore; it's almost impossible to get "lost" within an application.

Getting Started with Your PDA

9

§ 9.1 Terminology and Conventions

One of the beauties of the Palm OS is that there are usually multiple ways of completing basic tasks such as inputting or deleting a piece of information. Once you understand the official way of doing a task, you can choose your favorite method from among the various shortcuts available. To minimize repetition in describing these methods, I will use the following conventions:

1. *Tap* means to touch with the tip of a stylus. (Never use a pen or other sharp object that could scratch your handheld's touch-sensitive screen.) When various items are to be tapped in succession, *tap* will appear only before the first item.
2. *Select* means to indicate text by tapping anywhere on the word, sentence, or paragraph.
3. *Write* means to input characters using either Graffiti or the on-screen keypad.
4. / means to draw a slash (from the lower left to upper right). This is the command shortcut stroke that is followed by either writing a letter or tapping an icon.
5. *Arrows (→)* are used instead of "then" or "next" to indicate a series of taps, selections, and so on.
6. ▼ means the downward-pointing triangle on the screen that indicates the existence of a pop-up menu[1] that ap-

pears when you tap the triangle or the text next to it. For example, one such triangle appears in the screen shot in Figure 9-A in the upper right corner next to the word "System." To close a pop-up menu without selecting one of its items, tap anywhere else on the screen.

9-A:

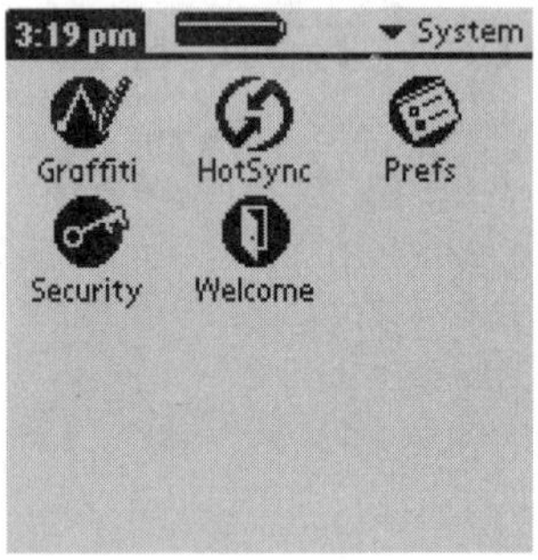

7. *Quotation marks* indicate words that appear verbatim on the handheld's screen, sometimes surrounded by a curve-cornered rectangle that forms a button (such as "Done" and "Details" in the screen shot in Figure 9-B), and sometimes contained in a pop-up menu. This is important since some buttons have icons rather than names, so you should not hunt for a button that has the word "Home" on it. The Home button has an icon of a house or, on earlier models, a curved arrow and the word "applications."

9-B:

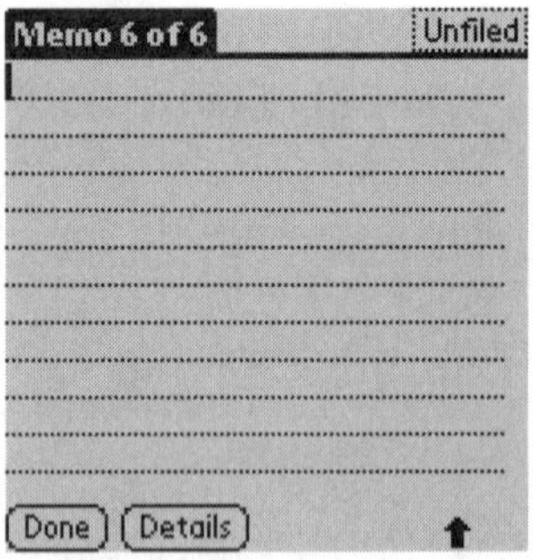

So instead of the cumbersome "Tap the Home button, then open the Graffiti application, then tap the downward-pointed triangle in the upper right corner, then tap where it says 'Tips,' " we have "Tap Home → 'Graffiti' → ▼ → 'Tips.'"

§ 9.2 First Things First

When you turn on your handheld, you see a screen full of icons representing the preinstalled applications. It should look something like Figure 9-C. If your screen looks completely different, tap Home. If fewer than twelve icons appear, you are viewing only one category of applications. The name of the category appears in the screen's upper right-hand corner, next to the ▼. To view all the applications, tap ▼ → "All" (or keep tapping Home to scroll through the various categories until you come to "All").

9-C:

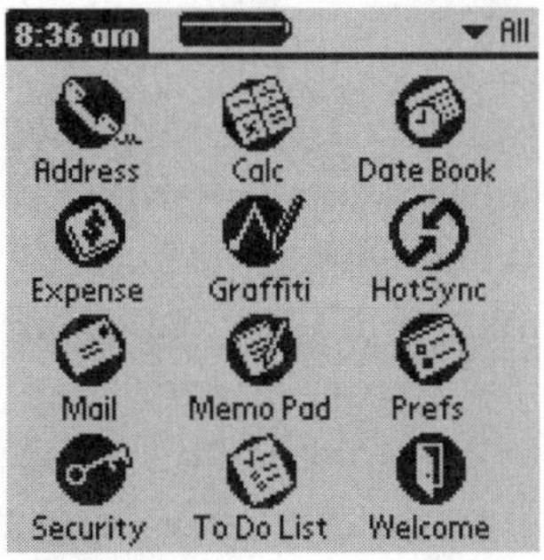

In addition to the icons representing the built-in applications, this screen contains three other useful elements:

1. The time indicator in the upper left corner
2. The battery icon which is actually a bar chart indicating how much power remains in the battery
3. The ▼ in the upper right corner, which indicates the category of items you are currently viewing

Tapping the ▼ or the text next to it opens a pop-up menu of all existing categories (see Figure 9-D). Move among categories by tapping the ▼, then choosing one of categories from the menu. Alternatively, repeatedly tapping the

9-D:

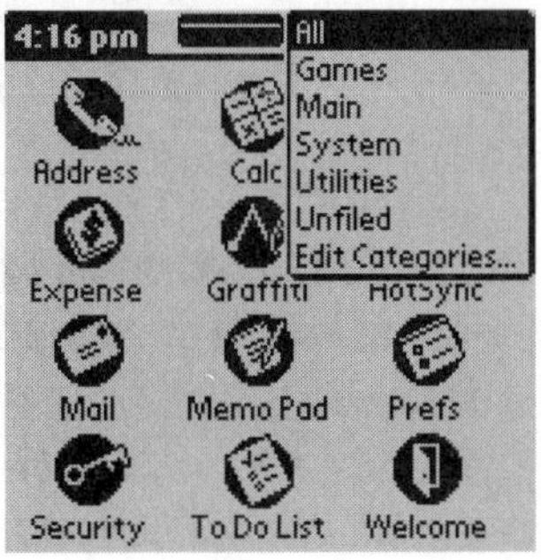

Home button scrolls through the categories. You will find that the Palm OS categorizes the four primary applications (Date Book, Address Book, To Do List, and Memo Pad), plus Calculator, Expense, and Mail, as "Main." Graffiti, HotSync, Prefs, Security, and Welcome are categorized as "System."[2]

§ 9.3 The Welcome Application

This application walks you through the few steps you have to take before using your handheld for the first time. It should open automatically when you first turn on your handheld. If it does not, tap the "Welcome" icon.

The first thing you must do is ensure that your handheld properly recognizes your stylus taps. Tap the center of the various targets that appear on the screen. This process is officially known as calibrating or digitizing the screen.

Next, set the time and date. In the Palm OS, whenever text is surrounded by dotted lines, as the time and date are in Figure 9-E, you can change that information. Tap anywhere within the dotted lines to bring up a dialog box, similar to the one shown in Figure 9-F. Tap on the number you want to change, then tap on the ▲ to increase the number, or on the ▼ to decrease it. Tap "OK" to return to the setup screen. Set the date by tapping within the dotted lines surrounding the date, then select the appropriate year (tap ▶ to move the calendar forward, ◀ to move it backward), month, and day. If you ever need to reset the date and time, you can use the Welcome application again (if you don't mind tapping the series of targets first), or tap Home → "Prefs" → ▼ → "General."

9-E:

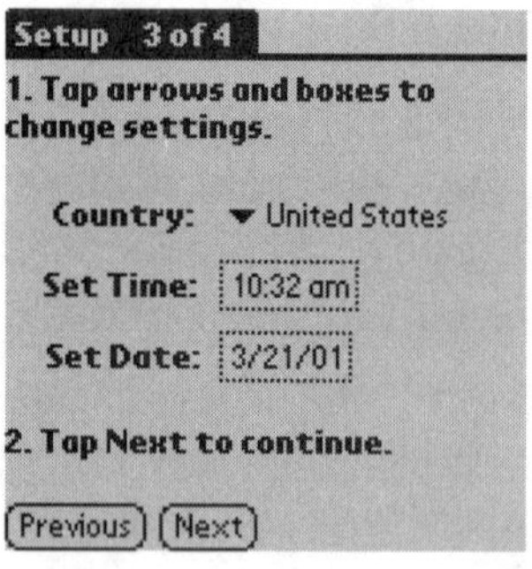

9-F:

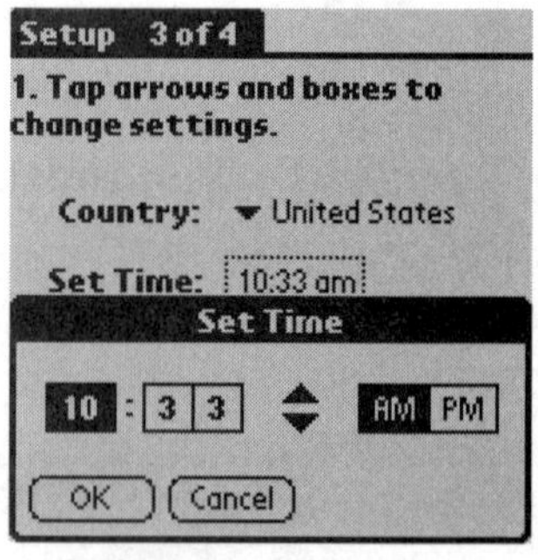

Over time, the screen calibration of some handhelds drifts slightly. If you notice that the screen is not responding as usual—or if it takes several attempts to hit an on-screen item—recalibrate the screen. Either go through the Welcome application again, or tap Home → "Prefs" → ▼ → "Digitizer," which presents you with the same series of targets as the Welcome application, but skips the time and date setup screen.

This completes the initial setup. At this point, the Welcome application gives you the option of going directly to the Graffiti tutorial (tap "Next"), or exiting the program (tap "Done").

§ 9.4 The Global Find Function

One of the most useful features of the Palm OS is the global Find function, which is accessed by tapping the silk-screened button on the lower right corner of the screen (the button with the icon of a magnifying glass). Tap the Find button, and insert (using Graffiti or the on-screen keyboard) the string of characters for which you are searching (see Figures 9-G through 9-I). All records that contain that string of characters are listed on the screen; tap on any of the items to go straight to it.

9-G:

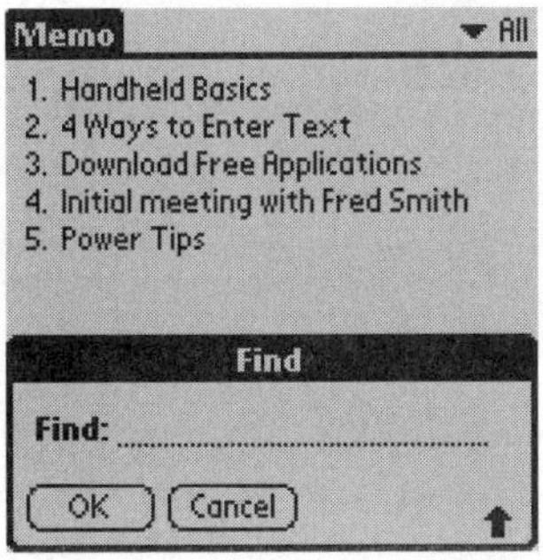

9-H:

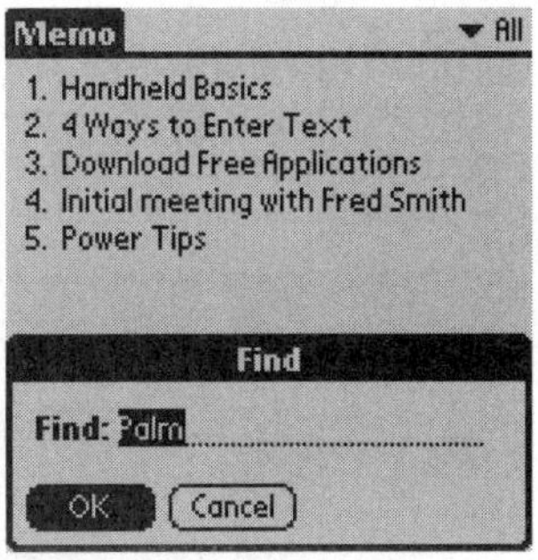

9-I:

When using the Find function, it is important to be aware that it is not case sensitive, but it does limit its searches to character strings that occur at the beginning of a word. The Find function begins searching with the application you are currently in, so if you are looking for text that you know appears in a particular application, you can save a few seconds by starting the search (by tapping the Find button) while you are in that application. Finally, if you highlight a word or phrase before tapping the Find button, the highlighted text automatically appears in the Find box (see Figure 9-J).

9-J:

§ 9.5 Security[3]

This application allows you both to assign various levels of privacy to specific records on your handheld, and to lock your handheld so that no one can turn it on without the proper password. To open the program, tap Home → "Security" (Figure 9-K).

9-K:

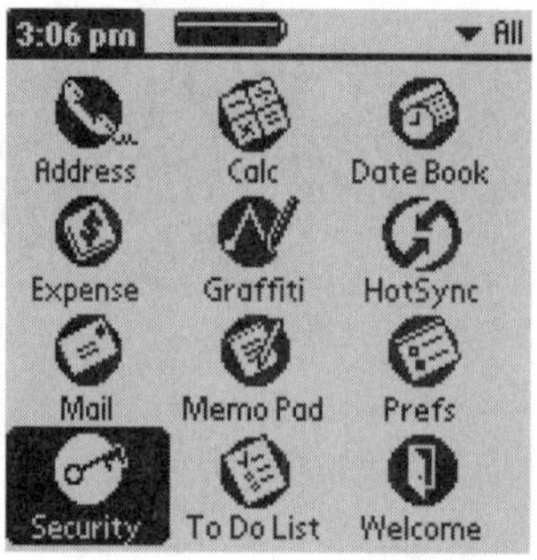

To set the privacy level, open the Current Privacy pop-up menu (Figures 9-L and 9-M).

9-L:

9-M:

The options are (1) Show Records, (2) Mask Records, and (3) Hide Records. These options apply consistently to all records you mark as private throughout Date Book (Section 11.5), Address Book (Section 12.5), To Do List (Section 13.7), and Memo Pad (Section 14.5); in other words, you cannot have some private records showing while others are masked or hidden. When you select "Mask Records," the lines where the text of private records would normally appear are replaced with gray hatch marks. When you select "Hide Records," the items become invisible. When you select "Show Records," the private items appear as if you had not marked them "Private" in the first place, so revert to "Show Records" when you want to read your private items.

To set, change, and delete your password, tap within the dotted rectangle next to the word "Password," and follow the instructions in the dialog boxes (see Figure 9-N).

9-N:

If you assign a password to your handheld and then forget the password, you can create a new password, but doing so also deletes all of your private records. (Not to worry: you can restore previously synchronized private records with a "Desktop overwrites Handheld" HotSync; see Section 10.2.)

Once you have set a password, you can use the "Lock & Turn Off" feature so that no one can view anything other than your handheld's owner information screen without inserting the password; see Figures 9-O and 9-P. (Section

9-O:

9-P:

22.2 explains how to insert owner information.) If you forget your password when this feature is activated, the only way to make your handheld operable is to perform a hard reset (see Section 22.1), which erases all of the information on your handheld, not just the private records. You can still restore previously synchronized records at your next HotSync, but it is like starting over with an entirely new handheld.

Notes

1. Also known as pick-lists, pop-up menus are also called drop-down menus when they appear at the top of the screen.

2. If "Main" and "System" are insufficiently descriptive for you, rename the categories and recategorize the applications any way you like, subject only to the limitation—typical in the Palm OS—that you cannot have more than fifteen categories. See Section 16.4 on categorizing applications.

3. As noted in Chapter 8, this discussion covers the basic features of version 3.5 of the Security application, which is the version native to a Palm Vx. More recent versions of the Security application contain more features and even greater security.

How to Get Information into Your PDA

10

§ 10.1 Graffiti®

Graffiti is the Palm OS version of handwriting recognition. You use Graffiti to input text into your handheld, so you have no need for a keyboard. Unlike the popular conception of handwriting-recognition software that recognizes your handwriting, Graffiti requires you to write letters, numbers, and punctuation marks in a form that it will recognize. This is not as difficult as it sounds; most Graffiti characters are fairly intuitive, and closely resemble the block version of the letter or number they represent.

Begin by tapping Home → "Graffiti" to access the Graffiti tutorial. (You can always return to this tutorial to remind yourself of Graffiti's finer points.) As the tutorial explains, the Graffiti writing area consists of the rectangle at the bottom of the Palm's touch-sensitive screen. It is divided into two parts delineated by an imaginary line connecting the small triangles at the top and bottom of the rectangle. The larger part on the left is for writing letters; the smaller part on the right is for writing numbers. You can write punctuation in either area.

Each Graffiti character consists of one continuous stroke, beginning at the point indicated by the heavy dot (see Figure 10-A).

Most of the characters are similar to the upper-case, hand-printed version; others (A, F, K, T, and 4) look like only part of their usual selves. The one exception to the "one continuous

10-A:

stroke" principle is the letter "X," which consists of two strokes: a diagonal slash from the upper left to the lower right of the letter area, followed by a diagonal slash from the upper right to the lower left.

To write a capital letter, first write the Caps Shift character (equivalent to pressing the Shift key on a keyboard), which consists of a vertical line drawn from bottom to top (see Figure 10-B). This line must be drawn in the letter side of the writing area. After you have drawn the Caps Shift stroke, a solid arrow pointing upwards appears in the lower right corner of the screen to indicate that you are in Caps Shift mode. Caps Shift mode disappears automatically after you input one letter, or you can cancel Caps Shift mode by inputting the Back Space character (a horizontal line drawn from right to left; see Figure 10-B).

10-B:

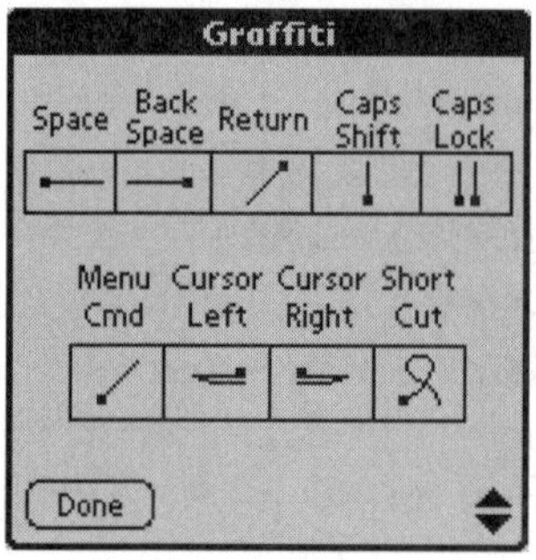

To write a series of capital letters without having to repeat the Caps Shift stroke, use the Caps Lock character (two upward strokes; see Figure 10-B). This is equivalent to the Caps Lock key on a keyboard, and is indicated by a two-part, upwards-pointing arrow in the lower right corner of the screen. Inputting the Caps Shift character again turns off the Caps Lock mode.

The Space character is a horizontal line drawn from left to right; imagine that you are moving the cursor along the line of text (see Figure 10-B). Similarly, the Return character is a diagonal line drawn from the upper right to the lower left (see Figure 10-B), which mimics the effect of pressing the Return or Enter key on a keyboard.

To move the cursor to the right (or left) without deleting existing text, draw the Cursor Right (or Cursor Left) character, which consists of tracing a line back over the Space (or Back Space) stroke without lifting the stylus from the screen (see Figure 10-B).

Tap "Try It!" → "Next" to take you to the Practice Letters screen (Figure 10-C), which shows you exactly what you have drawn with your stylus, as well as the resulting Graffiti character. (You can use this screen to practice numbers and punctuation in addition to letters.) The visual feedback is extremely helpful when you are learning Graffiti, since the shape you think you have drawn and the shape you have actually drawn can differ significantly. For optimal accuracy, write as large as possible within the letter or number area, write at a normal speed, and avoid writing on a slant. You can tap the "Tips" button to review these hints.

10-C:

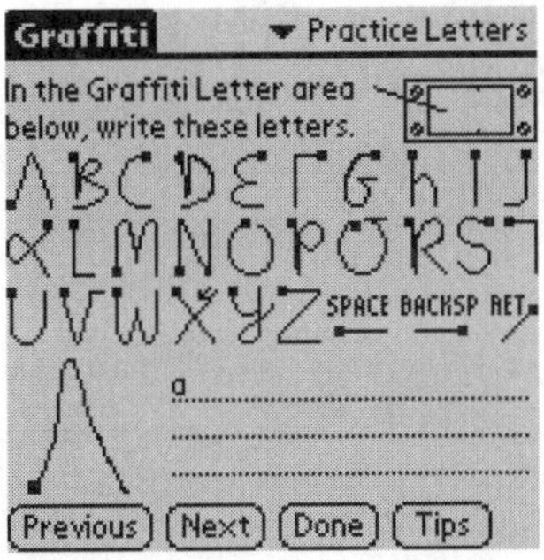

To input punctuation marks, enter Graffiti punctuation mode by tapping once on either side of the Graffiti writing area. A black dot will appear in the lower right corner of the screen when you are in punctuation mode. Insert punctuation marks by following that initial tap with the appropriate Graffiti punctuation character. See Figures 10-D and 10-E. You insert less-common

10-D:

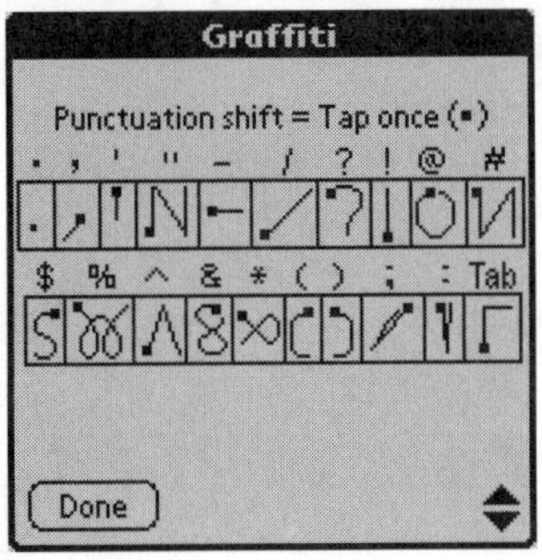

10-E:

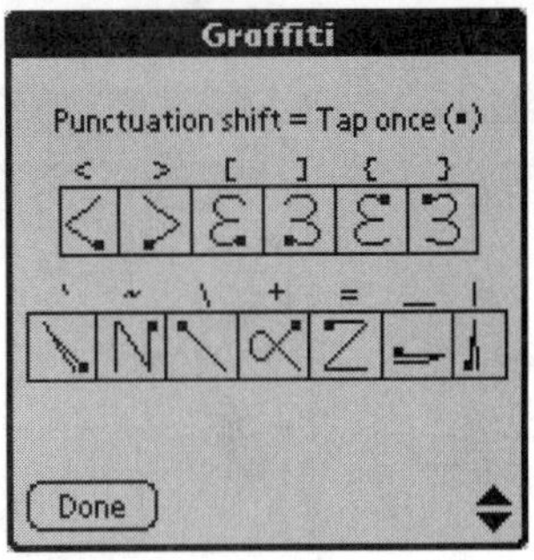

punctuation marks and characters by using the extended shift stroke (a diagonal line drawn from upper left to lower right), followed by the appropriate character (see Figure 10-F).

10-F:

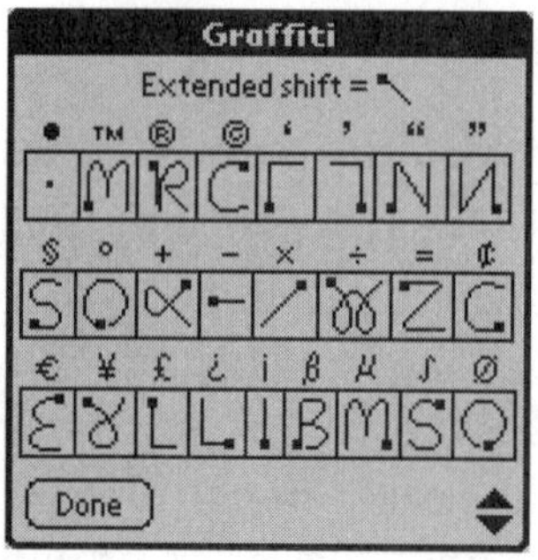

If at any point you prefer to enter text without using Graffiti, call up the on-screen keyboard by tapping one of the dots in the lower corners of the Graffiti writing area. Until you have mastered Graffiti, and even then when you want to input less common characters, hunting and pecking with your stylus can be more convenient than Graffiti (see Figure 10-G).

10-G:

A common convention in Palm OS programs is that tapping on the letter "i" in the upper right corner of a screen or dialog box reveals helpful information and reminders. For example, the screen in Figure 10-H appears when you tap the "i" in Figure 10-G.

10-H:

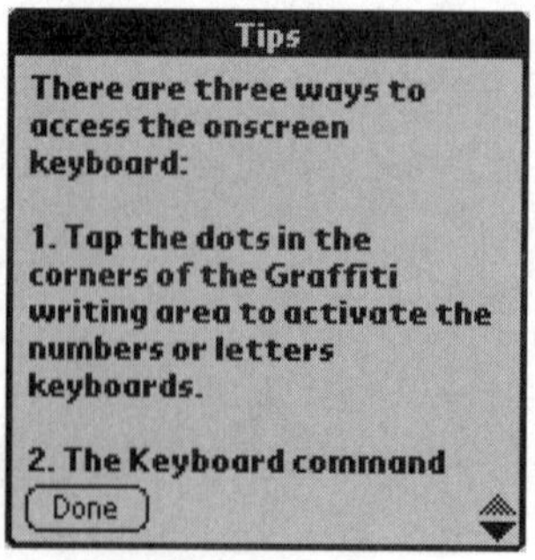

To become proficient at Graffiti:

1. Practice, practice, practice. Write out the alphabet several times to identify the characters that cause you the most trouble, then focus on mastering those. Actually, there are multiple ways to draw most Graffiti characters; see Appendix C for some alternatives that may work better for you.
2. Remember the basics: write at a normal speed, as large as possible within the prescribed area, not on a slant, and with a firm pressure.
3. Learning Graffiti can be fun if you use Giraffe, a Space Invaders-type game in which Graffiti letters and numbers drop from the top of the screen and crash if they reach the bottom before you input them correctly. If Giraffe is not already on your handheld, you can find it on your desktop (usually in the C:\Palm\Add-on folder) and install it at your next HotSync. See Chapter 17 on installing add-on programs to your handheld.
4. Remember that much of the information on your handheld can be installed by inputting it on the Palm Desktop program on your PC, then HotSyncing the information to your handheld. Since keyboard entry is usually much faster than Graffiti, you should use your computer's keyboard to input information whenever you are at your computer, or an add-on keyboard when you are away from it. See Section 10.3 below.
5. A handy alternative when you are having a bad Graffiti day is to use the on-screen keyboard. Tap one of the dots in the lower left corner of the Graffiti area to pull up a tiny QWERTY keyboard on the screen of your PDA. There is also a numerical keypad accessible from this screen, or by tapping the dot in the lower right corner of the Graffiti area. There is also a keyboard for foreign letters and letters with foreign accents, and if you use these elements rarely, it's easier to insert them using the keyboard than it is to memorize their Graffiti equivalents.
6. If you have a great deal of trouble with Graffiti, investigate replacements such as Jot and Wordcomplete, which are discussed in Section 10.3 below.

§ 10.2 HotSync®

HotSync is the Palm OS term for synchronizing the information on your handheld with that on your desktop computer. When you install the Palm Desktop software, the comprehensive setup wizard guides you through a series of steps so that your handheld information synchronizes with the desktop programs of your choice. For example, you can synchronize Date Book, Address

Book, To Do List, and Memo Pad with Microsoft Outlook rather than with the Palm Desktop program. The setup wizard also guides you through all the basic HotSync configurations. If you require a custom configuration not covered by the wizard, you are probably a "techie" yourself or have access to experts in your organization's information technology department. If not, you can get help on line for a tricky HotSync configuration using Palm's e-mail help desk at **www.palm.com**.

Once you have installed the Palm Desktop software, you can customize a particular HotSync operation so that only certain applications are synchronized. You can also choose whether the operation will truly synchronize a program's data (so that changes run both from your desktop to your handheld and vice versa), or have the handheld files overwrite the desktop's, or have the desktop's overwrite the handheld's. The last permutation is particularly useful in case you lose your handheld or accidentally delete information from it; you can restore lost data with a "Desktop overwrites Handheld" HotSync.

To set up a customized HotSync, either (a) tap the HotSync icon on your computer's toolbar, or (b) click "Start" → "Programs" → "Palm Desktop" → "HotSync" Manager, or (c) open your Palm Desktop and click "HotSync." Then click "Custom." Select an application, click "Change," and select whether you want to (a) synchronize the files, (b) have the desktop overwrite the handheld, (c) have the handheld overwrite the desktop, or (d) do nothing for that particular application. You can apply any of the four HotSync options to any combination of applications in a single HotSync, so save time by using a custom HotSync whenever you want to update fewer than all of your applications.

Once the HotSync configuration is set up to your preference, press the HotSync button, which is the only button on the HotSync cradle. Alternatively, you can tap the on-screen HotSync button that appears in the middle of your handheld's screen when you open the HotSync application. (Tap Home → "HotSync" to access the HotSync application (see Figure 10-I). You may wonder why would you ever use the on-screen button instead of the physical button. The answer is this: it comes in handy when you use the travel HotSync

10-I:

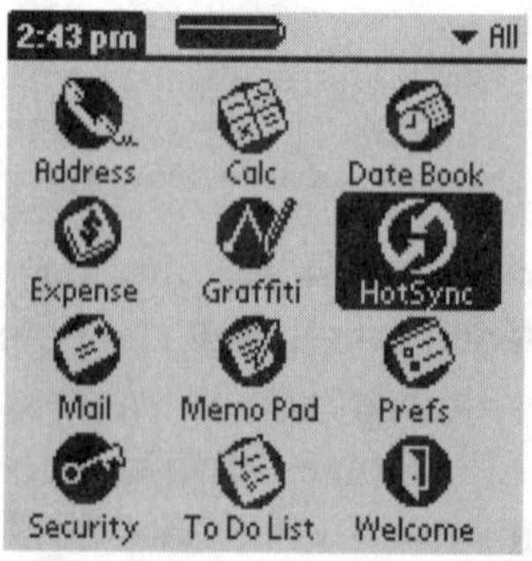

cord, which may not have its own HotSync button but is much easier to pack than the bulky, awkwardly shaped HotSync cradle.

After each HotSync, a comprehensive log appears in your desktop HotSync Manager detailing what happened during the operation. If you set an application to synchronize the files, but changed the same record in inconsistent ways on your desktop and handheld, the log informs you that both versions have been copied on both platforms, and that you should delete the incorrect version prior to your next HotSync. An abbreviated version of this log appears on the handheld as well (tap "Log").

You can also use the HotSync application to remind yourself of the name you assigned to your handheld, which appears in the upper right hand corner of the handheld's HotSync screen, and to set your preferences between a Local versus a Modem HotSync, and a Direct Serial versus an IR connection (see Figure 10-J).

10-J:

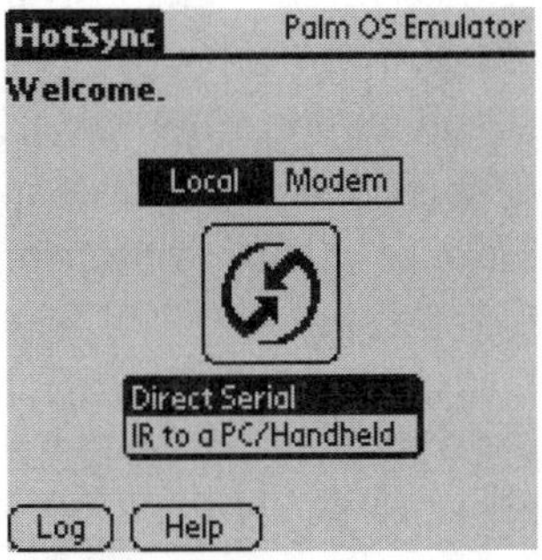

§ 10.3 Other Ways to Get Information into Your PDA

In addition to Graffiti, the on-screen keyboard, HotSync, and beaming, you can insert information into your PDA using a variety of add-on software programs and hardware devices.

Software options. There are currently three basic categories of software programs available to allow you to insert information into your PDA more quickly than with standard Graffiti. The first category consists of programs that allow you, to some extent, to customize your PDA so that it recognizes your Graffiti letters even when they don't fall precisely into the parameters required by standard Graffiti. For example, Jot[1] allows you to write anywhere on the screen (not just in the Graffiti area), and it allows you to see your characters as you write them. This visual feedback tends to improve accuracy. Jot also allows you to create shortcuts for frequently-used phrases, and to fine-tune its ability to recognize your own version of the traditional Graffiti characters. Other programs similar to Jot include RecoEcho Plus and TealEcho.

The second category consists of programs such as WordComplete, which offers you a pop-up list of applicable words as you enter each successive letter of any word. When the word you want appears on the list, tap it, and the word is automatically inserted in its entirety. WordComplete allow you a variety of convenient options, such as locating the pop-up list near the cursor or at the bottom of the screen; setting how many words to display in the list; whether to suggest words after one, two, three, or four letters; including only words with at least three, four, five, or six letters; and whether to include a space after the word is inserted. Another similar program is QuickWrite.

The third category consists of programs such as QuickNotes. These programs allow you to draw or sketch directly on the screen, with digital ink appearing wherever you touch your stylus to the screen. You can therefore use these programs to write short notes in your own printing or handwriting. These programs do not "translate" your writing into Graffiti. Other similar programs are InkSnap, and Palm's own NotePad, which comes preinstalled in devices using Palm operating systems 4.1 and above.

Hardware options. There is an ever-growing number of add-on keyboards available for Palm Powered™ PDAs, from full-size portable folding keyboards, to minikeyboards, ultrathin keyboards, and thumb-boards (see Section 20.10).

Note

1. See Appendix B on how to find Jot and other add-on software.

Using Date Book 11

§ 11.1 Overview

Like any calendar, Date Book helps you keep track of events, appointments, deadlines, reminders, birthdays, and anniversaries. Unlike a paper calendar, Date Book lets you set alarms to remind you of upcoming events; insert repeating events quickly with no rewriting; reschedule events easily; hide certain events from prying eyes; attach notes to an event; view your calendar by the day, the week, the month, or with your to-do list; schedule events up to thirty years in advance; and find specific events quickly without flipping through any pages.

You can launch Date Book most easily by pressing the physical button furthest to the left on the front of your handheld. Alternatively, you can tap Home, locate the Date Book icon, and tap it. This opens the Date Book program and takes you directly to the daily calendar page for today (Figure 11-A).

11-A:

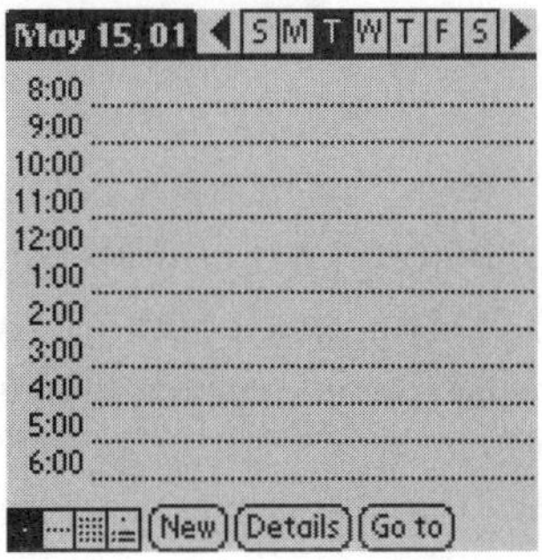

§ 11.2 Views in Date Book

There are four views in Date Book: Day View, Week View, Month View, and Combination View. You can scroll through these four views by repeatedly pressing the Date Book button, or by tapping one of the little boxes in the lower left corner of the screen (Figure 11-A). The box farthest to the left is for Day View, the next is for Week View, and so forth.

Day View (Figure 11-A) shows your schedule for a single day, and is the view in which you input new events. From Day View, you can move to other days of the current week by tapping the day indicators at the top right of the screen. You can move forward in one-week increments by tapping the arrow to the right of the day indicators, and backward in one-week increments by tapping the arrow on the left. The "Go to" button at the bottom of the screen opens the Go to Date box, where you can go to any date[1] by selecting the desired year, month, and day. You can select either the month or the year first, as long as you select the day last. Return to the current date by tapping "Today" in the Go to Date box. Finally, you can scroll from day to day with the physical scroll button. Scrolling down moves Date Book forward in time; scrolling up moves it backward.

Week View (Figure 11-B) shows you a silhouette of the entire week, with events appearing as shaded gray boxes. When you tap on a shaded box, the date, time, and name of the event appear in a box at the top of the screen (Figure 11-C).

11-B:

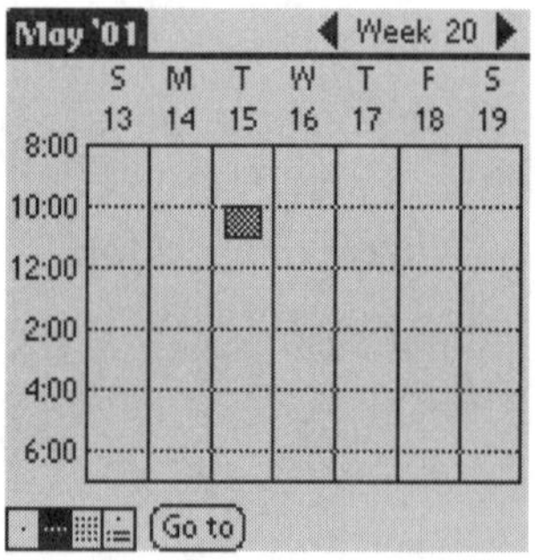

11-C:

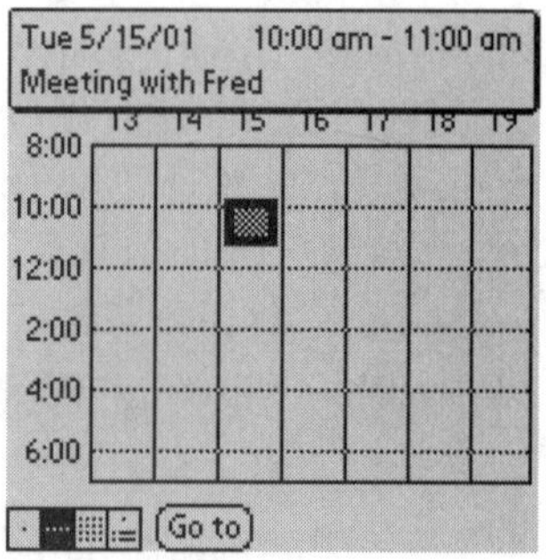

You can reschedule an event within the week by tapping on the shaded box and dragging it to another day or time. To scroll from week to week, tap the arrows on each side of the week indicator at the upper right of the screen, or use the physical scroll button. You can move to any other week's view by tapping the "Go to" button.

In Month View (Figure 11-D), timed events are indicated by small black marks on the right side of the square for each day, with morning events at the top, afternoon events in the middle, and evening events at the bottom. An un-

11-D: 

timed event is represented by a small black diamond in a square's lower left corner. Events that last more than a day are illustrated by a dotted line along the bottom of the appropriate squares. To view other months, tap the arrows in the upper right corner of the screen, use the scroll button, or tap the "Go to" button.

Combination View (Figure 11-E) consists of a list of that day's appointments, plus a list of that day's tasks imported from To Do List. Tapping on any item takes you directly to it, so this view is a handy way of moving back and forth between Date Book and To Do List.

11-E: 

§ 11.3 Inserting an Event

In the Palm OS, there are usually several different ways to do the same thing. For example, you might reasonably assume that the first step in inserting a new event in Date Book would be to tap the "New" button at the bottom of the Day View screen, and indeed this is one way to begin.[2]

When you tap "New," the Set Time box appears (Figure 11-F). To set the event's starting time, tap within the Start Time box, then tap on the hour, and—if the start time is not on the hour—the minute indicator. The default length of time for an event is one hour. If your event has a different duration, tap inside the End Time box, then tap the appropriate hour and minute. The "All Day" button automatically sets the start and end time to correspond to the first and

11-F:

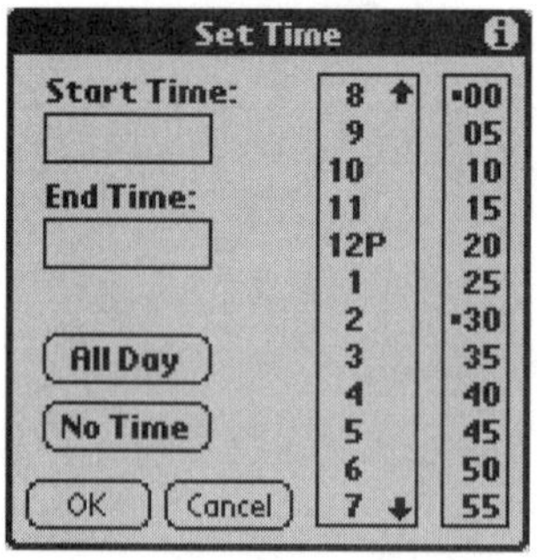

last times shown in Day View. (You can customize these times; see Section 11.12 below.) Use the "No Time" button for birthdays, anniversaries, and other events that have no specific start or end time. Tap "OK." Immediately insert the name of the event on the line indicated by the flashing cursor. If you tap elsewhere on the screen before you enter the name of the event, Date Book assumes you have changed your mind about inserting the event, and deletes all the start-time and end-time information you just input.

You can avoid this pitfall by using an easier way to insert an event. You can either (a) tap a line at or near the starting time of the event, then insert the name of the event, or (b) just begin writing the name of the event in the Graffiti area, which Date Book records as an untimed event. Once you have inserted the name of the event, tap the "Details" button to bring up the Event Details box, then tap on the time indicator to bring up the Set Time box.

Your event should now appear in Day View with the start and end times marked with a bracket at the left margin of the screen. Untimed events appear at the top of the schedule next to a black diamond (Figure 11-G).

All day events are compressed to show only their start and end times (Figure 11-H).

11-G:

11-H:

§ 11.4 Setting an Alarm for an Event

Date Book's alarm function is sufficiently flexible so that you can use it to give you ten-minutes' warning before an office meeting, or sixty-days' notice of a major deadline. The alarm consists of an audible tone (except for untimed events) and an on-screen reminder box complete with a snooze button. You can set the alarm's advance time to be different for different events.

To set an alarm, make sure you are in Day View, then tap anywhere on a line containing the description of an event, tap "Details," then tap the Alarm checkbox (Figure 11-I). You can set the alarm to go off anywhere from 0 to 99 minutes, hours, or days before an event. Once you set an alarm for an event, an alarm clock icon appears at the right edge of the screen on the same line as the description of the event (Figure 11-J). Tapping on this icon will take you directly to the Event Details box again. This is faster than the alternative, which is to select the event, then tap "Details."

11-I:

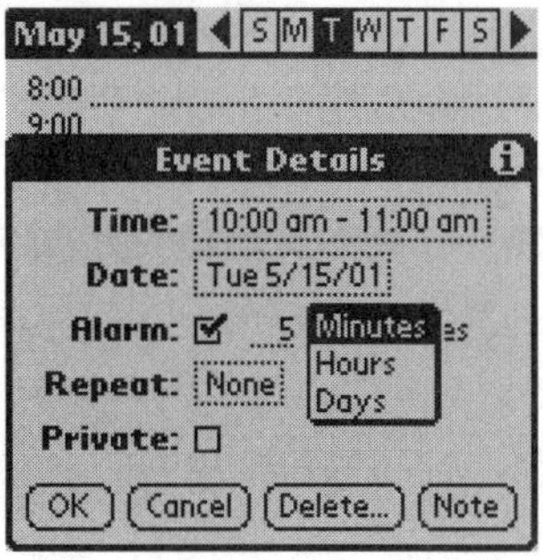

11-J:

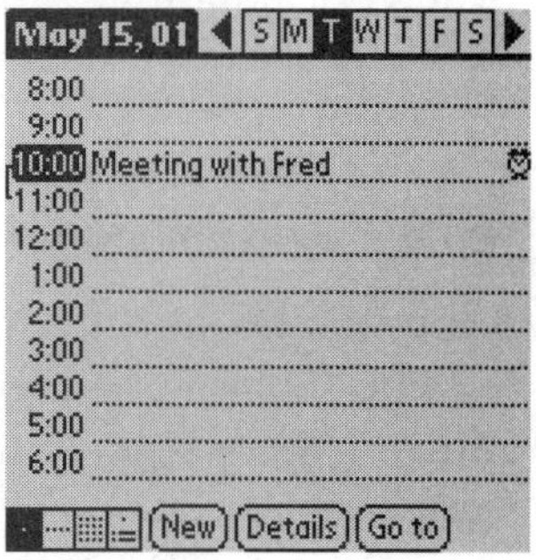

You can customize various characteristics of the alarm. You can set the default option so that an alarm is automatically set whenever you insert an event. Tap Menu → "Options" → "Preferences" and the Alarm Preset checkbox, and set the advance time to 0 to 99 minutes, 0 to 99 hours, or 0 to 99 days. (You can always change this for a specific event.) Tap the Alarm Sound pop-up menu to listen to and select one of the seven alarm sounds; tap the Remind Me pop-up menu to select how many times you want the alarm to sound if you don't turn it off (once, twice, three times, five times, or ten times); and tap the Play Every pop-up menu to select the interval between the times the alarm will sound (one, five, ten, or thirty minutes). The alarm sound, frequency, and interval are universal throughout Date Book, and cannot be changed for specific events.

§ 11.5 Making an Event Private

If you want to keep your event hidden from prying eyes, select the event (by tapping anywhere on a line containing its description), tap "Details," and then the Private checkbox in the Event Details box (Figure 11-K). You can mask the event (Figure 11-L), or make it entirely invisible by tapping Menu → "Options" → "Security" and selecting your preference. If you have not yet inserted a password, the program prompts you to do so now.

11-K:

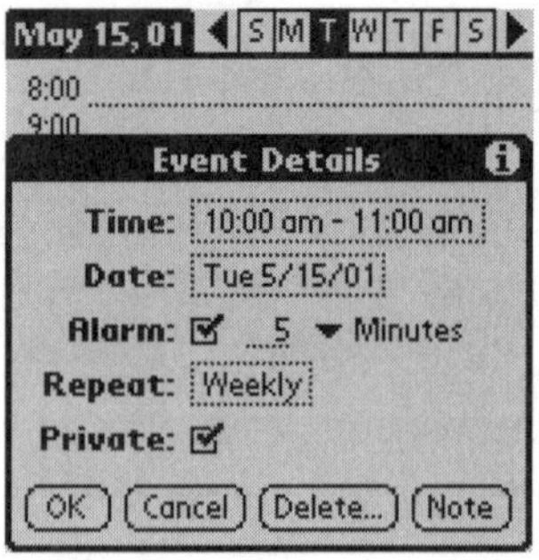

11-L:

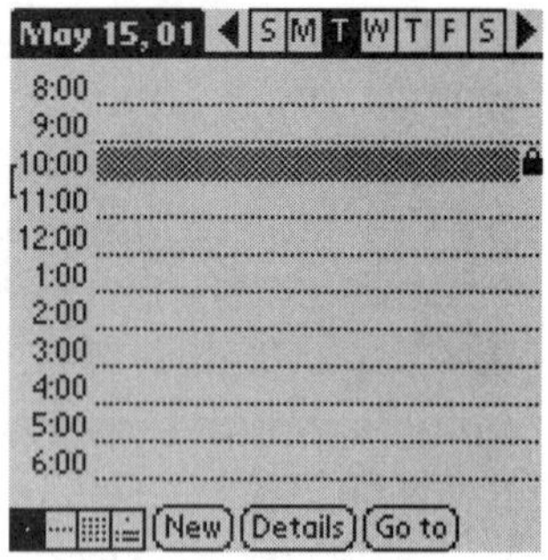

This option, while handy, provides only limited security, since private events are still visible on the desktop calendar program with which you Hot-Sync your handheld.

§ 11.6 Attaching a Note to an Event

Select the event, then tap "Details" → "Note." This creates a note with room for 4,096 characters (about two double-spaced pages of 12-point type), an excellent spot to park directions, reminders, and miscellaneous information concerning the event (see Figures 11-M and 11-N).

11-M:

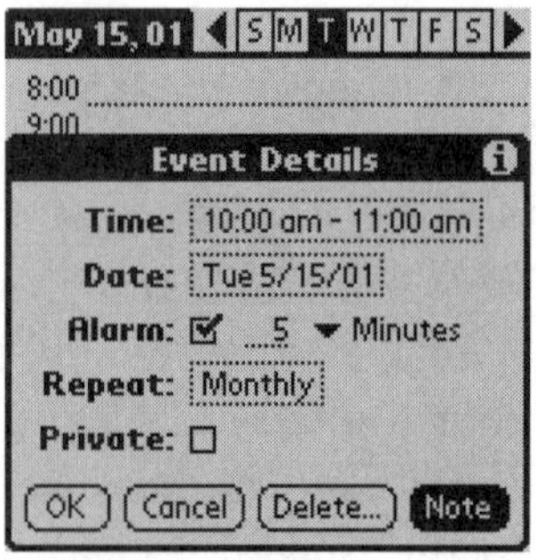

11-N:

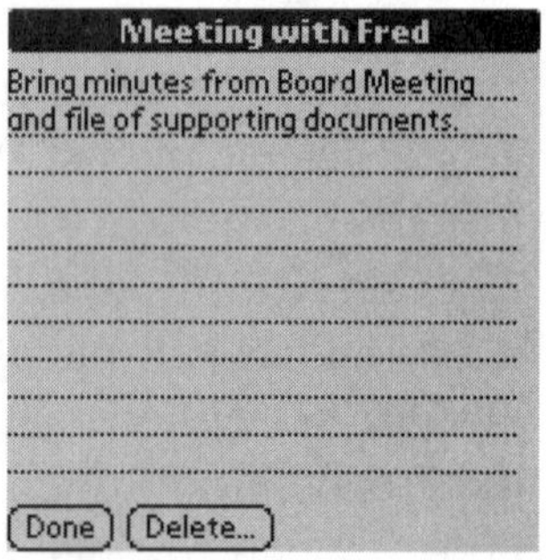

Once you have attached a note to an event, a note icon appears on the same line as the description of the event (Figure 11-O). Tapping the icon brings up the note itself (not the Event Details box, as is the case when you tap the alarm or repeat icon). This is faster than the alternative, which is to select the event, then tap "Details" → "Note."

§ 11.7 Inserting a Repeating Event

You can insert a series of repeating events without inserting each one separately. After inserting the first event, tap "Details" to bring up in the Event De-

11-O:

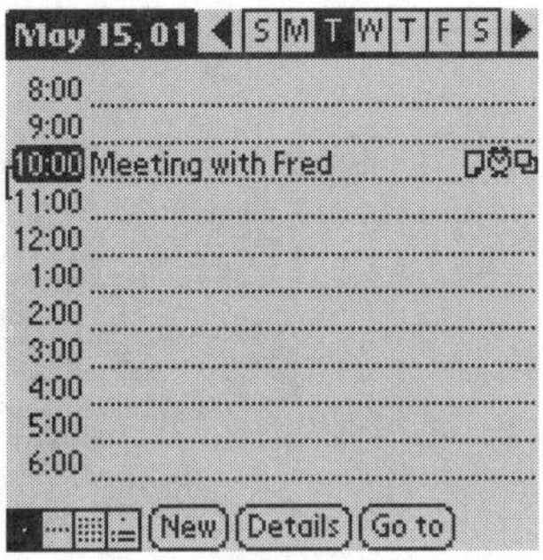

tails box, then tap within the Repeat box to bring up the Change Repeat box (Figure 11-P). Select whether the event recurs on a daily, weekly, monthly, or yearly basis. The Change Repeat options are flexible: you can set an event to repeat once or several times a week (Figure 11-Q).

11-P:

11-Q:

A monthly event can be scheduled for a specific date, or for a specific day during the first, second, third, fourth, or last week of the month (Figures 11-R and 11-S).

11-R:

11-S:

You can schedule a repeating event to recur indefinitely, or you can choose a specific end date (Figures 11-T through 11-V) using the date selector screen.

11-T:

11-U:

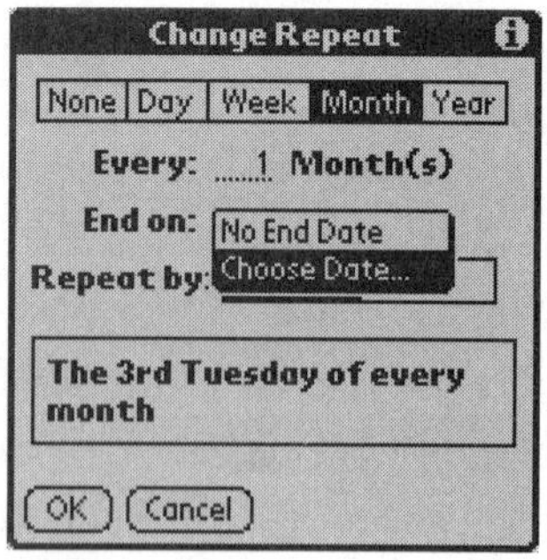

11-V:

Once you have set up a repeating event, the repeat icon appears at the right edge of the screen on the same line as the description of the event (Figure 11-W). As with the alarm icon, tapping the repeat event icon takes you straight to the Event Details box, which is quicker than selecting the event, then tapping "Details."

11-W:

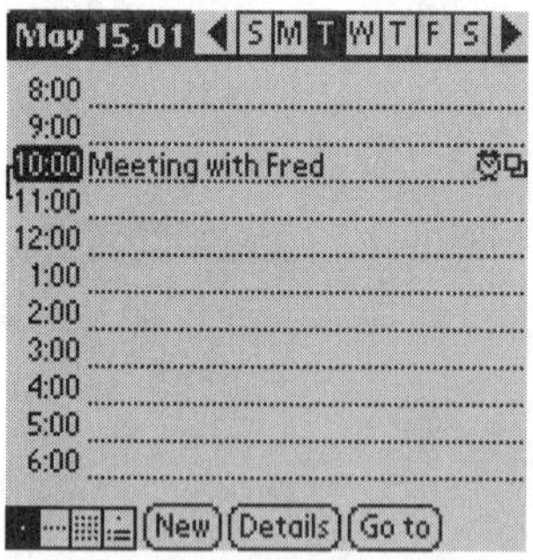

When you change the name of one of a series of repeating events, Date Book automatically changes the name for each event in the series. However, when you add a note, add or change the alarm setting, or make one of the series private, you have the option of limiting that change to that event, or applying it to the entire series.

§ 11.8 Changing the Details of an Event

You can change an event's details at any time. Select the event, then tap "Details" to bring up the Event Details box (Figure 11-X). From this box, you can change the event's start time, end time, date, alarm, recurrences, and privacy level. You can go straight to the Set Time box by tapping the event's time in the left column of Day View, or straight to the Event Details box by tapping the alarm or repeat icon.

11-X:

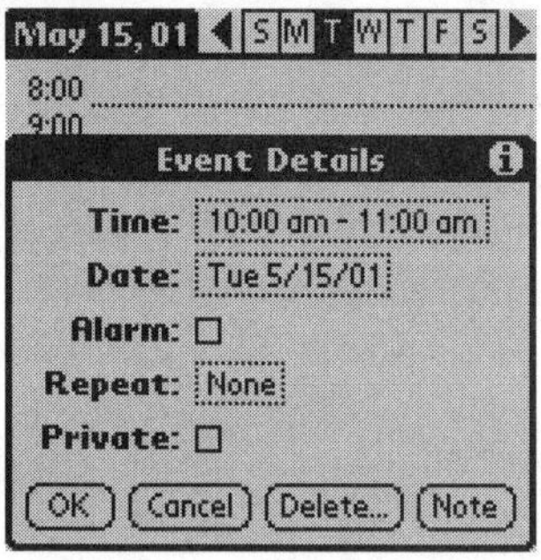

In addition, you can always edit the name of the event (plus the text in an attached note), using Graffiti, Graffiti ShortCuts (see Section 15.5), or the on-screen keyboard. In addition, the standard edit commands (undo, cut, copy, paste, and select all) are available on the pull-down menu (tap Menu → "Edit") or by using the associated command shortcuts or the floating command icon bar (see Section 15.7).

§ 11.9 Deleting an Event

Deleting an event is another operation that you can accomplish in many ways. One straightforward method is to select the event, then tap "Details" → "Delete" → "OK" (see Figure 11-Y).

11-Y:

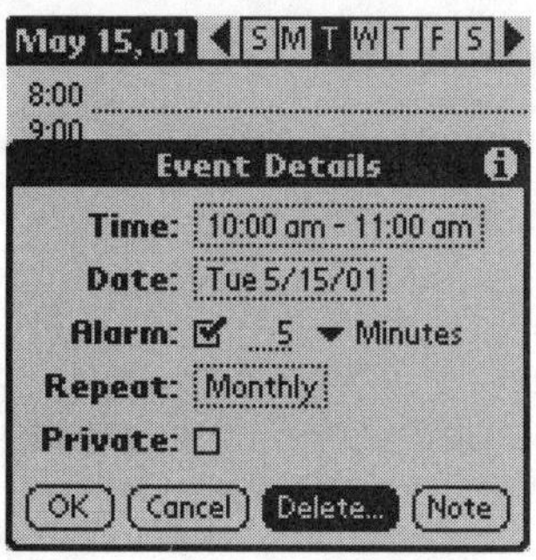

The other ways are to:

1. Select the event, tap the Menu button, and tap "Delete Event"
2. Select the event, tap the date indicator, and tap "Delete Event"
3. Select the event and write the command shortcut /D
4. Select the event, write /, and tap the trashcan icon
5. Backspace over the name of the event
6. Highlight the name of event and backspace once
7. Highlight the name of the event, write /, and tap the scissors icon
8. Highlight the name of event and write /D
9. Highlight the name of event and write /X

There are various ways to highlight the name of an event:

1. Drag the stylus over the text
2. Double-tap (if the description consists of one word)
3. Triple-tap (if the description consists of more than one word)

These various choices means that there are more than a dozen different ways to delete an event. However, Date Book gives you the option of saving an archive copy on your PC only when you delete an event using some variation of the Delete button or command (as opposed to erasing the name of the event). When you choose to save an archive copy, the event no longer appears in Date Book, although it remains in your handheld's memory until after your next HotSync.

§ 11.10 Purging Events

You can delete multiple events simultaneously by purging events that are older than a week, two weeks, three weeks, or one month. From Day View, tap the Menu button and select "Purge" (or use the command shortcut /E), select the time frame and back-up option, and tap "OK." Again, Date Book gives you the option to save archive copies on your PC.

§ 11.11 Beaming an Event

There are three ways to beam an event. Select the event, then do one of the following:

a. Tap Menu and select "Beam Event."
b. Write the command shortcut /B.
c. Write / and tap the beam icon in the pop-up command bar.

Beamed events appear in a recipient's handheld exactly as they appear in yours, along with any associated recurrences, alarm settings, and notes.

§ 11.12 Options in Date Book

Date Book allows you to customize Day View in four ways:

1. You can display events in one of three fonts. Tap Menu → "Options" → "Font" (or use the command shortcut /F) and tap the font you want. This change applies to all events in Date Book; you cannot apply a font change selectively to some events but not to others. However, you can apply one font to all events and another font to all notes in Date Book. To change the notes font, open any note, then tap Menu → "Options" → "Font" (or use the command shortcut /F as discussed in Section 15.07).
2. You can hide the time brackets that appear on the left side of the screen. Tap Menu → "Options" → "Display Options" and tap the checkbox to deselect the "Show Time Bars" option.
3. You can turn off the default Compress option, which hides unscheduled time as necessary to show the day's events. The default setting in the Palm OS is to have the Compress option on, since then you need not scroll down to view an evening event if there are few events scheduled during the day. To turn off this option, tap Menu → "Options" → "Display Options" and tap the checkbox to deselect the "Compress Day Views" option.
4. You can reset the default start and end times shown in Day View (and used for All Day events). Tap Menu → "Options" → "Preferences" and tap the arrows next to the start-time and end-time boxes to scroll to the times you want (Figure 11-Z).

11-Z:

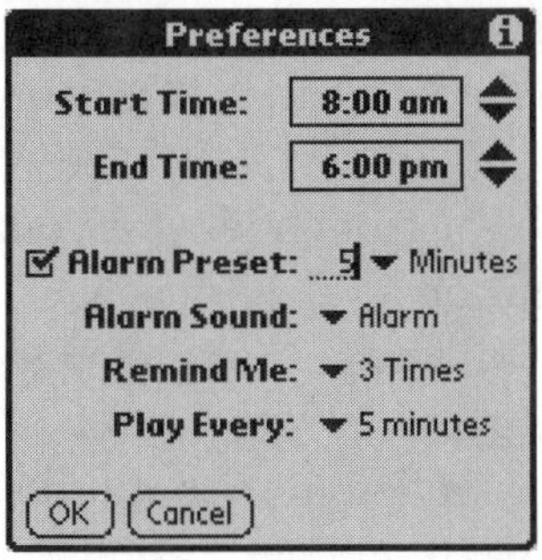

In Month View, you can choose whether to show or hide timed events, untimed events, or daily repeating events. Tap the Menu button → "Options" → "Display Options" and select or deselect the appropriate box. This option is handy if you do not want Month View cluttered with birthdays or reminders.

Another handy option in Date Book is Phone Lookup, which gives you easy access to names and telephone numbers in Address Book. Here is how it works: if you have scheduled a meeting with Mr. Smith, select the word "Smith" by tapping anywhere in the word, then write the command shortcut /L (or tap Menu → "Options" → "Phone Lookup"). "Smith" is replaced with a full name and telephone number. If you know more than one Smith, Phone Lookup takes you to a pick-list of Smiths in your Address Book so you can tap the correct one.

§ 11.13 Suggestions for Using Date Book

You can get the most out of Date Book with the following techniques:

1. With a little creativity, you can make the global Find feature even more useful. For example, when you insert deadlines for a particular project, begin each item with an abbreviation or acronym unique to that project, such as "SvJ" for Smith v. Jones, as well as the date ("5/1/02"), so that a global find search for "SvJ" yields a list of matching terms that is in effect the timetable for the project. Since you can tap any item to go directly to it, this is a convenient way to review and revise the schedule for that project. Similarly, for annual repeating events such as birthdays and anniversaries, begin the entry with "B-day" or "Anniv," and include the entire date of the original event ("10/15/85") so the list of matching items contains the maximum amount of information. This is also a convenient way to indicate which birthday or anniversary it is, since you can insert the identical item as a series of annual repeating events. Repeating events must have the same title, so this technique is easier than having separate events for "Firm's Seventh Anniversary," "Firm's Eighth Anniversary," and so on.
2. Use the repeating-event option to create reminders for yourself to accomplish important tasks that occur on a regular basis, such as paying your bar dues and keeping up with your continuing legal education credits.
3. When you beam an event with an attached note, both the event and the note appear on the receiving handheld, so beaming events is a

convenient way of sharing important information, such as driving directions or meetings agendas.

4. Customize the alarms setting for specific events to give you the appropriate amount of advance warning: ten minutes before a meeting in your office, forty minutes for meetings across town, at least several days before all-day conferences or business trips.
5. You can silence an alarm quickly by using your finger to tap the large "OK" or "Snooze" button instead of fumbling for your stylus.
6. If you have trouble hearing the alarm, be sure it is set as loud as possible. Tap Home → "Prefs" → ▼ → "General" → "Alarm Sound" → "High." If the alarm is still too quiet, place your handheld face down, since on most models the sound comes from the back of the device.
7. Insert multiday conferences (such as ABA meetings) as repeating events instead of inserting a separate event for each day.
8. Purge your Date Book periodically to prevent old events from clogging your handheld's memory. However, when you use the "Purge" command, you cannot pick and choose which events to purge; it applies to all events older than the time period you specify. (See Section 11.10 above.) This can cause problems if you want to keep some important event permanently on your handheld for future reference. To prevent a special event from being purged, make it a repeating event occurring once every 99 years, since Date Book purges events based upon the date of the last of a series of repeating events.
9. Be careful when hiding private events in Date Book, since invisible entries are easy to forget, thereby defeating one of the main purposes of keeping a calendar. It is better to mask events than to hide them entirely; the gray strip alerts you that something is coming up, even though you may have to unmask the event to recall the specifics.
10. Develop the habit of keeping your handheld with you as much as possible, and input items as soon as you think of them. During otherwise unproductive time (commuting, waiting in line, waiting on hold on the phone, waiting for a long document to download from the Internet), scroll through your calendar to keep upcoming events fresh in your mind.
11. Remember that your handheld is only one part of your overall organizational system. Many people like having a monthly paper calendar in view at all times. Using a handheld does not mean you cannot avail yourself of this option as well. After HotSyncing, print out your monthly calendar from your desktop program.

12. If you find the month view in Date Book to be insufficient for your needs, replace it with a more comprehensive program such as DateBk5 from Pimlico Software (**www.pimlicosoftware.com**; $24.95), which offers an improved week view as well as distinct icons for different kinds of events.

Notes

1. Date Book 3.5 covers dates from January 1, 1904 through December 31, 2031.

2. Sometimes the Palm OS takes user-friendly to extremes: in case you forget the purpose of the "New" button, you can create a new event by using the pull-down menu (in Day View, tap Home or the date indicator at the top left corner of the screen, then tap Record → New Event), or the command shortcut /N (see Section 15.7 on command shortcuts).

Using Address Book 12

§ 12.1 Overview

Address Book is where you keep information about the people and organizations in your life. With Address Book you can find telephone numbers in seconds, store lots of information about people, organize your contacts into customized categories, update information easily, and create an electronic business card you can beam to other handhelds in one step. The views in Address Book acknowledge the realities of modern life by having room for multiple telephone numbers and e-mail addresses, and placing them before the mailing address.

You can open Address Book most easily by pressing the physical button second from the left on the front of your handheld, or you can tap the Address Book icon. The first view you see is the list view, which looks something like Figure 12-A.

12-A:

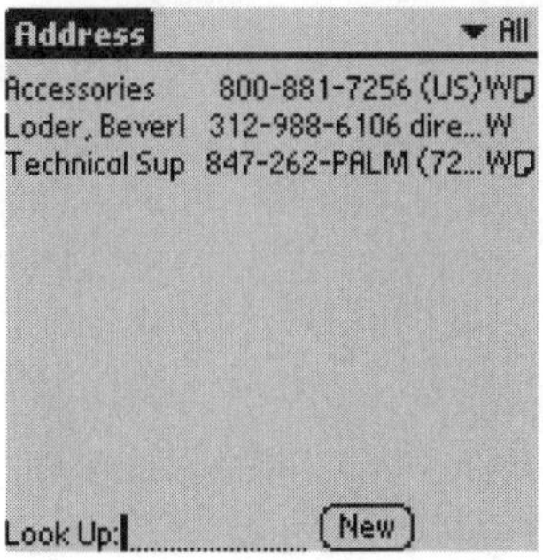

§ 12.2 Views in Address Book

Address Book has three basic views: List View, Address View, and Address Edit View. In List View, you see the names of your contacts, along with one telephone number for each contact, and a note icon if you have attached a note to the contact's record. In Address View, you see the detailed information about one contact. You insert and edit information in Address Edit View.

Address Book always opens into List View. To access the detailed Address View for a particular contact, tap anywhere on the line of text containing that contact's name and telephone number. To return to List View from Address View, tap the "Done" button in the bottom left corner of the screen.

To open Address Edit View, go to Address View and tap "Edit." (Actually, you can get to Address Edit View by tapping anywhere on the Address View screen.) To return to Address View, tap "Done." You cannot go directly from List View to Address Edit View for an existing contact.

You can customize List View in two ways. (1) You can specify whether your contacts appear in alphabetical order by last name or by company. Tap Menu → "Options" → "Preferences" and make your selection. If you list contacts by company, contacts without companies are listed by their last name. (2) You can also select which of the contact's telephone numbers appears in List View. By default, the telephone number in the first telephone number field appears in List View. To change this, select the contact, tap "Edit" → "Details" → Show in List pop-up menu, and make your selection.

§ 12.3 Inserting a Contact Record

In Address Book (unlike Date Book, To Do List, and Memo Pad), you have to use the "New" button to insert a new record. (If you just start writing, Address Book thinks you are using the Look Up feature; see Section 12.9.) When you tap "New," the Address Edit screen appears (Figure 12-B).

12-B:

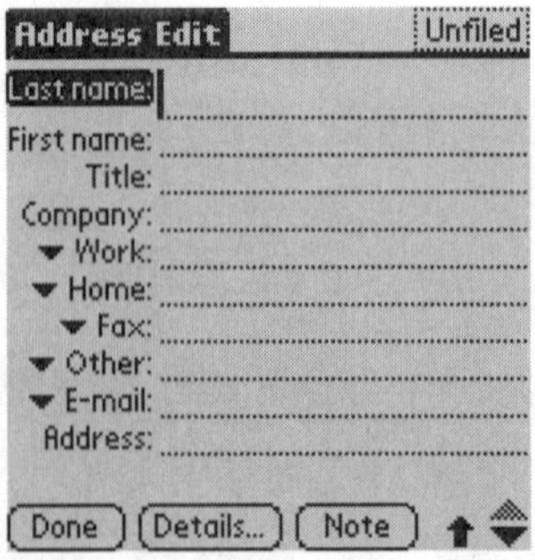

Using Graffiti or the on-screen keyboard, write the appropriate contact information on each line. The first letter in each field is automatically capitalized, so you can skip the initial Caps Shift stroke. To move to another field, tap anywhere within the dotted lines delineating the field. A field can contain more than one line of text; just keep writing, or insert a Graffiti Return character.

You can change the name of any of the five telephone number fields by tapping on the triangle next to the name of the field, then selecting another name from the pop-up menu (see Figures 12-C and 12-D). You can choose the same name for two (or more) of these fields. Tap the shaded gray triangle at the bottom right corner of the screen to scroll down or up to the rest of the fields (Figure 12-E).

12-C:

12-D:

12-E:

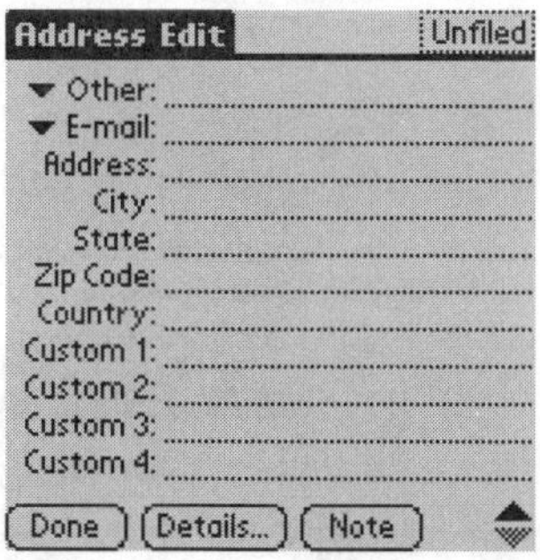

You can choose which phone number to show for a contact in List View. In Address Edit View, tap "Details" → the ▼ next to "Show in List:" and select the phone number you want to see in List View (see Figure 12-F).

Address Book is the only one of the four main Palm OS applications that allows you to create customized field names. This option makes Address Book extremely flexible, since you can create fields for such handy identifiers as client-matter number, case name, project name, professional organization, or any other descriptor that will allow you to identify contacts who share a common quality. For example, if you name a field something like "How we met,"

12-F:

and for each contact insert a word, phrase, or acronym describing your common bond, such as ABA, ABA-LPMS (Law Practice Management Section), your law school, or the professional organization through which you met, then a search for that word, phrase, or acronym yields a list of everyone you met through that organization, which would be handy to review as you travel to the next meeting. A search by client-matter number yields the cast of characters for that matter.

You can give the four custom fields any names you want. Tap Menu → "Options" → "Rename Custom Fields" and edit the text in the box (see Figures 12-G and 12-H).

12-G:

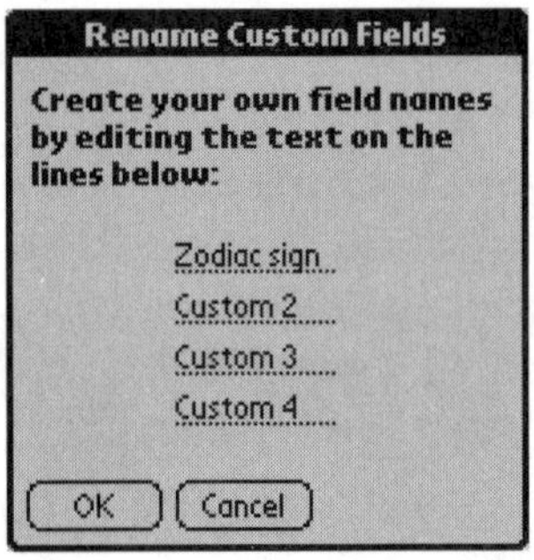

12-H:

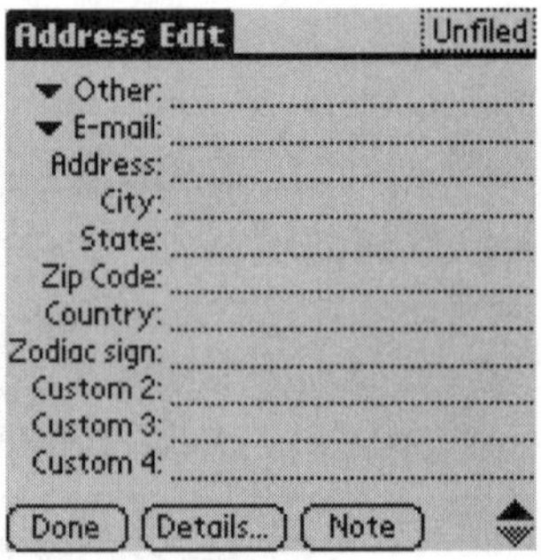

When inserting a contact with the same address as an existing contact (such as a partner, colleague, or family member), save time by using the Duplicate Address option. In List View, Address View, or Address Edit View, tap Menu → "Record" → "Duplicate Address" or use the command shortcut /D, which creates a copy of the contact showing on the screen or which you have selected from List View.

§ 12.4 Categorizing Records

In Address Book (as in To Do List and Memo Pad, but not in Date Book), you can put records into up to fifteen categories of your own creation. Four categories—All, Business, Personal, and Unfiled—are preinstalled. You can delete or rename "Business" and "Personal," but "All" and "Unfiled" are unalterable, and are not included in the fifteen-category limit.

To create a new category, tap "Details" → the ▼ next to "Category" → "Edit Categories" → "New" (Figures 12-I and 12-J). Insert the name of the new category and tap "OK" (Figures 12-K and 12-L). Your new category now shows up in the pop-up menu.

12-I:

12-J:

12-K:

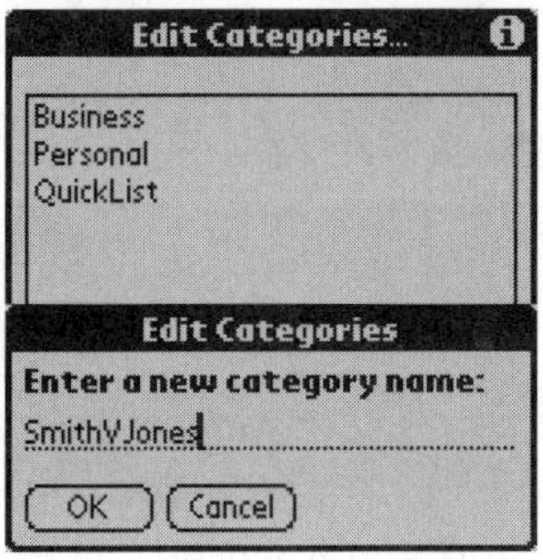

12-L:

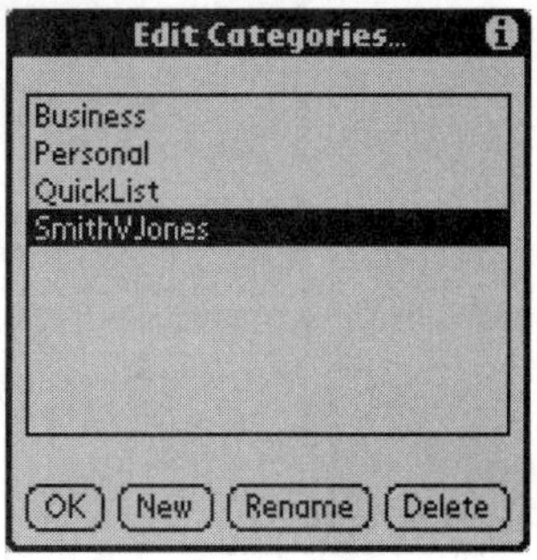

To delete a category, tap the pop-up menu → "Edit Categories" → the category name → "Delete." (When you delete a category, its tasks are not deleted, but are recategorized as "Unfiled.") To merge two categories, tap the pop-up menu → "Edit Categories" → the name of one of the two categories → "Rename" and give that category the same name as another existing category.

You can categorize a record or change its category at any time. In Address Edit view, tap the name of the category in the upper right hand corner to bring up the pop-up menu of available categories. Select the category in which you would like the record to appear, or create a new category using the method described above (see Figure 12-M).

The default category for new contact records is "Unfiled." You cannot change this default setting, but can bypass it by inserting the record while viewing only the desired category.

12-M:

In the Address View (Figure 12-N), the category for a particular contact appears in the upper right corner of the screen. You cannot change categories from this view, but must first tap "Edit" to get into Address Edit view.

12-N:

Categories are specific to each application; creating a category in Address Book does not also create it in To Do List or Memo Pad. This is convenient because you will find contacts, tasks, and memos tend to fall into different kinds of categories. Categories are also a handy way to group contacts for ease of reference, since you can view individual categories. In List View, tap the triangle in the upper right corner of the screen for a pop-up menu of categories, and select the category you want to view (Figure 12-O). Or press the physical Address Book button repeatedly to scroll through all the categories.

12-O:

Handy category names in Address Book include Airlines, Clients, Doctors/Medical, Entertainment, Experts, Family, Firm, Friends, Hotels, Restaurants, Stores/Services, and Taxis.

§ 12.5 Making Records Private

As in Date Book, you can mask or hide a record (Figure 12-P). In Address Edit View, tap "Details" and the Private checkbox. You can change the universal privacy level on your handheld by tapping Menu → "Options" → "Security" and making your selection (or by leaving Address Book to go to the Security application to make the same selection there).

12-P:

§ 12.6 Attaching a Note to a Record

In Address Book (as in Date Book and To Do List, but not in Memo Pad), you can attach a 4,096-character note to a record. In Address Edit view, tap the "Note" button and insert the text of your note (Figure 12-Q). This is a handy place to keep miscellaneous information about the contact. Once you have attached a note to a contact record, the first few words of the note appear at the bottom of the Address View for that contact (Figure 12-R), and a note icon appears next to the contacts name in List View (Figure 12-S). As in Date Book, tapping the note icon takes you directly to the text of the note. Moreover, Address Book offers a further convenience: you can create a note just by tapping in the right margin of List View (the spot where the icon is going to appear).[1]

§ 12.7 Editing a Record

You can edit an existing contact record only in Address Edit view. In List View, select the contact to go to Address View. In Address View, tap "Edit" (or any-

12-Q:

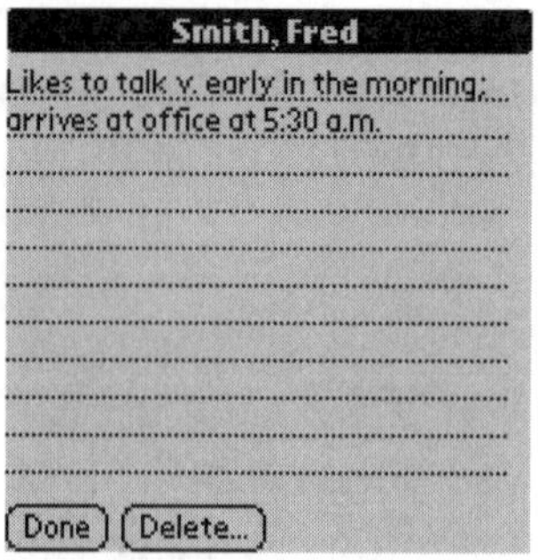

12-R:

12-S:

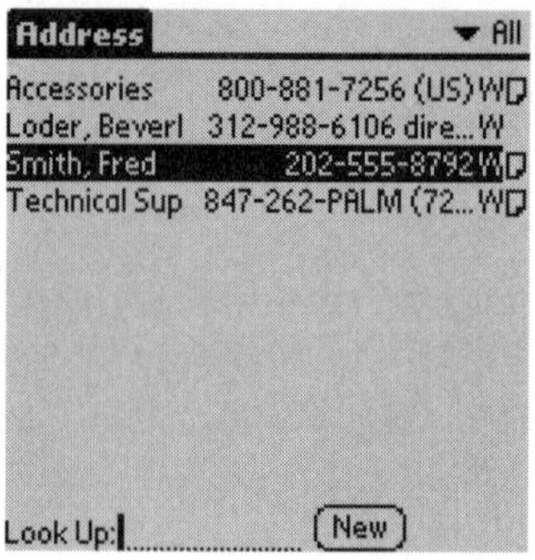

where on the screen). Use the standard edit menu options (undo, cut, copy, paste, and select all) or the associated command shortcuts or the floating command icon bar (see Section 15.7).

§ 12.8 Deleting a Record

As in Date Book, there are multiple ways to delete a record. In either Address View or Address Edit view, tap Menu → "Delete Address" or write the command shortcut /D. In Address Edit view, you can also delete the record by tapping "Details" → "Delete." The deletion methods described in Section 11.9 also work in Address Book.

§ 12.9 Using the Look Up Feature

At the bottom left of the List View screen are the words "Look Up" followed by a dotted line (Figure 12-T). In List View, when you write a letter in the Graffiti area, the letter appears on the dotted line at the bottom of the screen, and the list itself moves to the first name beginning with that letter. Each time you write another letter, the list moves to the first contact beginning with that string of letters. This feature means you can look up a contact as quickly as you can write that contact's name.

12-T:

§ 12.10 Beaming Records

You can beam either individual records or entire categories of records. To beam one record, enter Address View for that contact, and either (a) tap Menu → "Beam Address," (b) use the command shortcut /B, or (c) write / followed by tapping the beam icon in the floating command icon bar.

To beam a category, get to a List View of only that category by tapping the appropriate category in the pop-up menu in the upper right hand corner (or pressing the Address Book button repeatedly), then tap Menu → "Beam Category." There is no command shortcut for beaming a category in Address Book.

§ 12.11 Creating and Beaming Your Business Card

You can designate one record (presumably your own) as your electronic business card, after which you can beam it in one step. Select your record and tap Menu → "Select Business Card" (Figure 12-U). A Rolodex card icon appears at the top of the screen (Figure 12-V).

12-U:

12-V:

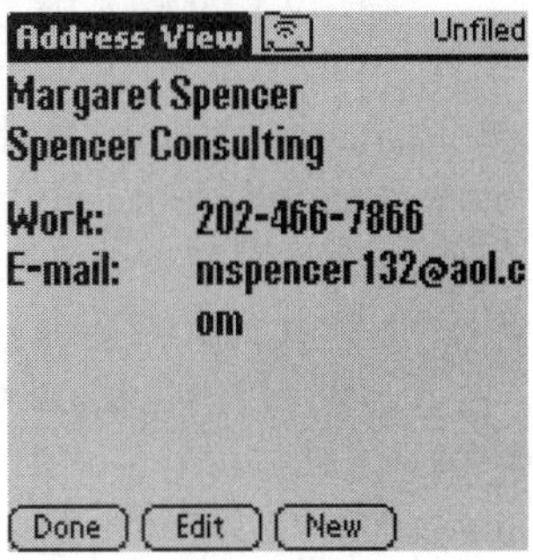

You can beam your business card from anywhere in the Address Book application by tapping Menu → "Record" → "Beam Business Card." Simpler still is the one-step method (which works even when your handheld is off): press the Address Book physical button and hold it down for a few seconds.

§ 12.12 Options in Address Book

As in Date Book, you can display Address Book records in your choice of three fonts. In either List View, Address View, or Address Edit View, tap Menu → "Options" → "Font" (or use the command shortcut /F) and tap the font you want. You can use different fonts for each of the three different views, but the font option for each view applies to all the records throughout Address Book.

You can make Address Book open into whichever category you were viewing last. In List View, tap Menu → "Options" → "Preferences" → "Remember last category" checkbox. When this option is off, Date Book automatically opens to "All."

§ 12.13 Suggestions for Using Address Book

1. The Phone Lookup function works only for a contact's last name (or company, if you selected the "List by Company" option). If you forget someone's last name but remember anything else, use the global Find function instead. If you have trouble remembering names, insert memorable reminder words in a note ("discussed CLE training issues" or "wrote article on prenuptial agreements in DC Bar journal") for which you can search using the global Find function.
2. Use the global Find function to ascertain whether you know anyone who works for a particular organization—useful as part of a conflicts check or when a colleague distributes an e-mail asking, "Does anyone know anyone at the Brown & Black firm?"
3. Your handheld can save you time and frustration if one of your recurring tasks is to correlate long-distance telephone numbers with the client-matter number to which the call should be billed (not all telephone systems do this automatically): just do a global find search for each telephone number.
4. Use Address Book to keep track of more than just contact data. For example, if you want an easy way to look up a client-matter number, insert the name of a case or project in the "Last name" or "Company" field, and put the client-matter number in the first telephone field (use the pop-up menu to make the name of that field read "other" if

you like.) Once you have done this, you can use the Phone Lookup function in another Palm OS application to automatically add the client-matter number to the project name—extremely handy if you use your handheld to keep track of your billable time (see Chapter 19).

5. Use Address Book to keep track of passwords and other confidential information. Insert the name of the computer program as the last name or company, and the password in a telephone number field. For security's sake, make the record private, or use a low-tech encryption technique such as transposing the third and fourth characters of each password. Hide your credit card numbers in your handheld by disguising them as telephone numbers of memorable fictitious contacts (such as favorite obscure literary characters).[2]
6. If you synchronize your handheld with a desktop program that has a notes field for each contact—such as Microsoft Outlook—those notes appear as an attached note on your handheld (up to 4,096 characters). You can quickly insert helpful information on both your desktop and handheld by copying and pasting relevant portions of documents and e-mails into this field. Putting this information on your handheld allows you to search for it with the global Find function, an option that is usually not available on your desktop.

Notes

1. This trick works only in Address Book, not in Date Book or To Do List.

2. Be cautious about using add-on applications specifically designed to keep track of your passwords (they do exist), since it is possible for a programmer to write a program that uploads that information when you HotSync while your PC is on line (the same way programs such as AvantGo and Vindigo upload information from your handheld to their sites during online HotSyncing).

Using To Do List

13

§ 13.1 Overview

To Do List helps you keep track of tasks and projects. Unlike a paper to-do list, the Palm OS To Do List is a dynamic organizational tool allowing you to revise, categorize, and prioritize your tasks, and to display them in a variety of ways. You can attach notes to a task, beam tasks to fellow handheld users, and import telephone numbers from Date Book. You can check off completed tasks, delete outdated tasks, and purge all completed tasks with a few taps.

You can open To Do List by pressing the physical button second from the right on the front of your device, or by tapping the To Do List icon.

§ 13.2 Views in To Do List

While To Do List has just one view—a list of tasks—you can customize this list in various ways. The simplest version consists of two elements: a description of the task, and a checkbox to indicate whether you have completed the task. Even in this simple view, tasks with attached notes display a note icon (see Figure 13-A).

As discussed in Section 13.10, you can customize this view by adding the priority, due date, and category for each task. You need not assign any of these elements to a task, but using priorities, due dates, and categories judiciously can help you manage your tasks more effectively.

13-A:

§ 13.3 Inserting a Task

Tap "New," or just start writing (this works only with Graffiti, not the on-screen keyboard). When you have finished entering the description of the task, tap anywhere on the screen other than a line containing the description of your new task. The task joins the list in the order in which you inserted it, not alphabetically by the description of the task. (You can change this order by giving a task a priority, due date, or a category; see Section 13.10).

When you complete a task, tap the checkbox next to it to mark it as completed. You can choose whether to keep completed tasks on the screen, or make them disappear (see Section 13.10).

§ 13.4 Setting a Priority for a Task

Select a task and tap "Details" to open the To Do Item Details box (Figure 13-B). Tap on a number from 1 (highest priority) to 5 (lowest priority). By default, To Do List assigns new tasks a priority of 1. While you cannot change this default setting, there is a sneaky way to get around it: if you select an existing task before you tap "New," the new task has the same priority level (and category and due date) as the first task.

13-B:

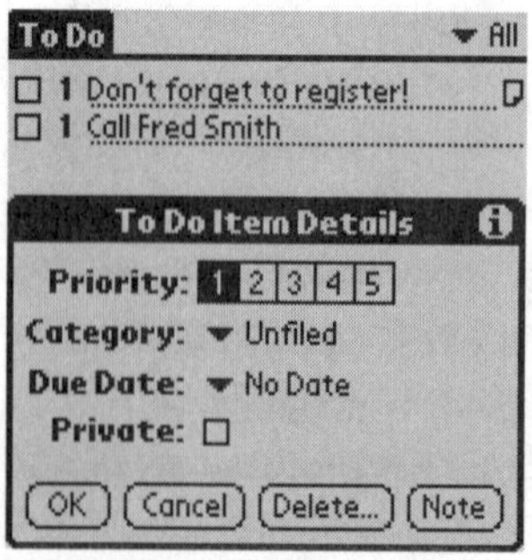

§ 13.5 Categorizing Tasks

The Category function in To Do List works just as it does in Address Book and Memo Pad. To categorize a task, select it, tap "Details" and the category pop-up menu in the To Do Item Details box, and tap the category you want.

The default category for new tasks is "Unfiled." You cannot change this default setting, but there are two ways to bypass it: (a) enter the task while viewing only the desired category; or (b) before inserting a new task, tap an existing task in the category you want your new task to be in. The new task has the same category (and due date and priority level) as the task you tapped.

To view one category at a time, tap the pop-up menu in the upper-right corner and select a category, or press the To Do List button repeatedly to scroll through the categories in alphabetical order. To view all categories, select "All" from the pop-up menu, or scroll through the categories until you reach "All."

Create, edit, rename, and delete categories as described in Section 12.4.

§ 13.6 Setting a Due Date for a Task

To assign a due date to a task, select the task, then tap "Details" and the Due Date pop-up menu. You can access the standard Choose Date box, set "No Date," or make the program do the figuring by tapping "Today," "Tomorrow," or "One week later."

The unchangeable default setting for due dates is "No Date." However, if you select an existing task before you tap "New," the new task has the same due date (and category and priority level) as the first task.

§ 13.7 Making Tasks Private

Select the task, and tap "Details" and the "Private" checkbox. As in Date Book and Address Book, you can mask the task or make it entirely invisible by tapping Menu → "Options" → "Security," and selecting your preference. If you have not yet inserted a password, the program prompts you to do so. As always, private events remain visible on the desktop calendar program with which you synchronize your handheld.

§ 13.8 Attaching a Note to a Task

As in Date Book and Address Book, you can attach a note to an item; simply tap "Note." Although the description of the task itself can be up to eleven lines long, put detailed information in a note (rather than in the description of the task) to make your To Do List easier to read (see Figure 13-C).

13-C:

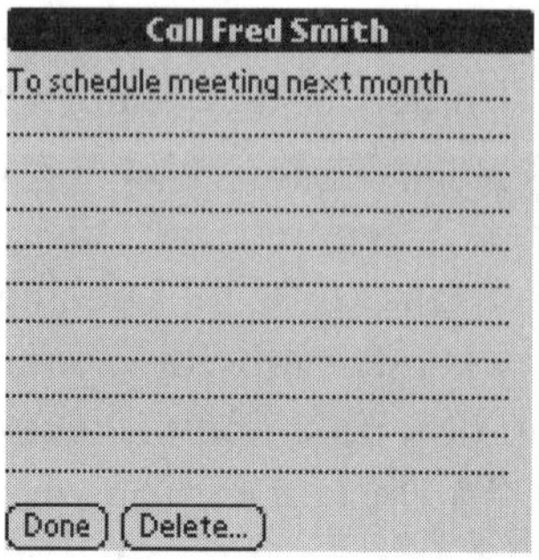

As in other applications, tapping on the resulting note icon takes you directly to the text of the note (see Figure 13-D). However, unlike Address List, tapping where a note icon would be does not create a note.

13-D:

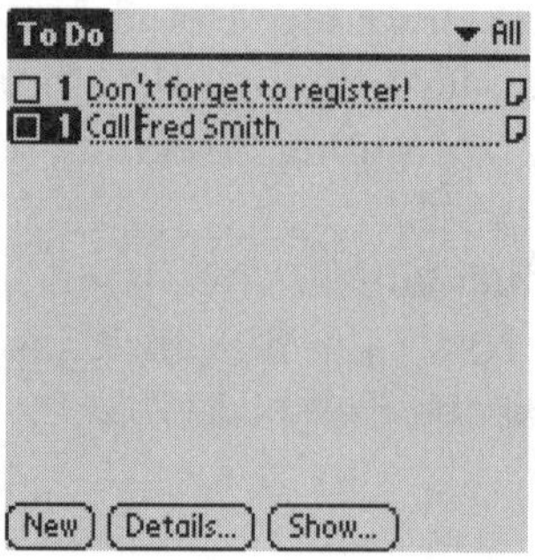

To delete a note, either bring up the note and tap "Delete," or erase the text of the note. Neither alternative allows you the option of saving a backup copy on your PC.

§ 13.9 Editing a Task

You can always edit the description of a task; just select it and edit as usual with Graffiti, menu commands, or command shortcuts. To change the details of a task (its priority, category, due date, and privacy), select it, tap "Details" to bring up the To Do Details box, and change the task's details as you prefer.

§ 13.10 Preferences in To Do List

To Do List has a unique way of accessing the Preferences box. Instead of having a “Preferences” option in the pull-down menu at the top of the screen, there is a “Show” button at the bottom of the screen. Tap it to bring up the To Do Preferences box (Figure 13-E).

13-E:

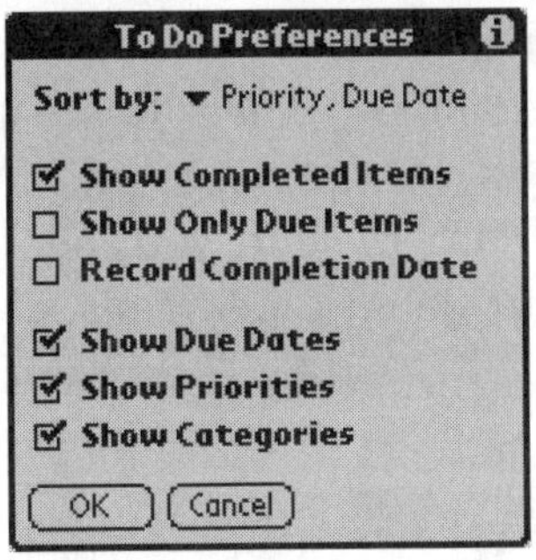

You should configure these settings depending on how you think about your tasks. Consider the suggestions below, and experiment with the various options to determine what works best for you.

The “Sort by” pop-up menu gives you four options (Figure 13-F). Your tasks can appear on the screen in one of the following orders: (a) by priority, and then by due date within each priority level; (b) by due date, and then by priority within each due date; (c) by category, and then by priority within each category; or (d) by category, and then by due date within each category. Actually, you can sort by all three elements simultaneously if you choose one of the first two options, then view one category at a time (see Section 13.5).

13-F:

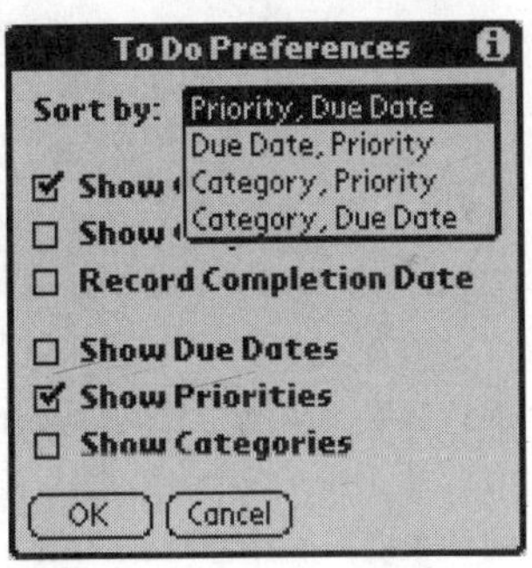

Select “Show Completed Items” if you want to leave completed tasks visible on the screen, and deselect it to make them invisible. If you choose not to show completed items, enjoy the entertaining effect of seeing a task disappear from the screen the moment you check it off. Note that deselecting "Show Completed Items" merely hides completed tasks; it does not delete them. To delete hidden completed tasks, you must either purge them (see Section 13.12), or, much more cumbersome, reselect "Show Completed Task" and delete them individually as described in Section 13.11.

Select "Show Only Due Items" to show only those items that are due today, overdue, or have no due date. Some Palm OS users like to see evidence of their progress; others prefer to keep only pending items visible on their lists. Incidentally, if you cannot find a task that you know you have inserted (a common problem among newcomers to the Palm OS), check to see if you have inadvertently selected the "Show Only Due Items" option.

When you select "Record Completion Date," the date you check off a task as completed thereafter shows up at its "due date." Unless you select "Show Completed Items," there is really no point to selecting "Record Completion Date" either. You cannot retrieve a task's original due date once you have checked off the task as completed while this option is on.

Select "Show Due Dates," "Show Priorities," and "Show Categories," to make those elements appear on the main screen next to the description of the task. When due dates appear on the screen, To Do List adds an exclamation point to due date for overdue tasks. There are advantages and disadvantages to showing due dates, priorities, and categories. For example, the screen is harder to read when it has more elements. Compare Figure 13-G (which includes all three optional elements) with the streamlined version in Figure 13-H (which shows none).

13-G:

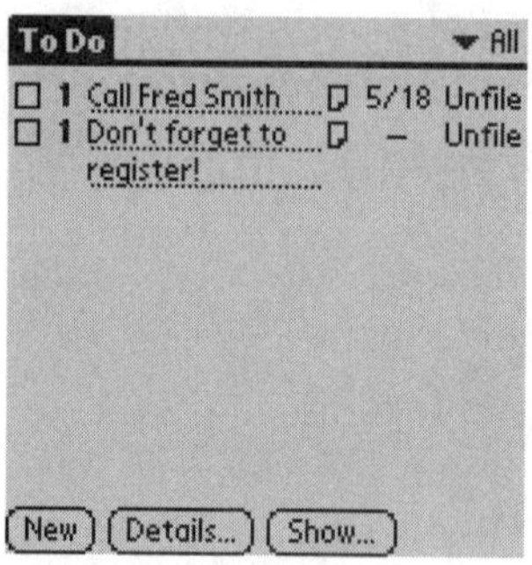

13-H:

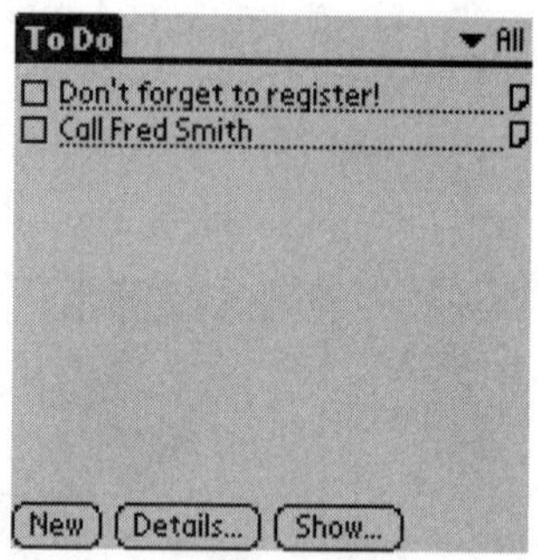

However, showing an element means you can change that element without opening the Details box, since tapping the element opens the associated pop-up menu. (When "Show Due Date" is selected, items without due dates have a dash in the due date column. You can tap on the dash to bring up the pop-up menu of due date options.)

Selecting the "Show Category" option is helpful only when you are looking at more than one category at a time. You might as well save screen space by selecting this option only when looking at "All" categories (see Section 13.5).

§ 13.11 Deleting a Task

Select the task, tap "Details" → "Delete" and, if you like, tap the "Save archive copy on PC" checkbox. The deletion methods listed in Section 11.9 also work in To Do List. You can delete a task (and save an archive copy on your PC) whether or not you have marked the task as completed.

§ 13.12 Purging Tasks

Since checking off a task as completed does not remove it from To Do List, you should purge completed tasks periodically to free up room on your handheld's memory. (It is easy to forget to do this if you have rendered completed tasks invisible by selecting the "Show Only Due Items" option.) Tap Menu → "Record" → "Purge" and indicate whether you want to save archive copies on your PC. If you do save archive copies, your handheld's memory is not freed up until after your next HotSync, when the items are archived on your PC and deleted from your handheld.

§ 13.13 Beaming Tasks

In To Do List (as in Address Book and Memo Pad), you can beam items individually or by category. To beam one task, select it, then tap Menu → "Record" → "Beam Item" or use the command shortcut /B (or the command icon for beaming). To beam a category of tasks, use the category pop-up menu in the upper-right corner (or press the To Do List button repeatedly) to get to the category you want, then tap Menu → "Record" → "Beam Category." There is no command shortcut or icon for beaming categories.

§ 13.14 Options in To Do List

You can use Phone Lookup in To Do List (and in Date Book and Memo Pad[1]) to automatically insert the last name, first name, and phone number of a contact as follows: Select the person's last name, then tap Menu → "Options" → "Phone Lookup" (see Figures 13-I through 13-K).

13-I:

13-J:

13-K:

If there is only one person with that last name in your Address Book, the person's full name and first telephone number automatically appears in the text. If there is more than one person with that last name, a pop-up menu offers you a pick-list of everyone with that last name.

§ 13.15 Suggestions for Using To Do List

You can make To Do List the bedrock of your organizational system by using the following techniques:

1. Use To Do List for both your work and personal tasks, since it is more efficient to have all your tasks in the same system than to juggle two separate systems. Segregate work and personal items by putting them in different categories.
2. Keep your handheld with you as much as possible, and strive to adopt the habit of inserting To Do items (at least a cursory version) as soon as you think of something to do.
3. Use what would otherwise be downtime (mass-transit commuting, waiting in line, waiting for a meeting to begin) to read through your To

Do List. This helps you remember lower-priority tasks, which is handy in case you find yourself in a situation or location where you can accomplish the task with minimal extra effort. For example, maintain a To Do task such as "Office Supply Store" and attach a note listing all the items you want to get there. If you keep your handheld with you at all times, the list is handy the next time you happen to find yourself near an office supply store.

4. There are no alarm settings in To Do List, so if a task must be done by or at a specific date or time, enter the item in Date Book instead of To Do List.
5. For tasks such as business calls, include the agenda for the call in an attached note.
6. You can set due dates far in the future, so insert To Do tasks to remind you to schedule or complete tasks that should recur on a regular basis, such as tax filings; annual physicals; dental appointments; and vehicle maintenance, registration renewals, and inspections.
7. When you select "Show Only Due Items," the list includes items having no due date in addition to due and overdue items. To avoid cluttering up today's to-do list with undated items, use one specific date far in the future (December 31 of next year, for example) as a holding tank for undated items.
8. For items such as "Call George Galifianakis" you can use the Phone Lookup feature to speed up insertion of the person's name, since you need not insert the entire name before using Phone Lookup. If you write "Gali," then use Phone Lookup, the pop-up menu consists of every name beginning with those letters. This is handy if you cannot remember how to spell someone's name, or if you don't want to insert the entire name. You can even use Phone Lookup as a kind of Graffiti shortcut for unique names in your Address Book, since you can always delete the telephone number and leave just the name, so you never have to write out long, tricky-to-spell names more than once.
9. If To Do List's features and configuration options are insufficient for your needs, try a more comprehensive third-party alternative such as ToDo Plus by High Hands Software (**www.highhands.com**), which allows you to filter your tasks in many useful ways, create templates to facilitate inserting new tasks, and add alarms to items.

If you synchronize your handheld with a desktop program that has a notes field for each task—such as Microsoft Outlook—those notes appear as an attached note on your handheld (up to 4,096 characters). You can quickly insert helpful information on both your desktop and handheld by copying and pasting relevant portions of documents and e-mail messages into this field. Putting this information on your handheld allows you to search for it with the global Find function, an option that is usually not available on your desktop.

Note

1. Actually, you can also use Phone Lookup in Address Book itself to insert information in a note attached to a contact record.

Using Memo Pad 14

§ 14.1 Overview

Use Memo Pad, the last of the four main Palm OS applications, to record and maintain notes, memos, lists, reminders, ideas, random musings, quotations, and anything else you can think of. Memo Pad is perfect for material not specifically relevant to an entry in Date Book, Address Book, or To Do List. With relatively few features, the straightforward Memo Pad is the simplest of the four main Palm OS applications, and therefore the most versatile.

You can start Memo Pad by pressing the physical button furthest to the right on the front of your device, or by tapping the on-screen Memo Pad icon. This produces the List View of Memo Pad (see Figure 14-A), where Palm Computing has left some memos for you with tips on using the Palm OS.

14-A:

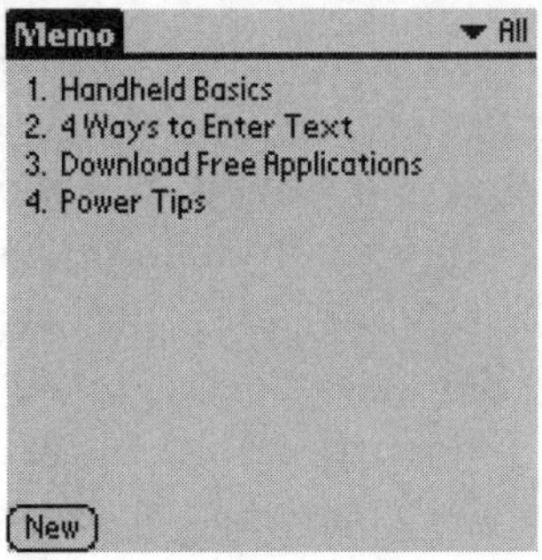

§ 14.2 Views in Memo Pad

There are only two views in Memo Pad: a numbered list of existing memos (List View), and the contents of an individual memo (Memo View, shown in Figure 14-B).

14-B:

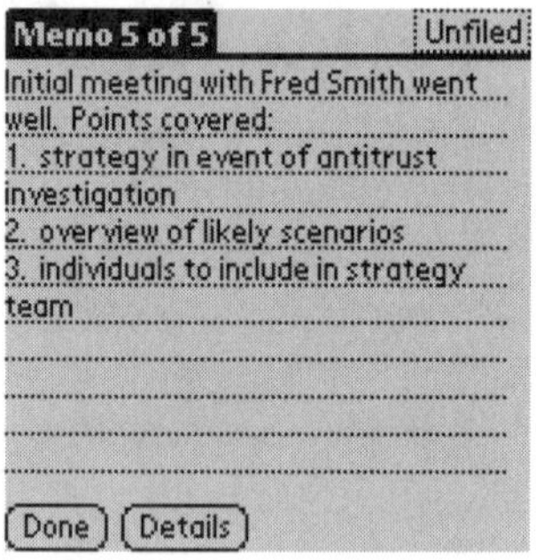

Memo Pad automatically shows List View when you open the application. To move from the list to an individual memo, tap the title of the memo you want to view. To return to List View, tap "Done."

When your list of memos—or the text of one memo—grows too long to fit in one screen, a vertical scroll bar appears along the right side of the screen. This scroll bar is simultaneously a means of navigating through a lengthy list or memo, and an indicator of the proportion of the existing list or memo appearing on the screen. There are arrows at the top and bottom of the scroll bar; the bar itself consists of a shaded gray bar containing a shorter black bar. The black bar represents the proportion of the list or memo appearing on the screen.

Tap one of the arrows to scroll the text one line in that direction. Tap and hold your stylus on an arrow to scroll line-by-line continuously in that direction. Tap once in the gray area above or below the black bar to scroll the text up or down one screen. (Actually, it's slightly less than one screen: when you scroll by screenfuls, there is a one-line overlap, so when you scroll down, the last line of one screen becomes the first line of the next, and vice versa for scrolling up.) Tap and hold your stylus on the gray area to scroll screen-by-screen continuously. Or tap and hold the black bar and drag it up or down to go directly to a specific part of the list or memo. Finally, you can always use physical scroll button to scroll up or down one screenful at a time; this is probably the easiest method to use most of the time, since using the scrollbar requires a high level of accuracy and dexterity with the stylus.

§ 14.3 Inserting a Memo

From list view, tap "New" or just start writing using Graffiti. If you are already in Memo View and want to create another memo without returning to List View, tap Menu → "Record" → "New Memo" or use the command shortcut /N. Memo Pad uses the first line of the memo as a sort of title to represent the memo in List View. You can create a memo with actual titles (if you do, insert a return after the title to keep the List View tidy), or let the first line of text serve that purpose.

In List View, each memo is automatically numbered according to the order in which it appears on the screen. When you change the order in which the memos appear (see Section 14.9), Memo Pad automatically renumbers the memos to reflect the new order.

Memos are subject to the same length limitation (4,096 characters) as notes in Date Book, Address Book, and To Do List.

§ 14.4 Categorizing Memos

Categories work in Memo Pad just as they do in Address Book and To Do List. To categorize a memo, go to Memo View, tap on the pop-up menu in the upper-right corner of the screen or tap "Details" and the category pop-up menu in the Memo Details box (see Figures 14-C and 14-D), and select or create a category as described in Section 12.4.

14-C:

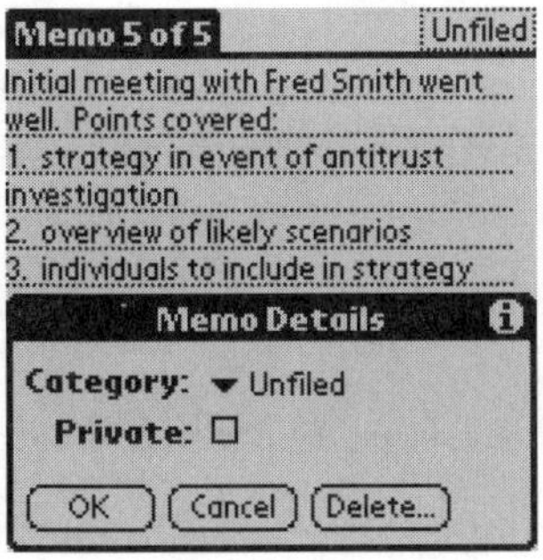

14-D:

Follow the usual procedures for editing the Memo Pad category list (see Section 12.4). Scroll through the categories by repeatedly tapping the Memo Pad button, or go directly to a category by tapping the pop-up menu in the upper-right corner in List View.

By default, Memo Pad categorizes new memos as Unfiled, but when you create a new memo while viewing just one category, the memo is automatically put in that category. Similarly, when you create a new memo while viewing an existing memo, the new memo is put in the same category as the existing one.

§ 14.5 Making Memos Private

Privacy works in Memo Pad just as it does in Date Book, Address Book, and To Do List. To make an item private, tap "Details" and the Private checkbox (see Figure 14-C). Access the Security application to change the privacy level to mask an entry or hide it completely. You can either leave Memo Pad to go to the Security application, or you can open the Security function while in Memo Pad by tapping Menu → "Options" → "Security" or using the command shortcut /H.

§ 14.6 Editing a Memo

In Memo View, use the familiar edit menu commands (tap Menu and "Edit") or the associated command shortcuts. When you alter the opening characters of a memo, the placement of the memo may change if you have selected the alphabetical sort option (see Section 14.9).

§ 14.7 Deleting a Memo

To delete a memo, go to Memo View, then either (a) delete all of its text; (b) tap "Details" → "Delete"; (c) tap Menu → "Record" → "Delete Memo"; or (d) use the command shortcut /D. All methods except the first give you the option of saving an archive copy on your PC. The various deletion methods listed in Section 11.9 also work in Memo Pad.

§ 14.8 Beaming Memos

In Memo Pad (as in Address Book and To Do List), you can beam one item individually or you can beam an entire category of items together. To beam one memo, select it, then tap Menu → "Record" → "Beam Memo" or use the command shortcut /B (or the command icon for beaming). To beam a category of memos, use the category pop-up menu in the upper-right corner (or press the To Do List button repeatedly) to get to the category you want, then tap Menu → "Record" → "Beam Category." There is no command shortcut or icon for beaming categories.

§ 14.9 Options in Memo Pad

There are only two things you can do to customize the views in Memo Pad: (1) choose from among the same three fonts as in the other three main applications (although you can use one font in List View and a different font for Memo View), and (2) choose whether to sort memos into alphabetical order instead of leaving them in the order in which you inserted them.

To change the font in either List View or Memo View, go to that view and tap Menu → "Options" → "Font."

To set your preference of alphabetical or manual sort order, tap Menu → "Options" → "Preferences" (Figure 14-E). If you choose the manual alternative, you can rearrange your memos by dragging them up or down in the list. A gray horizontal line hovers at the point where the memo ends up when you lift the stylus (Figure 14-F). Before trying to drag a memo, be certain you have selected "Manual" in the Memo Preference box; otherwise you cannot drag a memo anywhere. The sorting method you choose applies to all categories in Memo Pad; you cannot keep some categories sorted alphabetically and others manually. Each time you choose the alphabetic sort option, your manual sort order is irretrievably lost. Fortunately, Memo Pad reminds you of this before you confirm the change.

14-E:

14-F:

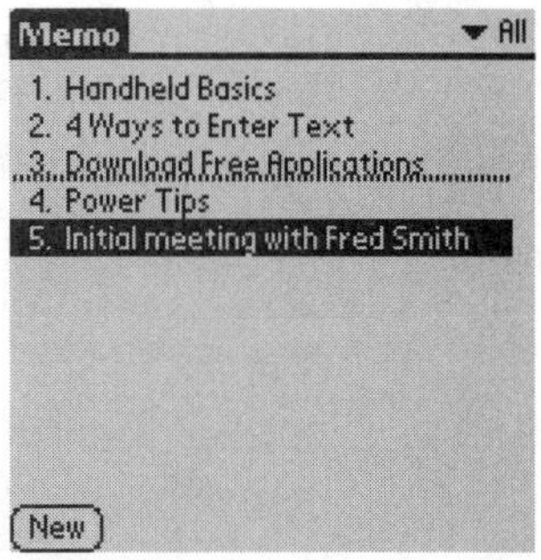

Memo Pad is the only one of the four main Palm OS applications that does not allow you to attach a note to a memo, which makes sense since a memo is pretty much a free-floating note unattached to an event, contact record, or task.

§ 14.10 Suggestions for Using Memo Pad

With the following techniques, Memo Pad can become a convenient place to store and retrieve all kinds of information:

1. Memo Pad is where the global Find feature comes into its own. Since you can locate any item in your handheld by using the Find feature to locate any word contained in the item, you do not need an elaborate system of categorizing or naming your files in order to retrieve them quickly. For example, if you think of a question you want to ask a witness at a deposition scheduled months in the future, jot the idea down in a memo. When the time comes to prepare for the deposition, use the Find feature to look for a word (ideally an uncommon one) used in the memo. Find looks first at records contained in the application you are currently in, so save a few seconds by selecting Memo Pad before you begin the search.
2. Alternatively, you can create a category such as Ideas, Depo Prep, or Smith Case, then go to that category and scroll down until you find the memo you want. If you have more than fifteen ways to categorize your memos, begin each memo with a word or two describing the grouping, then apply the alphabetic sort option. Your memos will not be in separate categories officially defined by the Memo Pad program, but they appear together in the alphabetical list so you can find items easily, which is the point of categorizing items in the first place
3. Make longer memos more readable by including a blank line between paragraphs. It has become a common format in the Palm world to indicate paragraphs by skipping a line, not by beginning the paragraph with a tab. (Although you can certainly use a tab if you prefer; see Figure 10-D, which includes the Graffiti character for Tab.)
4. Unless you are both extremely proficient at Graffiti and a lousy typist, you can input text much more quickly with a keyboard than with Graffiti, so whenever possible, input longer memos with a keyboard (either your PC's keyboard prior to HotSyncing, or a portable keyboard; see Section 20.10).
5. Do not use Graffiti or a keyboard to input text that already exists (or that you can get) in electronic form on your PC. Instead, copy and paste the material from your word processor, e-mail program, or Web browser into a note on your Palm Desktop, then HotSync it onto your handheld. When you use this method to input text that exceeds Memo Pad's 4,096-character limit, Memo Pad automatically creates multiple memos with appropriately numbered headings.
6. When taking notes on the fly in Memo Pad, remember you can always edit and expand the memo on your PC after HotSyncing, so save time by abbreviating and using your usual note-taking shortcuts whenever possible. After HotSyncing the memo onto your PC, you can copy and paste the text into a word-processing program and use its

find-and-replace feature to replace your abbreviations with complete words or phrases.

7. Copy and paste text from notes attached to records in other applications to jump-start note-taking for that item. For example, if you have inserted the agenda for a meeting as a note attached to the meeting (which you inserted as an event in Date Book), use the existing memo as a template to facilitate further note-taking.
8. Put frequently used memos at the top of an alphabetical list by putting a blank space, a number, or a punctuation mark before the first word of the memo. A variation of this technique lets you keep items in chronological order: use the date as the first element of the title, in numerical year-month-day format (for example, May 25, 2002 would be 020525).
9. Think of beaming notes as a high-tech, silent way of passing notes and ideas to colleagues in court and at depositions. Watch your aim to avoid letting opposing counsel intercept information.
10. If you want to beam several memos that are in different categories, you can set up a category called something like "To Beam," and put items temporarily in that category in order to beam them in one step.
11. Keep a log of your phone messages in a memo, and copy and paste material to substantive documents as needed. Use the Palm OS built-in Graffiti shortcuts for date stamp, time stamp, or date-and-time stamp (see Section 15.5). While some word-processing programs automatically update time and date stamps each time you save or print a document, in the Palm OS the date and time remain what they were at the moment you input them.
12. If Memo Pad is insufficient for your needs, replace it with Memo PLUS by Hands High Software (**www.handshigh.com**).

Preferences and Shortcuts

15

§ 15.1 Preferences

Now that you are familiar with the four main Palm OS applications, it is time to customize your handheld and to learn some timesaving techniques applicable in all Palm OS applications.

Most of these techniques begin in the Preferences application. To open that program, tap Home → "Prefs" (see Figure 15-A).

15-A:

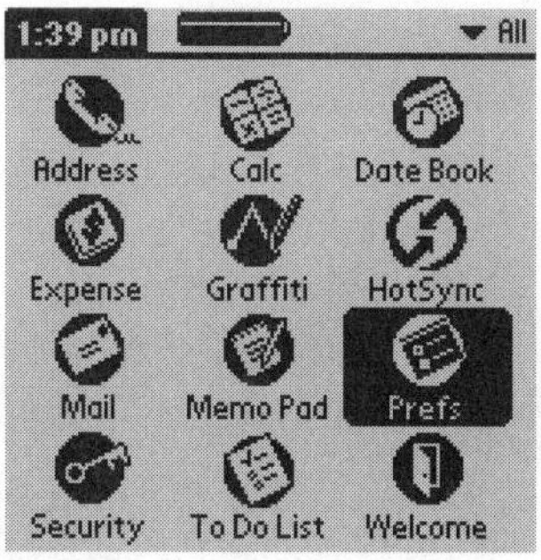

There are eight categories of preferences for you to set to your liking: Buttons, Connection, Digitizer, Formats, General, Network, Owner, and ShortCuts. Tap the ▼ in the upper right-hand corner to open the pop-up list and navigate through the items (see Figure 15-B).

15-B:

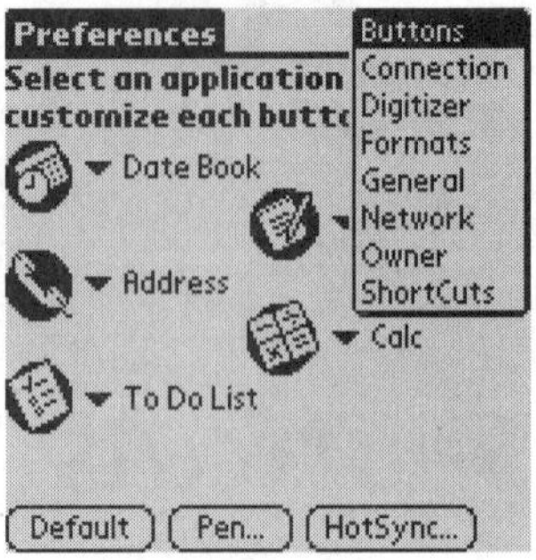

§ 15.2 Customizing the Buttons

Each of the four physical application buttons, as well as the soft calculator button and the HotSync button on your handheld's cradle, can be set to launch any application on your handheld. If you find that you use certain applications more than the four main programs or the calculator, you may find it convenient to reset the buttons to launch your preferred applications. Tap Home → "Prefs" → ▼ → "Buttons" (see Figures 15-B and 15-C). Tap the ▼ next to each button's icon and select an application from the pick-list. You can easily undo button customizing by tapping "Default," which resets the buttons to their original configuration.

15-C:

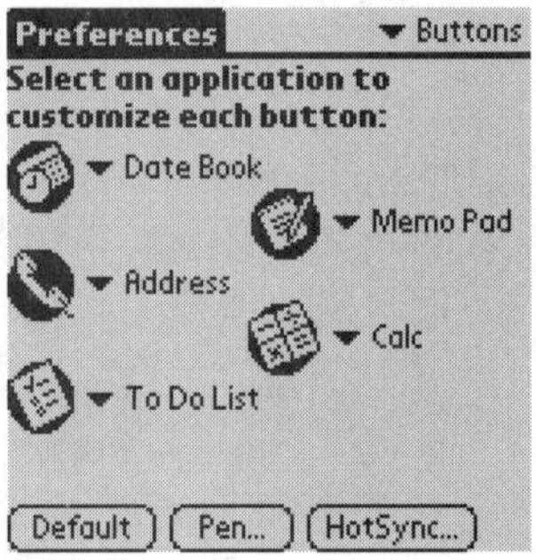

To reset the physical button on your HotSync cradle, tap "HotSync" (Figure 15-D), then on the ▼ next to each button's icon (see Figure 15-E) and select an application from the resulting pop-up menu.

There is yet another way to access certain helpful features. Tap "Pen. . ." (Figure 15-F) and select which of five features you want to activate whenever you swipe your stylus from the bottom to the top of the screen (see Figure 15-G).

15-D:

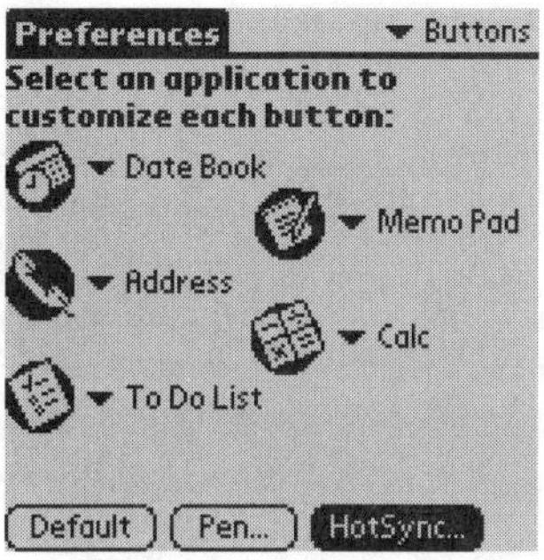

15-E:

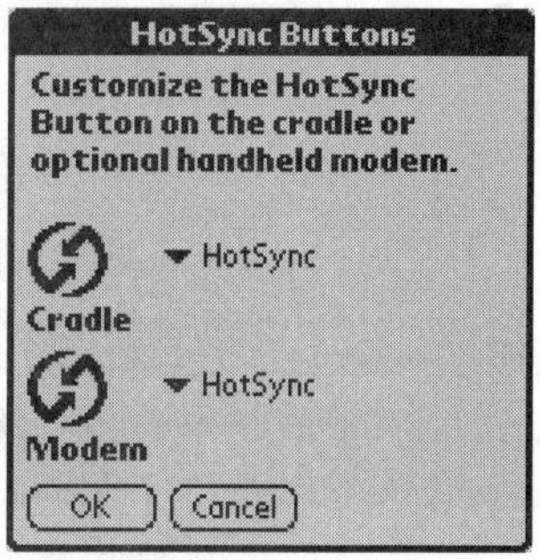

15-F:

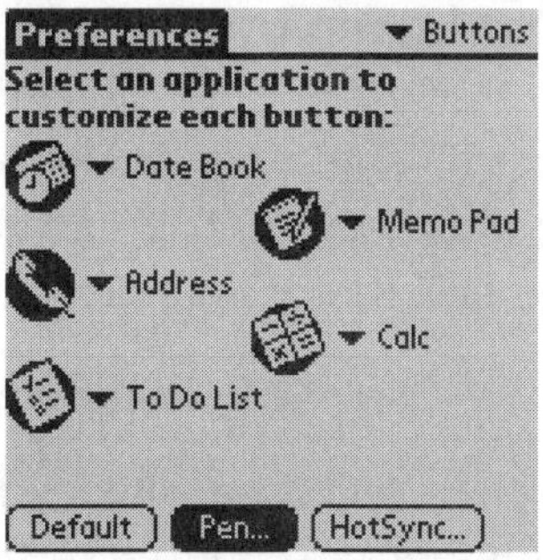

15-G:

If you use primarily the four main Palm OS applications, the option that makes the most sense is "Turn Off & Lock," since each of the other alternatives is easily accessible while you are in the main programs: you can turn on the backlight by pressing and holding the on-off button; the keyboard appears when you tap one of the dots in the bottom corners of the Graffiti area; Graffiti Help is a menu option in all four of the main programs (tap Menu → "Options" → "Graffiti Help" or use the command shortcut /G); and data in all four programs can be beamed using either the menu options (see Sections 11.11, 12.10, 13.13, and 14.8), the command shortcut /B, or the beam icon on the floating command bar.

§ 15.3 Customizing General Preferences

Tap Home → "Prefs" → ▼ → "General" (see Figures 15-H and 15-I). From this screen you can set the time, date, auto-off duration (for internal battery models), sound volume levels, and the beam receive feature.

Your handheld should automatically update the time and date whenever you turn it on. If this feature fails,[1] you can reset the clock and calendar from this screen, which is faster than the alternative of wading through the Welcome application again.

15-H:

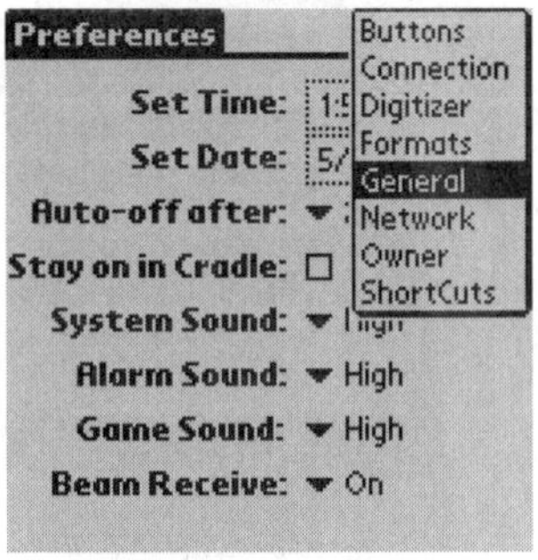

15-I:

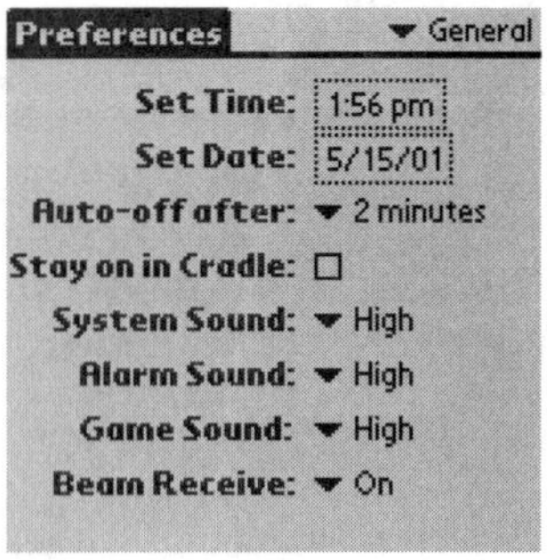

To determine which auto-off option (thirty seconds, or one, two, or three minutes) is right for you, begin by selecting thirty seconds, then increase the duration if you find that you have to keep turning your handheld back on frequently during normal use. The shorter durations save battery power, but the longer durations are more convenient if you find that you look a screen without touching it for minutes at a time.

For most recent Palm models you can select “Stay on in Cradle,” without worrying about draining the battery, since they recharge whenever they are in the cradle. Your handheld’s LCD screen is not susceptible to the burn-in phenomenon.

The System Sound provides auditory feedback confirming that your handheld recognizes your taps. The low setting is quiet enough so that usually others cannot hear it, but you can turn the sound entirely off in situations where you want to maintain complete silence, such as in court or in meetings.[2] In such situations, you should also turn off the alarm sound. Do not forget to turn it back on, or else you will not notice an alarm until the next time you turn on your handheld. Turn the Game Sound on only when you have the auditory privacy to enjoy the stress relief of playing games complete with sound effects.

You might as well set the Beam Receive to On, since there is no risk of receiving any unwanted beams; your handheld asks you to confirm the receipt of each attempted beam.

§ 15.4 Customizing Owner Information

This is the place to insert your name and contact information so that your handheld stands a chance of finding its way home should it go missing. As handhelds become more common, individuals—including personnel in charge of lost-and-found departments—are learning to go to this screen to identify a handheld’s owner. It cannot hurt to add “Reward for safe return” along with your name and telephone number.

Tap Home → “Prefs” → ▼ → “Owner” (Figure 15-J) to insert your identifying information (Figure 15-K).

15-J:

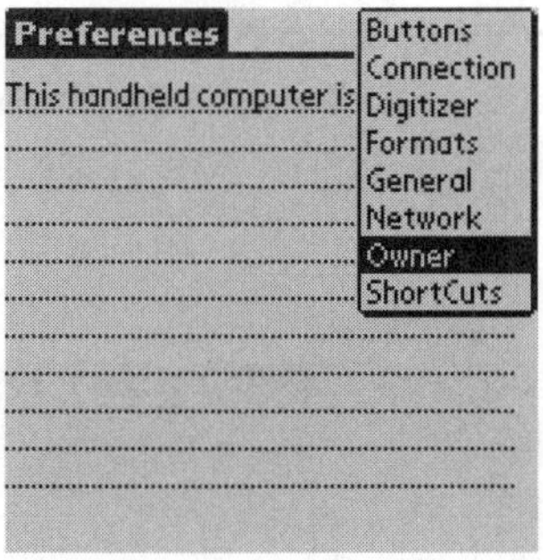

15-K:

If you "Turn Off & Lock" your handheld, this information appears as soon as the device is turned on (see Figure 15-L), and is the only information accessible without the password.

15-L:

§ 15.5 Graffiti® ShortCuts

Graffiti ShortCuts are the Palm OS version of shorthand, except that you can create your own. To view the built-in, editable ShortCut list, tap Home → "Prefs" → ▼ → "ShortCuts" (Figure 15-M).

15-M:

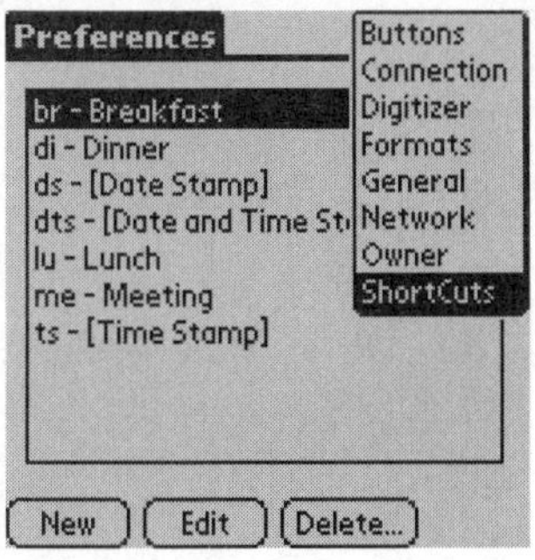

To input the word "breakfast" using the existing ShortCut, write the corresponding abbreviation (see Figure 15-N) after first writing the Graffiti Short-

Cut character, which looks like a fat, lower-case, cursive "e" (see the example in Figure 15-O), and which I will indicate in this text by the symbol ℓ. In any Palm OS application, when you write "ℓbr," the entire word "breakfast" appears on the screen.

15-N:

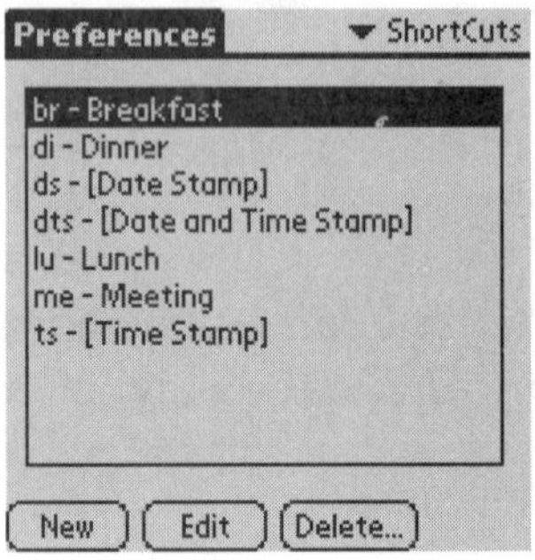

15-O:

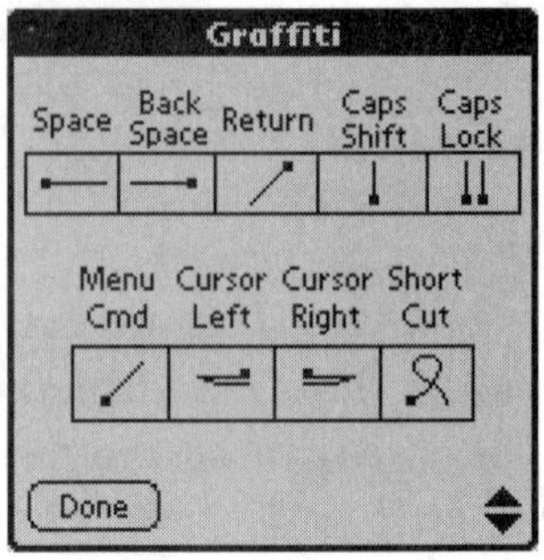

The preinstalled ShortCuts include time and date stamps as well.

To create your own Graffiti ShortCuts, tap "New" (Figure 15-P), insert the abbreviation and text of your shortcut, then tap "OK" (see Figure 15-Q).

15-P:

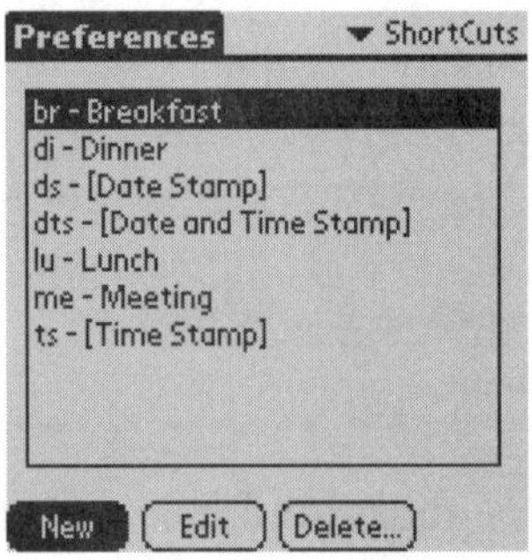

15-Q:

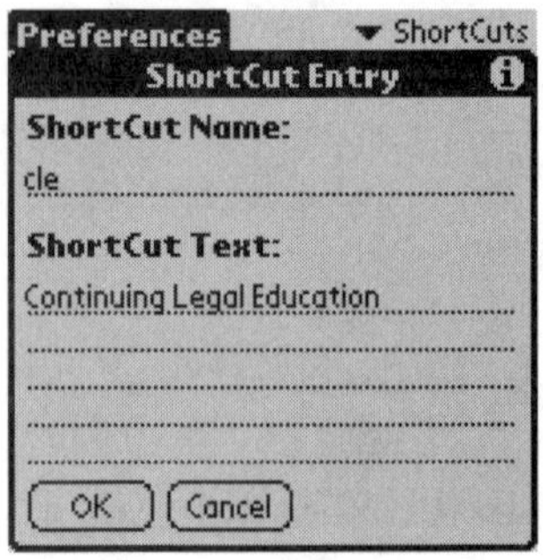

Your new Graffiti ShortCut appears on the ShortCut list, where it is available for editing or deletion (see Figure 15-R).

15-R:

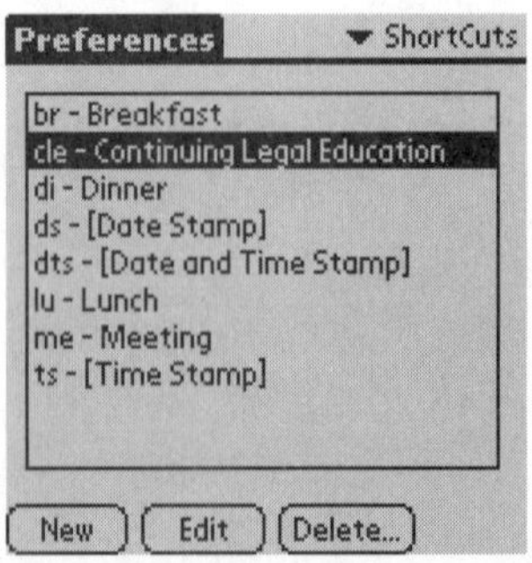

You should use at least two (preferably three) letters for your shortcut name, because using only one letter prevents you from creating a multiletter ShortCut beginning with that letter.

Use Graffiti ShortCuts for words and phrases you use frequently, such as firm names, legal terminology, case and project names, and even templates for lists. The text associated with a Graffiti ShortCut can contain multiple lines of text, and can include returns and tabs.

§ 15.6 Other Customizing Options

Connection

Use this option—which should be set on "direct serial" for normal HotSyncing—to set up special HotSync configurations when you want to HotSync using an attachable modem, or using the infrared ports on both your handheld and desktop computers. You can also configure a HotSync between two handhelds, by dialing into a network or by using a cradle connected to a computer on your organization's local-area network (LAN) or wide-area network (WAN). The handbook that came with your handheld contains the directions for configuring both your Palm Desktop and handheld prior to one of these specialized HotSync operations.

Digitizer

This opens the same calibration screen featured in the Welcome application. Recalibrate your screen if the setting drifts, and after a hard reset.

Formats

You can set the time on your handheld to appear in a twelve-hour format punctuated by a colon or period, or a twenty-four-hour format punctuated with a colon, period, or comma. You can configure dates to appear as month/day/year, day/month/year, or year/month/day, separated by slashes, hyphens, or periods. Tap "Week starts" to select whether all calendars in Date Book and elsewhere on your handheld begin the week on Sunday or Monday. Tap "Numbers" to select whether a period or a comma serves as the decimal point, and whether numbers over a thousand are shown as 1,000, 1.000, 1 000, or 1'000. Tap "Preset to" to see a pop-up menu of thirty-three countries; choosing a country sets the time, date, weekly calendar, and numbers to conform automatically to the conventions of a particular country. (This is the same pop-up menu that appeared in the Welcome application.)

Network

Use this option in conjunction with the "Connection" preferences to configure a HotSync via a connection with your internet service provider (ISP) or a dial-in server.

§ 15.7 Command Shortcuts

Many of the common tasks on your Palm can be accomplished more quickly using command shortcuts, which are different from Graffiti ShortCuts. Graffiti ShortCuts are a faster way to insert text; command shortcuts are a faster way to edit text or manipulate records or applications. On the right side of every pull-down menu is a list of one-letter codes that can be used instead of opening the menu and tapping the command. To use command shortcuts, write the command stroke (a diagonal slash drawn from the lower left corner to the upper right corner), followed by the Graffiti letter. (You cannot use the on-screen keyboard with command shortcuts).

The command shortcuts, arranged by function as they appear on most of the pull-down menus, are shown in Figure 15-S. (Not all command shortcuts

15-S:

	Date Book	Address Book	To Do List	Memo Pad
Record				
N New	√	no	no	√
D Delete	√	√	√	√
A Attach Note	√	√	√	no
O Delete Note	√	√	√	no
E Purge	√	no	√	no
B Beam	√	√	√	√
T Duplicate Address	no	√	no	no
Edit				
U Undo	√	√	√	√
X Cut	√	√	√	√
C Copy	√	√	√	√
P Paste	√	√	√	√
S Select All	√	√	√	√
K Keyboard	√	√	√	√
G Graffiti Help	√	√	√	√
Options				
F Font	√	√	√	√
R Preferences	√	√	no	√
Y Display Options	√	no	no	no
L Phone Lookup	√	no	√	√
H Security	√	√	√	√

work in all applications, as indicated by the √ marks and "no's.") Figure 15-T is an alphabetical version of this chart.

15-T:

Command	Code	Date Book	Address Book	To Do List	Memo Pad
Attach Note	/ A	√	√	√	no
Beam	/ B	√	√	√	√
Copy	/ C	√	√	√	√
Cut	/ X	√	√	√	√
Delete	/ D	√	√	√	√
Delete Note	/ O	√	√	√	no
Display Options	/ Y	√	no	no	no
Duplicate Address	/ T	no	√	no	no
Font	/ F	√	√	√	√
Graffiti Help	/ G	√	√	√	√
Keyboard	/ K	√	√	√	√
New	/ N	√	no	no	√
Paste	/ P	√	√	√	√
Phone Lookup	/ L	√	no	√	√
Preferences	/ R	√	√	no	√
Purge	/ E	√	no	√	no
Security	/ H	√	√	√	√
Select All	/ S	√	√	√	√
Undo	/ U	√	√	√	√

Another technique is not officially a command shortcut, but comes in handy in locating an application. When you write a letter in the Graffiti area when the Applications Launcher screen is showing (tap Home → ▼ → "All"), all the applications beginning with that letter move to the top of the screen.

§ 15.8 Editing Text

Once you have mastered command shortcuts, you will find that you can edit text quickly in any of the main four Palm OS applications, since they share the same command shortcuts for the five basic editing functions: /U to undo; /X to cut; /C to copy; /P to paste; and /S to select all the text in an item. Many add-on programs for the Palm OS use this edit menu as well.

There is an even faster way to accomplish certain commands and editing functions. When you write the command stroke, a long, thin rectangle with icons appears at the bottom of the screen, and hovers there for several seconds before disappearing. It contains icons for certain common commands applicable when you write the command stroke. For example, if you selected text prior to writing the command stroke, the floating command bar includes the icons for undo (a curved arrow), cut (scissors), copy (two overlapping pages), and paste (a clipboard). Tap the icon to perform the corresponding function. Other icons are a padlock (to open the Change Security screen), a handheld with waves radiating from it (to beam), and a trash can (to delete).

There are even more techniques in addition to using command shortcuts and the command icon bar to edit text quickly. To select an entire word, you do not have to drag your stylus through the word; just tap twice quickly anywhere in the word. To select an entire paragraph without dragging, triple tap anywhere in the paragraph.

Notes

1. I know of several handheld owners who complain that the automatic update feature fails when they do not turn on the device for day or two.

2. Or when you are reading documents on your handheld at night and do not want to disturb a bed partner. The backlight is perfect in this situation too.

Manipulating the Applications

16

§ 16.1 Overview

The Palm OS allows you to categorize, beam, and delete entire applications as well as individual records and categories of records. In addition, you can customize how the applications appear on your handheld's screen. Learning how to manipulate the applications helps you customize your handheld in the way that is most useful for you.

The subjects covered in this chapter are those items appearing on the menu bar in the Applications Launcher view. Tap Home → Menu to view the options: Delete, Beam, Category, and Info.

§ 16.2 Deleting an Application

Tap Home → Menu → "Delete" to show a list of items that may be deleted (see Figure 16-A).

In addition to applications, this list may include items that are accessible through multiple applications, such as documents (see Section 18.3). While the built-in applications cannot be deleted (and therefore are not on this list), it is important to know how to delete other programs so you can experiment with a variety of add-on applications, then remove programs that you do not find useful.

16-A:

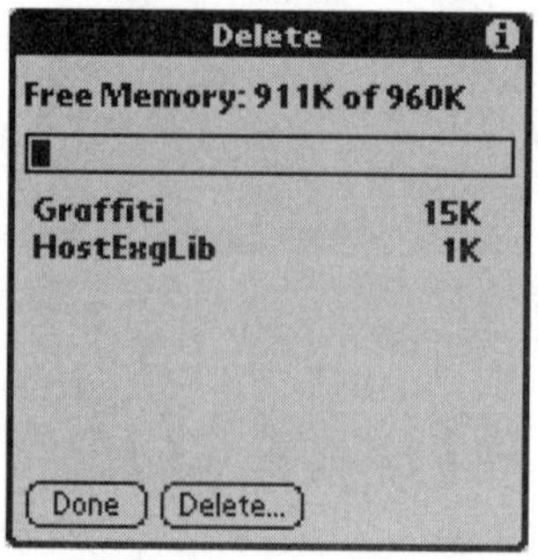

Across the top of the screen, the Palm OS helpfully provides a bar chart showing the memory available on your handheld, so that you can determine when it is time to free up some memory by deleting unused applications. It is a good idea to keep at least 10 percent of your memory free and available for running the Palm OS.

Select the item you want to delete. The Delete Application box appears, cautioning that continuing will delete the application "and all data." Proceed carefully at this point, since you may want to delete an application without deleting its data, if that data that can be accessed through other programs remaining on your handheld. For example, many documents can be read on several different document reader programs, and deleting one such reader deletes those documents as well. If you decide to delete the application (or if you confirm the deletion too quickly to grasp the consequences), you can restore the lost documents by configuring a "Desktop overwrites Handheld" HotSync for the program that is still on your handheld. Before deliberately deleting an application, it is a good idea to HotSync to ensure that you can restore any lost data.

§ 16.3 Beaming an Application

Tap Home → Menu → "Beam. . ." to show a list of items that may be beamed from one handheld to another via the built-in IR port (see Figure 16-B).

16-B:

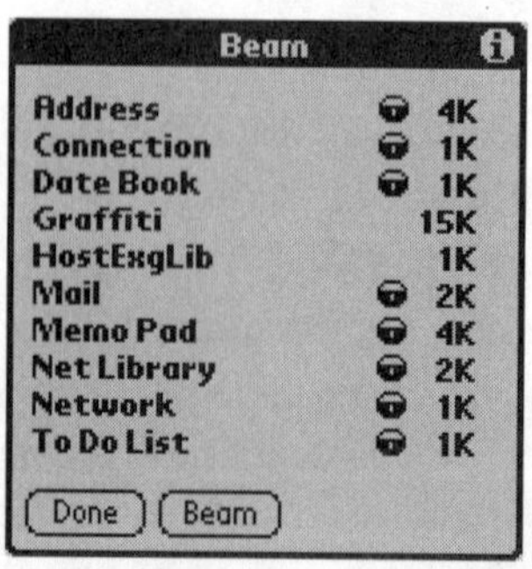

Applications that may not be beamed are indicated by a lock icon; these are either built in to the device, or—in the case of add-on applications—protected by copyright. To beam an application, select it, then tap "Beam" (see Figures 16-C and 16-D).

16-C:

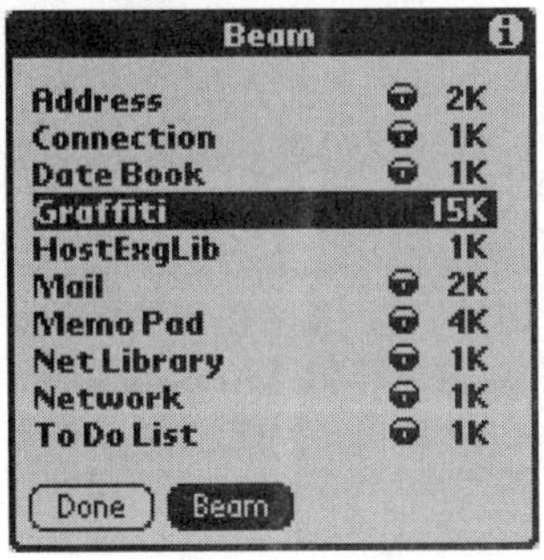

16-D:

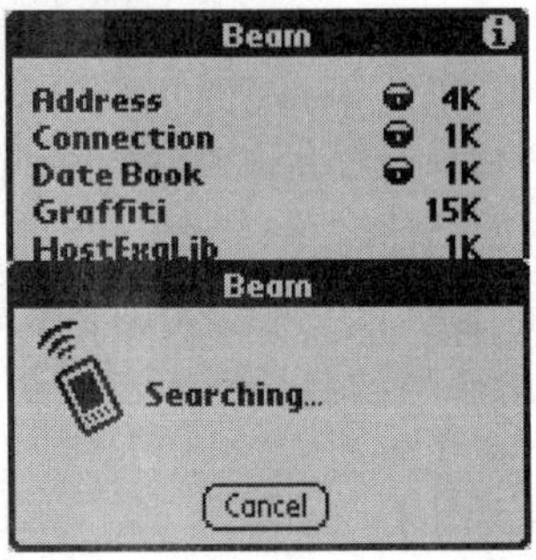

Your device lets you know whether the beaming was successful (see Figure 16-E).

16-E:

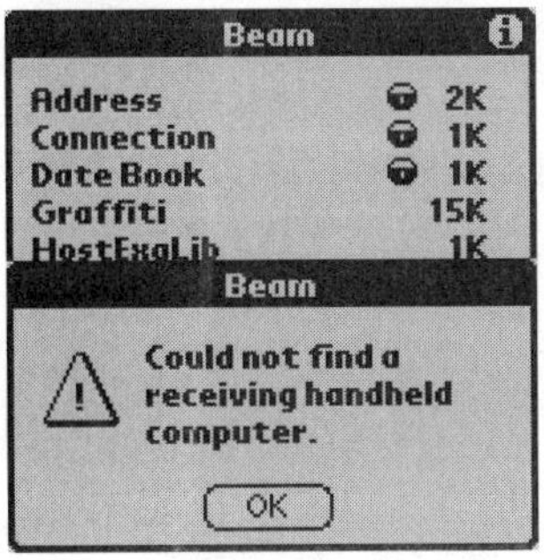

The optimal beaming length between two devices is from four to thirty-nine inches. To receive a beamed item, be sure that your Beam Receive preference is on. Tap Home → "Prefs" → ▼ in upper right corner → "General" → "Beam Receive" → "On." Although the beaming function was intended to send items to only one handheld at a time, experience has shown that multiple handhelds can receive the same beam simultaneously.

§ 16.4 Categorizing Applications

Categorizing applications involves a procedure similar to categorizing records in Address Book, To Do List, and Memo Pad. Tap Home → Menu → "Category" (Figure 16-F) to reveal an alphabetical list of applications and their categories (Figure 16-G). Tap any ▼ appearing on the screen (see Figure 16-G) and the

16-F:

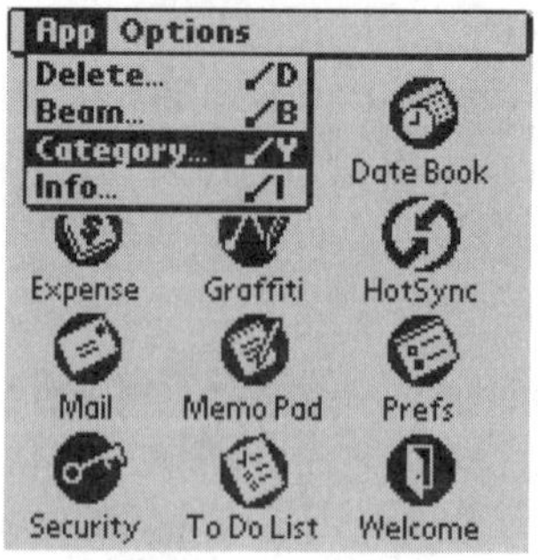

16-G:

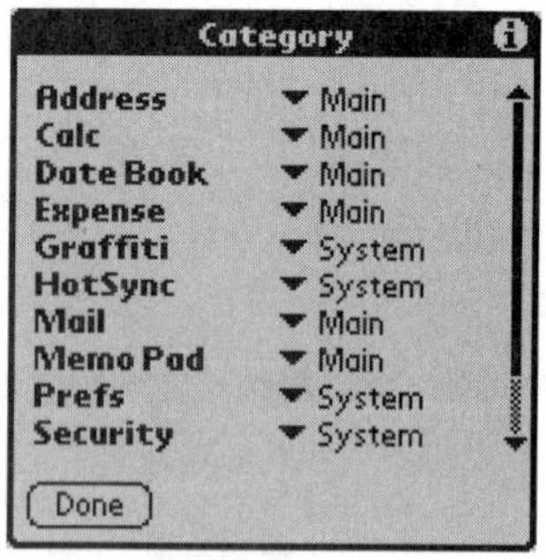

Category pop-up menu appears (Figure 16-H). Tap the ▼ next to an application to change its category, and tap any ▼ to edit the category list. As always, you can create up to fifteen categories and name them anything you wish (except that the name of a category cannot exceed the width of the screen). Think of category names that help you remember what kinds of applications are in each category, such as Add-Ons, Calculators, Main, Office Management, Readers, System, Timekeeping, and Utilities, or whatever names make sense to you. Tap "Done" to return to the Applications Launcher screen.

16-H:

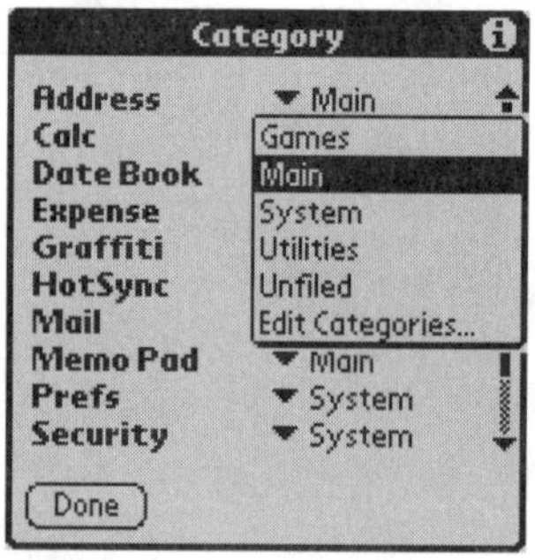

§ 16.5 Information about Applications and Memory

You should know how to do a few more things with the applications. To determine the level of available memory on your handheld, tap Home → Menu → "Info" (see Figure 16-I). The resulting screen (Figure 16-J) shows the level of free memory in your handheld as well as the size of your various applications.

Tap "Records" to show the amount of free memory as a percentage of total memory, plus the number of records in each application (see Figure 16-K). A record is the generic term for events (in Date Book), addresses (in Address Book), items (in To Do List) and memos (in Memo Pad).

Tap "Version" to show which version of the Palm operating system, as well as of each individual application, is installed on your Palm (see Figure 16-L). (You can also check the version from within an application. Tap Menu → "Op-

16-I:

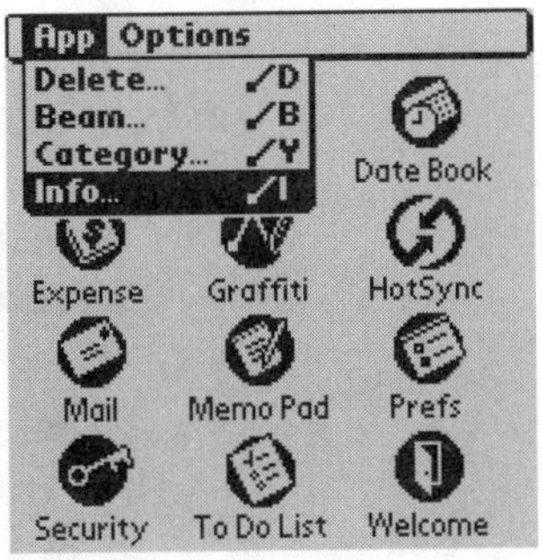

16-J:

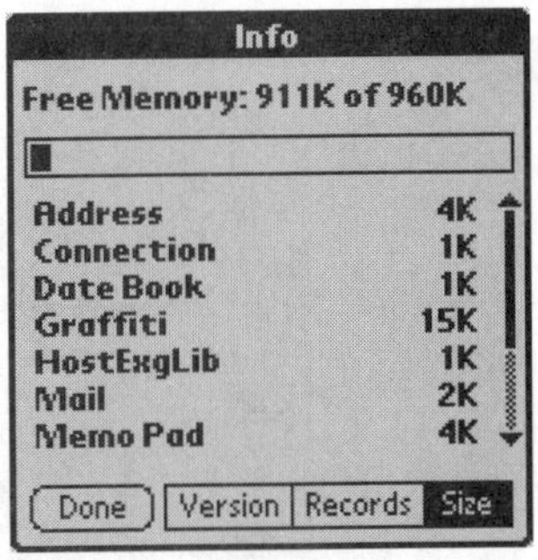

16-K:

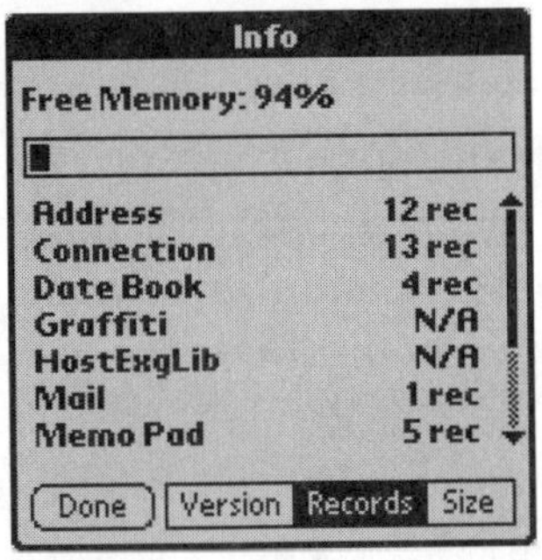

16-L:

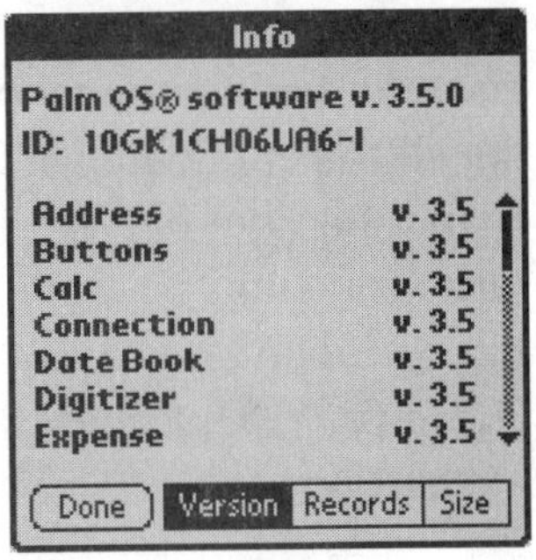

tions" → "About [name of application]"). This screen also shows the identification number assigned to your particular device.[1]

§ 16.6 Preferences

Finally, there are two ways you can customize the Applications Launcher. First, you can choose to view your applications in a list with small icons, which allows up to twenty-two applications to appear in a single screen (see Figure 16-M), instead of by the larger icons, which limits the number to twelve. Tap Home → Menu → "Options" → "Preferences" (see Figure 16-N), then tap on the ▼ next to "View By" and select your preference (see Figures 16-O and 16-P).

16-M:

16-N:

16-O:

16-P:

Second, you can opt to have the Applications Launcher open to the category of applications you view most often, instead of the default view showing all the applications. Select this option if you move frequently among more than a handful of applications. (If you use no more than five programs regularly, you should assign the four physical buttons and the soft calculator button to those programs. See Section 15.2 on customizing buttons.) Tap Home → Menu → "Options" → "Preferences" to tap the Remember Last Category checkbox.

Note

1. This number should also be printed on the back of the device, but the ink may be rubbed off over time.

Adding Programs to Your Handheld

17

§ 17.1 Overview

With over 275,000 registered Palm OS developers, thousands of add-on programs have been created for use on handhelds running the Palm OS, and more are being written every day. They run the gamut from office management tools, document readers, Web clipping programs, travel organizers, specialized calculators, and timekeeping programs to games, doodle pads, diet and exercise diaries, biorhythm calculators, and others that are totally cool but completely useless except for their stress-relieving entertainment value.[1]

In order to make your handheld as useful as possible for you, experiment with add-on programs until you find ones that fit your personality and work style. This chapter explains where to find add-on programs (beyond those mentioned in this book), the kinds of programs available (freeware, shareware, and commercial), the varieties of demonstration versions, and how to download, unzip, install, and uninstall programs on your handheld.

§ 17.2 Where to Find Add-On Programs

Palm OS add-on programs are available on thousands of sites on the World Wide Web. I have provided the Web address for many of the programs mentioned in this book; frequently the same site carries many other programs as well. In addition, many of the Web sites listed in Appendix B either provide add-on programs themselves, or give links to others sites where programs are available. Larger sites generally have a search feature for that site, so you can find particular categories of programs easily, without having to scroll through the site's entire inventory. You can usually find a specific program quickly by doing a keyword search with a search engine such as Yahoo! or Google, using the exact name of the program and the word "Palm."[2] In addition, several of the books listed in the bibliography come with a CD-ROM containing add-on programs. You can even hire a programmer to write a customized program for you.

Add-on programs are available by two methods of delivery. Either you download them from the Web, or you purchase them on a CD-ROM. Use the download method whenever possible since it is faster and cheaper.

§ 17.3 Categories of Add-On Programs

In addition to the various categories of subject matter, add-on programs fall into three categories in terms of cost: freeware, shareware, and commercial.

Freeware is, of course, free. While you generally get what you pay for, many Palm OS freeware programs are surprisingly excellent—useful, versatile, and reliable—as illustrated by AvantGo (see Sections 2.14 and 18.5) and BigClock (Section 20.9). Some freeware contains advertising. While you can distribute freeware programs freely (in their unadulterated form and with their original documentation), they are not in the public domain, and so may not be sold or modified without the developer's permission.

Shareware depends upon the honor system: it is free initially, and you pay for a particular program only if and when you decide you like it. Like most Palm OS programs, shareware usually includes a menu option headed "About [name of program]" listing the developer, the developer's e-mail address, the cost of the program, and a Web site for credit-card payments. Shareware is usually modestly priced (in the $5 to $20 range).

Commercial programs cost anywhere from twenty to several hundred dollars. However, most commercial programs offer a trial or demonstration version so you can decide if you like the program before you pay for it. Most demo versions differ from the full program in one of several ways: (a) limited functionality (for example, a timekeeping program that allows you to enter only five client-matter numbers), (b) limited duration (after thirty days—the usual trial period—the program stops working; tapping on its icon yields only a screen urging you to purchase the program), or (c) an initial warning screen (when you open the program, a screen informs you that you should pay for the program if you continue to use it).[3]

§ 17.4 Downloading Programs

Getting an add-on program onto your handheld usually involves three steps: (1) getting the program onto the PC with which you synchronize your handheld, (2) getting the program in line to be installed at your next HotSync, and (3) performing a HotSync.[4] This section describes the first step.

Most Palm OS programs on the Web are downloadable directly to your PC. Somewhere near the description of each program is a link labeled "download," "click here," "trial," or "zip." Click the link. A "File Download" box appears, asking whether you want to open the file from its current location, or save it to disk. Select the latter option and click "OK." A "Save As" box appears next. Use the pull-down menu in this box to navigate to the folder in which you want to store the add-on program. You can put the program in any folder you want, but a convenient and logical place is the "Add-on" folder that came with your Palm Desktop (you can find it at C:\Palm\Add-on). The "Save As" box also allows you to rename the file. If the original name is an obscure abbreviation or acronym (and some are), feel free to give the file a name you will recognize easily. Click "Save."

At this point the "File Download" box appears to show you the progress of the downloading. Palm OS files are relatively small, and usually download quickly (often in less than a minute). When the "Download Complete" box appears, click "Close" (or "Open" if you want to go directly to the next steps described in Sections 17.5 and 17.6).

If you downloaded the program onto a computer other than the one with which you synchronize your handheld, you can get it onto that computer by sending it attached to an e-mail, or by copying it onto a disk.

§ 17.5 Unzipping Programs

Although most Palm OS files are small, some arrive compressed. If the program's name has a "zip" suffix, and its icon is a two-drawer file cabinet clenched in a monkey wrench, that means it has been compressed with WinZip.[5] If WinZip is not already installed on your computer, you can download it at **www.winzip.com**.

Once you have installed Winzip, double-click on the zipped file. The WinZip Wizard guides you through the brief process of decompressing the file.

Normally, you need click only "Next," "Yes," and "Unzip Now." The unzipped program shows up in a folder titled "Unzipped" on your C drive (C:\Unzipped).

§ 17.6 Installing Programs

Go to the CD-ROM, the folder where you stored the downloaded file, or the Unzipped folder, and locate the downloaded Palm program. Some Palm programs consist of a single file; others are contained in folders along with supporting documentation such as a user's guide, set-up directions, and a file named ReadMe containing basic information. Glance through any supporting documentation before installing the program in case it is one of the few Palm programs requiring a special installation procedure.

Double-click the file containing the actual program, which is the item with the install icon (a red arrow encircling a green-screened computer). This simultaneously opens your Palm Desktop's Install Tool and puts the program on the list of add-ons to be installed at your next HotSync. Confirm that the name you assigned to your handheld appears in Install Tool's Username box.[6] (If you synchronize only one handheld with your PC, that handheld's name will be the only one in the Username pulldown menu.) Click "OK."

The Install Tool now informs you that the file will be installed on your handheld the next time you HotSync. Should you change your mind about installing the program before your next HotSync, you can remove it from the Install Tool by selecting it, then clicking "Remove."

You can install multiple programs during a single HotSync. To add programs to the list of those to be installed, either (a) locate the file, double-click it, and repeat the procedure described in the second paragraph of this section, or (b) open the Install Tool (by clicking "Start" → "Programs" → "Palm Desktop" → "Install Tool"),[7] click "Add," and locate the program by navigating through your PC's folders using the pull-down menu in the Install Tool. The first place the Install Tool looks is the Add-on folder in your Palm folder, which is why that is an excellent place to store add-on programs.

§ 17.7 Beaming Programs from Handheld to Handheld

Installing a program during a HotSync is not the only way to get a program onto your handheld. As described in Section 16.3, many applications can be beamed from one handheld to another. If a colleague has already installed a program you wish to try, ask him or her to beam it to you. The program arrives on your handheld in its pristine form, devoid of any information your colleague may have put into the program. Freeware and shareware are usually beamable in their entirety, while commercial programs are usually designed to beam only demo versions to other handhelds. Programs can take up to a minute or so to beam, unlike individual records or categories of records that can be beamed in seconds.

§ 17.8 Registering and Paying for Programs

If you decide you like a shareware or commercial program, go back to the Web site from which you downloaded it. The address is usually contained in the program itself, in the menu option titled "About [name of program]." The Web site tells you how to pay for the program by credit card over the Internet or by telephone. Once the company processes your order, it will e-mail you a registration code for you to input in the program. Inserting the registration code removes the limitations of the demo version, transforming it into the full-featured version. In shareware, installing the registration code turns off any nag features, and usually adds a "Thank you for registering" to the "About" screen.

§ 17.9 Removing Add-On Programs from Your Handheld

If you decide you do not want to continue using an add-on program, you can delete it from your handheld without paying for it. Use the procedure described in Section 16.2.

§ 17.10 Suggestions for Adding Programs to your Handheld

1. You can purchase a handheld with a variety of add-on software preinstalled from pdaJD's "Built to Order" customizing service (**www.pdaJD.com**).
2. While most add-on programs work well, the quality can vary for all aspects, such as ease of use, reliability, and helpfulness of the user's guide. If you are not satisfied with a program, try others that perform the same functions until you find one you like.
3. Once you have used several different add-on programs, you will be able to learn how to use others much more easily. Most Palm programs use the same icons and elements as the main applications, such as views, menus, buttons, scroll bars, checkboxes, preferences,

and command shortcuts. Frequently the edit menu is identical to the edit menus in the main applications (undo, cut, copy, paste, select all, keyboard, and Graffiti help).

4. Periodically browse Web sites that offer add-on programs to see what is new, especially **www.pdaJD.com** and the law sections of **www.palm central.com** (now **www.handango.com**) and **www.memoware.com**.
5. Revise your application category list (see Section 16.4) periodically to create descriptive category names for your new add-ons.

Notes

1. Since this is a serious book for lawyers I will mention only one program in the last category: Tricorder II, which allows your handheld to "scan" the surroundings for geological, meteorological, and biological phenomena, accompanied by high-tech graphics and computerized blips. Diehard Trekkies should use this program on a handheld with a flip-up cover for maximum verisimilitude. Available at **www.jeffjetton.com/tricorder** (free; charitable donation suggested).

2. For example, a Google search for "Tricorder" and "Palm" yielded the site mentioned in the previous footnote. See Appendix B for more ideas about how to find add-on software.

3. Popularly referred to as "nagware," these warnings can become extremely annoying if you use the program frequently—which is, of course, exactly what the developers intended. In the most effective versions of nagware, the warning screen has a built-in timer that prevents you from moving away from that screen for twenty or thirty seconds—a seemingly interminable delay in the Palm OS world, and one that is generally long enough to motivate you to pay for the program.

4. While some complex add-on programs require extra steps—including special configurations on your PC or multiple HotSyncs—such programs come with an installation guide detailing the required procedures.

5. The Macintosh version is Stuffit, available at **www.shareware.com**. The Stuffit suffix is "sit."

6. The name you assigned to your handheld when you first began using it appears on your handheld in the upper right corner of the screen when you open the HotSync program.

7. Or open the Palm Desktop and click the "Install" button.

Reading on Your Handheld

18

§ 18.1 Reading E-mail on Your Handheld

There are two ways to use your handheld for e-mail: (1) transfer your e-mails and replies between your desktop e-mail program and your handheld during HotSyncs using Mail, one of the built-in applications that came with your Palm OS handheld, and (2) send and receive e-mails wirelessly with a Palm with an internal modem or by attaching an external modem to one of the other models.

Off-Line E-mail

In order to use Mail, you must first set it up to connect with your existing e-mail program. You can synchronize Mail with many common e-mail programs (Microsoft Exchange 4.0 or higher, Microsoft Windows Messaging 4.0, Microsoft Outlook, Microsoft Outlook Express, Eudora 3.0.3 or higher, Lotus cc:Mail 2.5, Lotus cc:Mail 6.0, and Lotus cc:Mail 7.0).[1] On your desktop PC, click "Start" → "Programs" → "Palm Desktop" → "Mail Setup," and select your e-mail program from the pulldown menu. Confirm that your desktop HotSync Manager is set to "Synchronize the files" for the Mail program. Click "Start" → "Programs" → "Palm Desktop" → "HotSync Manager," and select Custom. If necessary, click "Change" to modify the HotSync setting for Mail to "Synchronize the files."

You can set your handheld's Mail program to handle your e-mail in several different ways: (a) synchronize all of the messages between your handheld and your desktop, (b) send messages only from the handheld to the desktop, (c) filter your messages so that your desktop sends to your handheld only messages meeting your specified criteria (such as messages marked high priority, messages containing—or not containing—certain character strings in the To, From, and Subject fields), or (d) send only unread messages to your handheld. You can also truncate long e-mail messages so that only the first 4,000 characters are sent to your handheld. To set up these preferences, open the Mail program on your handheld and tap Menu → "Options" → "HotSync Options."

Your handheld organizes your mail into five folders: Inbox, Outbox, Deleted, Filed, and Draft, and allows you to list them by date, sender, or subject (tap the "Show" button to select your preference). When you go to one of the five boxes, you see first a screen showing the sender, subject line, and date for each e-mail message in the box. Tap anywhere on the heading to bring up the text of the e-mail. When you are finished reading that e-mail message, tap "Done," "Reply," or "Delete." If you read or delete a message on your desktop or handheld, after your next HotSync the message shows up on the other platform as read or deleted as well. When you compose an e-mail on your handheld and tap "Send," it goes to Mail's outbox until your next HotSync, during which it is transferred to your desktop e-mail program and then sent. Mail offers you the usual e-mail options of blind carbon copies, forwarding, copying the text of the original e-mail into the reply, and a standard signature block. When you write e-mail, Mail also provides an e-mail address version of the Phone Lookup option, so that you can import e-mail addresses for contacts listed in Address Book.

In sum, the Palm OS Mail program is useful if you want to be able to read, write, and respond to e-mail off–line.

Online E-mail

With a wireless PDA, or by attaching an external modem to a nonwireless PDA, you can send and receive e-mail wirelessly, without synchronizing your handheld and your desktop.

With the Palm VII, for example, you can use Palm's built-in wireless e-mail application iMessenger, which sends and receives messages through your Palm.net account, or you can install an add-on program to establish a wireless connection between your Palm VII and your existing e-mail account. Reading, writing, and responding to e-mail on iMessenger is much like using Mail, except that because your connection is wireless, you can send an e-mail immediately after writing it, instead of waiting until your next HotSync.

The Palm VII comes with the Mail program as well as iMessenger, so if you prefer to synchronize your Palm VII with your desktop e-mail program instead of using its wireless e-mail capability, you can do so.

You can make any handheld capable of wireless e-mail by attaching a modem and the appropriate add-on software to communicate with an e-mail account. For example, AOL members can use AOL for Palm OS, which is free to AOL members and requires only a Palm Powered™ handheld and a compatible modem (see **http://mymobile.aol.com/portal/pda/index.html**).

Some ISPs provide service for wireless devices, such as GoAmerica (**www.goamerica.net**) and Palm.net (**www.mypalm.com**).

§ 18.2 Document Readers

There are many programs that allow you to read long documents such as word-processed files and electronic books.[2] They contain a variety of features to facilitate reading on your handheld, including such basics as a choice of fonts, a selection of scrolling techniques (including automatic scrolling similar to that used on teleprompters), the ability to create bookmarks to delineate major chapters or sections, a compression scheme to save memory, and pop-up menus that allow you to go to beginnings of chapters or sections. Some readers allow you to create and edit documents on your handheld as well. There are a wide variety of downloadable documents to read on your handheld (see Section 18.3).

Popular document readers include the following:

- **Adobe Acrobat Reader for Palm OS** (**www.adobe.com**) lets you read PDF files on your handheld.
- **AportisDoc Mobile for Palm Powered Handheld** (**www.aportis.com**, $30) was the first full-featured document reader with extensive search capability and all of the features mentioned above. You can also get AportisDoc Converter for Windows ($19.95) to create a Palm-ready document from any document originally created in Microsoft Word, WordPerfect, rich text format, text, or Adobe Acrobat format.
- **Word To Go** (**www.dataviz.com**, $89.95 as part of the Documents To Go bundle[3]) lets you HotSync, create, read, and edit Word, WordPerfect, Word Pro, and text files on your handheld without affecting the desktop formatting (such as bold, italic, indentation, numbering, and tables).
- **Quickword** (**www.cesinc.com**, $19.95) is integrated with Microsoft Word, and allows you to create or HotSync what are effectively Word documents on your Palm, and then read and edit them there. Its features include word-count statistics, find and replace text, categorization as in the main Palm programs, and the ability to print documents to an IR printer using PrintBoy Office.[4] The Web site contains free downloadable e-books as well.

- **TealDoc** (**www.tealpoint.com**, $16.95) is a powerful reader for both standard Palm OS document files and enhanced TealDoc files. Its features include a special tiny font, hyperlinks, hidden bookmarks, encryption, and the ability to insert pictures created with its companion program, TealPaint.
- **Wordsmith** (**www.bluenomad.com**, $29.95), like Quickword, integrates with Microsoft Word, has the ability to print documents with PrintBoy, and features paragraph formatting (such as setting page breaks and indents), automatic compression of documents during HotSyncs, word-count statistics, and a "go to" command that takes you directly to a specific character, paragraph, or percentage of the document.

In addition to these commercial programs, there are a variety of free readers at **www.pdaJD.com**.

After you have installed a document reader, you can install and view a wide variety of documents. When you open a particular reader program, all the documents that can be read with that program appear in a list view. Tap on the document to open it.

If you find that you are using a document reader such as Quickword or Word to Go instead of the built-in Palm OS Memo Pad, reset the Memo Pad button to launch your favorite document reader instead (see Section 15.2).

§ 18.3 Palm-Ready Law Documents on the Web

The following federal, state, Supreme Court, and miscellaneous documents are among those available for download, most for free (available at **www.memoware.com** unless otherwise noted). You can use the regular Palm OS global Find function to locate specific words in these documents, which can help you pinpoint a specific section of the document for legal research purposes.

Federal Documents

- Amendments to the Constitution (annotated version)
- Americans with Disabilities Act (ADA) Accessibility Guidelines
- Bankruptcy Code
- Basic Copyright Law (**www.peanutpress.com**)
- Copyright Act, Title 17 of the U.S. Code (dated 1/5/99)
- Directory for the U.S. Court of Appeals for the Sixth Circuit
- Fair Credit Reporting Act
- Fair Debt Collection Act
- Federal Aviation Regulations 2001 (parts 61, 67, 91, 119, 121)
- Federal Food, Drug and Cosmetic Act

- Federal Patent Act
- Federal Power Act of 1992, Part II (Sections 201-214)
- Federal Rules of Appellate Procedure and Sixth Circuit Rules
- Federal Rules of Civil Procedure (**www.memoware.com** and **www.peanutpress.com**)
- Federal Rules of Criminal Procedure
- Federal Rules of Evidence (**www.memoware.com** and **www.peanutpress.com**)
- Federal Sentencing Guidelines 2000 (**www.memoware.com** and **www.thedefense.com**)[5]
- Federal Trademark Act
- Flag Laws and Regulations
- Individuals with Disabilities Education Act (IDEA) 1997 Reauthorization
- Military Grade and Rank
- United States Constitution (annotated version)
- United States Constitution (**www.memoware.com** and **www.peanutpress.com**)
- Uniform Code of Military Justice

Supreme Court Landmark Decisions

- *ACLU v. Reno* (striking down the Communications Decency Act)
- *Bivens v. Six Unnamed Federal Narcotics Agents* (establishing a right to sue the feds for violating the constitution)
- *Brown v. Board of Education* (striking down school segregation)
- *Dickerson v. United States* (upholding *Miranda v. Arizona*)
- *Marsh v. Alabama* (creating free-speech right in a company town)
- *N.A.A.C.P. v. Alabama* (protecting N.A.A.C.P. membership lists from the scrutiny of the state)
- *Reporters Committee for Freedom of the Press v. D.O.J.* (establishes a privacy interest in criminal rap sheets)
- *United States v. Nixon* (Nixon had to disclose documents demanded by the court)

State Documents

- Arizona State Constitution
- California Business and Professions Code
- California Civil Code 2000 and 2001
- California Code of Civil Procedure 2000 and 2001
- California Commercial Code 2001
- California Constitution (**www.memoware.com** and **www.peanutpress.com**)
- California Corporations Code 2001

- California Evidence Code 1999 (**www.peanutpress.com**)
- California Evidence Code and Index 2000
- California Family Code 2000 and 2001
- California Financial Code
- California Fish and Game Code
- California Food and Agriculture Code
- California Labor Code 2000
- California Local Rules of Court for Lassen County, California
- California Local Rules of Court for Shasta County, California
- California Local Rules of Court for Siskiyou County, California
- California Penal Code
- California Penal Code 2000 (annotated)
- California Penal Code and Uniform Controlled Substances Act of the Health Safety Code 2000
- California Probate Code 2000
- California Rules of Court 2000 and 2001
- California Uniform Controlled Substances Act, 2001
- California Uniform Retail Food Facilities Law
- California Vehicle Code 2000 (annotated)
- California Vehicle Code, License and DUI Codes, 2001
- California's 2000 Lanterman Act and Selected Portions of the Welfare and Institutions Code
- Declaration of Rights under the Constitution of California
- Florida Constitution (**www.peanutpress.com**)
- Florida Felony Criminal Statutes
- Florida Rules of Civil Procedure (as of 1/1/98)
- Florida Rules of Evidence
- Florida Common Statutes
- Georgia Uniform Rules of the Road
- Illinois: Traffic Violation Codes Used by the Chicago Police Dept.
- Illinois: Uniform Crime Reporting Codes Used by the Chicago Police Dept.
- Iowa Code of Professional Responsibility for Lawyers
- Massachusetts State Constitution
- Michigan Constitution 1963
- Michigan Criminal Sentencing Guidelines
- Mississippi Rules Civil Procedure
- Mississippi Rules of Ethics
- Mississippi Rules of Evidence
- Multistate Compilation: Automotive Lemon Laws (by State) and How to Apply Them

- New York Local Rules for the U.S. District Court for Northern District of New York
- Oregon Revised Statutes: Chapter 161, Crimes and Punishments
- Oregon State Constitution 2000
- Texas Alcohol Beverage Code, 1995 Legislative Update
- Texas Code of Criminal Procedure, 1995 Legislative Update
- Texas Constitution, 2000
- Texas Education Code, 1995 Legislative Update
- Texas Health and Safety Code, 1995 Legislative Update
- Texas Penal Code, 1995 Legislative Update
- Texas Rules of Evidence in Civil Cases (**www.peanutpress.com**)
- Washington State Constitution

Miscellaneous

- 10 Tips for Staying Sane in Court (**www.peanutpress.com**)
- Alternative Dispute Resolution: An Introduction (**www.peanutpress.com**)
- Charter of the United Nations (**www.peanutpress.com**)
- Daily Tip (**www.peanutpress.com**)
- Definitions of Legal Terms (**www.benc.hr/dpmodules.htm**)
- Federal Judiciary Frequently Asked Questions (**www.peanutpress.com**)
- Glossary of Legal Terminology
- Glossary of Legal Terms (**www.peanutpress.com**)
- Law-Related Graffiti Shortcuts (adds over 120 legal words and phrases as Graffiti ShortCuts, **www.palmlaw.com**)
- Lawyers Weekly: Hot News & Headlines (**www.peanutpress.com**)
- Legal Headlines (**www.peanutpress.com**)
- Privacy Survival Guide (**www.peanutpress.com**)
- Robert's Rules of Order, Revised (1917 version)
- United States Congress: Floor Activities This Week (**www.peanutpress.com**)
- United States Government Acronym Database
- Universal Declaration of Human Rights (**www.peanutpress.com**)
- Your Right to Federal Records (**www.peanutpress.com**)

§ 18.4 Bringing the Web to Your Handheld, Part 1

By attaching a modem to your handheld (unnecessary if you have a wireless model), you can surf the Web on your device.[6] Getting online with your handheld is similar in many ways to getting online with your desktop: you need to have an account with an ISP, and you need to install a Web browser program on your device.

One popular Web browser for the Palm OS is ProxiWeb (freeware available at **http://pdacentral.ii.net/index.html**). In addition to installing ProxiWeb or another Web browser on your handheld, you must configure your device to connect to your ISP. Tap Home and "Prefs," then select "Network" from the pop-up menu in the upper right corner. Insert your user name and—if you do not want to insert it each time you log on—your password. If your ISP is included in the "Service" pop-up menu, select it; if not, tap Menu and "New," and insert the name of your ISP. If the connection you will be using appears on the "Connection" pop-up menu, select it, or tap "Custom" to create your own. In addition to your ISP's telephone number, the "Phone Setup" screen allows you to insert a dial prefix (such as "9" to reach an outside line), a calling-card number, and the necessary pauses, as well as to disable call waiting. If your ISP requires any of the special settings available in the "Details" box, it should provide you with that information. When you are ready to go online, tap "Connect."

Once you have configured your network preferences and installed ProxiWeb using the procedures described in Chapter 17, launch it by tapping its icon. A toolbar at the bottom of the screen has icons for back, next, open URL, reload, view cache, bookmarks, and page information. To go to a specific Web site, tap the icon for opening a URL, insert the address, and tap "Go to." A pop-up menu of standard elements of Web addresses (such as http://, www, .com, .org, and .gov) facilitates writing the address. The bookmark function works just as it does on desktop Web browsers, so you can mark your favorite pages and return to them by selecting them from a pop-up menu, and tapping "Go to." A progress bar indicates that a Web page is loading onto your handheld. Eventually, a Palm-sized Web page appears on your handheld's screen.

You may be surprised at how quickly Web pages load onto your handheld. The trick lies in the way ProxiWeb works: it routes your request through a computer in California that removes from each Web page its non-Palm-friendly elements, such as animation, frames, and blinking lights, which are what make Web pages so slow to appear on your desktop PC.

To scroll through a Web page, you can use your handheld's physical scroll button, or you can drag your stylus around on the screen, which moves the page in the same direction. A dotted line underneath a word means that it is a hyperlink, just like underlined text on a desktop Web browser. Tap it to go to the linked Web page.

You can also store pages to read them after you go off line. Tap Menu → "Go" → "Lock in Cache." Tap Menu → "View" → "Cache" to see a pop-up menu of pages you have stored. To view a specific page, tap it.

Two options in ProxiWeb are particularly useful. You can choose to limit the size of cached pages to a reasonable level—the default size is 100 KB—so that they do not fill up your handheld's memory. You can also set your Address Book physical button to serve as a Previous Page button, and your To Do List physical button as a Next Page button.

§ 18.5 Bringing the Web to Your Handheld, Part 2

If you anticipate that you will be doing most of your Web page reading offline, a handy alternative to ProxiWeb is AvantGo. Unlike ProxiWeb, AvantGo does not require you to attach a modem to your handheld. Instead, it installs Web pages you have preselected onto your handheld whenever you perform a HotSync while your desktop PC is online. Go to **www.avantgo.com** and follow the directions to download and install its Palm OS program on your handheld, create your free account, and configure it to your preferences. You can create your own channels to download your favorite Web site, and select from a list of popular Web sites already set up to be delivered by AvantGo. These currently include:

- *ABA Journal Mobile Edition*
- CNN
- **Gigalaw.com** (information for Internet professionals and their lawyers)
- MSN Mobile
- PBS
- The Daily Report ("Wisconsin's construction, law and public record authority since 1897")
- The Law Marketing Portal ("where law firms find out how to get more business")
- *The New York Times*
- *The Wall Street Journal*

§ 18.6 Legal Research on Your Handheld

With an ISP account and a wireless PDA (or another handheld with a modem attached), you can do legal research on your handheld with Westlaw.

Westlaw's handheld-compatible version, Westlaw Wireless (**www.westlaw.com/wireless**), allows access to most Westlaw information. You can download and install Westlaw's own wireless Web clipping program, or point your handheld's browser to **www.wireless.westlaw.com** (or its shortcut:

http://wl-w.com). Once you are connected and have a Westlaw password, you can (1) cite-check your cases, (2) run a search in Westlaw's databases using terms and connectors, natural language, or case titles, (3) send URL links to a document or search result to others by e-mail, (4) forward up to five cases, statutes, or other documents to your e-mail address or Westlaw printer, and (5) use the West Legal Directory to locate a lawyer, law firm, courthouse, or legal vendor.

Clearly the ability to perform legal research anytime, anywhere, comes in handy—perhaps in court, should opposing counsel mention a case that did not appear in his or her brief.

You can also arrange to have Westlaw send e-mail to your handheld alerting you to developments affecting specific cases, statutes, regulations, and administrative decisions (via KeyCite Alert Wireless), and news or other information you request (via WestClip Wireless).

Westlaw Wireless charges are based on the terms of your existing Westlaw subscription; there are no extra charges for accessing Westlaw wirelessly (except for using the e-mail link option). See **www.westlaw.com/wireless** for details.

Apart from Westlaw Wireless, you can transfer Westlaw documents (such as cases, statutes, regulations, news, and topical materials) from your PC to your handheld with a reader such as DataViz Documents To Go.

Notes

1. Add-on applications can expand this list. Search the PalmSource Web site for software for other e-mail programs.

2. Electronic books (or e-books) are usually free if the text is no longer copyright-protected, hence the wealth of classics (such as Dickens, Shakespeare, and the Bible) available on–line.

3. The bundle includes Palm OS programs corresponding to Microsoft Excel and PowerPoint.

4. See **http://www.bachmannsoftware.com/pbprem.htm**; $39.99.

5. If you install Quicksheet on your handheld (see Section 20.6), you can insert the offense level and criminal history and this program will tell you the range of sentence.

6. The modem can be either wireless or attached to a land line.

Keeping Track of Time on Your Handheld 19

§ 19.1 Overview

There are numerous add-on timekeeping programs available for handhelds running the Palm OS. Aside from the freeware-shareware-commercial distinction, they fall into three basic categories: (1) stand-alone programs, which operate primarily on your handheld; (2) programs that come with their own desktop applications that synchronize with the handheld version; and (3) programs that synchronize with widely used commercial desktop or network timekeeping systems such as DTE or Timeslips.

Stand-alone programs are those you can access only on your handheld. However, most of these programs allow you to generate reports that are exported to another Palm OS application (usually Memo Pad), so after performing a HotSync, the report shows up on your corresponding desktop program. From that point, it is easy to copy and paste the report into a full-featured desktop program such as Microsoft Word or Excel to format and analyze the information as you wish. Reading these reports is generally easier on the desktop program anyway, since the reports are usually charts in a tab-separated format, which is hard to read on a handheld's small screen.

§ 19.2 Suggestions for Choosing a Timekeeping Program

The timekeeping program that is right for you is very much a matter of personal preference. There are many ways to configure the basic features, and many variations of additional features, so it is worthwhile to experiment with several programs before settling on one. You will probably find that a certain program feels more comfortable for you than others.

While the commercial programs tend to be more comprehensive and come with more documentation (such as user's guides and quick-start directions), some of the freeware and shareware programs are quite good, and can fully satisfy the basic timekeeping requirements of many lawyers, particularly those in solo or small firm practice. Using a simple program is also a good way to learn whether you like to keep track of time on your handheld before graduating to a more comprehensive (and expensive) program.

If your firm already has one of the timekeeping systems for which there is a companion Palm OS program, you may be tempted to go directly to that program. However, if your current timekeeping procedure is to give your handwritten time sheet to your secretary, who then puts the information into the firm's system, you can streamline the procedure for both of you by using even a basic timekeeping program. Once you have mastered a basic program with a simple report feature, you can create a word-processed version of your time sheet with accurate, complete time totals and descriptions more quickly than you can write a time sheet, and your secretary can then copy and paste the information from that document into the firm's system.

§ 19.3 Timekeeping Programs

Each of the following programs contains some variation of the basic features you would expect in a timekeeping program, such as:

- The ability to create a list of clients and projects that are then included in an editable pop-up menu to facilitate inserting time entries. Such lists can be edited using dialog boxes similar to the Edit Categories dialog boxes in the main Palm OS applications. Usually you can create as many projects as you require.
- Space to insert a description of a task, either as a field in the basic time record screen or as a separate note similar to notes in Date Book, Address Book, and To Do List.
- Three ways to insert time: (1) manually inputting total time (using the standard Palm OS "Set Time" box), (2) inputting start and end times, and (3) via timers that you can stop and restart as often as you like, so

keeping track of time you spend on a project is reduced to tapping on the timer at the start and end of a work session. These timers remain running even when your handheld is off.

- The ability to set the timer to round to increments such as minutes, tenths, or quarter-hours, according to your preference.
- The ability to edit your time totals, which is useful if you forget to start the timer when you begin working on a project, or to stop the timer when you finish.
- The ability to calculate total time by client, by project, and for all clients and projects within dates you specify.
- The ability to sort time records either chronologically or alphabetically by client or project.
- The ability to generate reports detailing or summarizing time worked (within dates you specify) on an individual client, for a specific project, or for all clients and projects.

Moreover, most of the programs use the basic elements of the Palm OS, so you can input and edit text just as in the main applications (using Graffiti or the on-screen keyboard), select dates using the standard Palm OS date selector boxes, and tap on the "i" in the upper-right corner of a box to learn more about a feature.

Many of these programs are available free for thirty days, and have free, detailed, screen-shot-laden user's guides either online or that you can download at any time. Complete and current information about these programs is available at the Web address provided for each program.

- **AllTime** is a basic time and expense tracking program. Useful features include Quickfill, which automatically completes an entry as you begin entering letters into a field, yet allows you to continue entering text if the proffered word is not the one you want. Handy views include lists of Clients, Projects, Activities, Expense types, Accounts, and Payees. AllTime also multiplies the amount of time spent on a project by your hourly billing rate. You can enter time by entering the total time directly into the duration field, by inputting the start and end times for a project, or by using a stopwatch-type timer (which remains running even when your handheld is off). You can create up to fifteen categories (the standard Palm OS category limit) to keep track of time and expense entries, and can append a note to each entry. AllTime allows you to view entries in various configurations such as sorting[1] entries by date, client, or project, or filtering entries to view only those for specific clients, projects, or activities. AllTime allows you to generate reports that cover the time and expense categories and dates you specify. Optional filters allow you to generate reports on just one client, project, or activity. The reports can be exported to either Memo Pad or Mail for transfer to your PC at your next HotSync, where they may be transferred to Microsoft Word or Excel. AllTime (**http://www.iambic.com/alltime/palmos**) costs $39.95 (free for a thirty-day trial period).

- **DTE InHand** by Advanced Productivity Software is the Palm OS companion program to the DTE timekeeping system. This version allows you to transmit billing data either wirelessly, or via HotSync. The View Entries screen shows time entries in chronological order, beginning with the most recent entry. The Time Entry screen includes fields for client, matter, task, start and stop time, hours worked, a four-line description, and a timer button. The program has room for tracking expenses as well. DTE InHand (**www.aps-soft.com**) costs $100, has a thirty-day trial version, and is usable only with the desktop DTE program, which starts at $125 per user, with quantity discounts available for multiple users.
- **HourzPro** is a flexible, multifeatured program that can be customized to suit a variety of work styles. Unlike most timekeeping programs, HourzPro time entries are not described by client, but only by task, although entries do have a field for the client name. In addition to the standard timekeeping functions (timer, start and end times, manual input), you can specify total break time during a work period, which the program subtracts from the gross hours to calculate the total time worked.

  HourzPro has two customizable list views: Project View, which provides a multi-day view of time entries for all projects or a specific project, and Day View, which shows all the time entries for a given day. A handy feature is Easy Entry, which allows you to create new time entries in just two taps, and automatically starts the timer for that task. You can choose whether HourzPro rounds up, down, or to the nearest time interval you select. You can hide infrequently used items to allow more room for more frequently used entries. In addition to allowing you to record fixed-rate items, HourzPro calculates the total amount to bill based on a customizable hourly billing rate, and determines mileage based on start and end odometer readings.

  HourzPro has two companion Palm OS programs: ExpenzPro (which shares a common project list with HourzPro) and Reportz, used to generate reports in your choice of date range, project, and format (Intuit Interchange Format [IIF], comma-separated value [CSV], or tab-separated format [TXT]). The resulting reports are then transferred to your PC at your next HotSync, where they are ready to be imported into QuickBooks Pro, or another spreadsheet or database program such as Microsoft Access, Claris FileMaker Pro, or FoxPro. HourzPro (**www.zoskware.com**) costs $49.95 (free for a thirty-day trial period).

- **PCLaw TE** software for the Palm OS, by Alumni Computer Group, can be used only with its companion desktop version, PCLaw. Its Time Entry view on the handheld displays the date, matter, task, and rate (with a pop-up menu for each), and includes a stopwatch timer that begins automatically when you start a new time entry. The program automatically calculates and displays the hours spent on the task and the corresponding fee, and has a pop-up menu for descriptive terms, as well as room for six lines of description. At each HotSync, entries are transferred to your PC and removed from your handheld. PCLaw TE is available from Alumni Computer Group (**www.pclaw.com**, **sales@pclaw.com**, 1-800-387-9785); contact the company for pricing options.
- **ProjecTrak** by Inertron Software contains all the basic features you would want in a timekeeping program. Its main view consists of four columns: (1) the name of the client or project, (2) today's cumulative time for each project, (3) the total time for the project since its inception (for those dates you have not yet purged), and (4) a checkbox to show whether a project has been finished. The list is alphabetical by project name or by client name, according to your preference. You can also sort completed projects to the end of the list. You can add a note of up to 4,096 characters to each day's time record for a project by tapping a button with the standard Palm OS note icon.

  Tapping on a project's accumulated time display in the "today" column of the main view starts or stops the timer for that project. Tapping on the time display for a second project simultaneously stops the timer for the first project and starts it for the second, thus facilitating switching back and forth between projects. ProjecTrak does not permit you to record more than twenty-four hours in a day (so if you are working around the clock on the day that daylight savings time ends, or while traveling west, you are out of luck). However, if you have a timer running past midnight, ProjecTrak automatically changes to the next day and continues timing.

  A detailed view for each project shows the client, project, total time, unbilled time, and the dates on which any time was recorded for the project. A handy button toggles the list between chronological and reverse chronological order.

  A summary view shows the total time for any or all projects between any two dates. Reports are exported to Memo Pad, with a choice between linear or spreadsheet options, and between a comma or a tab separator between data fields. In addition, all your ProjecTrak information (not just data contained in reports) is backed up each time you HotSync.

ProjecTrak (**www.inertron.com/palm**) is shareware with a $25 registration fee. There is a full-featured thirty-day demonstration version. The companion desktop program is called ProjecTrakDesk and costs $10.

- **TakeTime** is a very basic timekeeping program. It allows you to create client and task lists that appear as pop-up menus to facilitate inserting subsequent entries. You can track time by using a timer, or by entering the start and end time for the task. Each task screen has room for notes of up to two hundred characters. A display at the bottom of the screen shows the running total time for both the current task and the day. You can generate summary reports for all clients (showing total time for each client) and for each client (showing time totals for each separate task) for any day or date interval you specify. Detailed reports for all clients and tasks (including any notes, plus start time, end time, and total times for each task) can also be created. All reports are exported to Memo Pad. TakeTime (**http://www.geocities.com/salvisiuribus/palm.html**) is free.
- **Time Logger,** Responsive Software's Palm interface program, is a powerful application. Developed to complement Time Logger for PC, the Palm OS interface allows you to describe time records by up to ten linkable fields including client, project, subproject, activity, and hourly rate. After HotSyncing with the PC program, Time Logger can store data as Microsoft Access files, which are accessible by other standard commercial database applications such as Excel, and can be exported to Quicken (.aif) and QuickBooks (.iif) formats. The data can also be placed in your word-processing files. Even on the handheld, you can analyze time records by sorting and filtering the list of time records to view totals for duration, fees, expenses, and mileage. The program includes extensive help available by tapping the standard Palm OS "i" button.

  Time Logger's Palm interface (**www.responsivesoftware.com**) is currently free (under a "limited-time offer," warns the Web site) when you purchase the Time Logger for PC, which costs $89. You can download free demo versions of both the PC program and the Palm program; however, the Palm OS demo version does not allow you to HotSync your records to your PC, and the PC demo version, which automatically expires after sixty days, allows you to store no more than forty time records, and does not allow you to print out reports.
- **Time, Expense, and Automobile Keeper (TEAK)** comes with a powerful companion desktop program, and you can create entries either on

your handheld or on your PC. In the handheld version, the View Entries screen shows a list of existing time, expense, and mileage entries. The Time Entry screen shows the details: client, project, task, start and stop time, hours worked, hourly billable rate, amount billable (hours worked multiplied by the billable rate), and has a four-line description field. The Expense Entry and Auto Mileage Entry screens are similarly straightforward. The desktop program lets you create reports (plus a variety of pie charts and graphs) using TEAK's extensive variety of templates, or you can create your own using Crystal Reports 5.0 by Seagate Software. TEAK also allows you to export data into a variety of standard programs such as Excel, Word, Lotus 123, and CSV format.

TEAK (**www.eb7.com**) costs $79.95 for both the Palm OS and PC versions (free for a forty-five-day trial period).

- **TimeCompanion** by Inmotion Mobile Software Solutions consists of companion Palm OS and PC programs. You can input entries on your handheld or your PC, and the data is synchronized between the Palm and PC platforms during each HotSync. The Palm OS program has a view listing projects alphabetically by name, with a brief description and daily time totals for each project. You can edit the project list and individual project descriptions, and can beam projects to other TimeCompanion users. The desktop program can create reports and export data to files for use in common applications such as Excel, in CSV format, as well as in more advanced formats. Designed for use by workgroups, the desktop program can create reports based on data from multiple TimeCompanion users. Data from different users can be input by HotSyncing multiple handhelds with one desktop TimeCompanion program, or by HotSyncing to separate PCs and then e-mailing the data to one computer for consolidation. TimeCompanion (**www.inmotion.se**) costs $30.
- **TimeReporter** is a full-featured program for both your PC and handheld. It tracks both time and expenses, and is compatible with Microsoft Access, Microsoft Excel, QuickBooks, and Quicken. It has multiple filtering and sorting capabilities, and allows you to assign time to clients, projects, activities, or users; to import information from Date Book and Address Book when making time entries; and to format your reports in a variety of ways.

  Both programs are available from Iambic Software (**www.iambic.com**) for $149.95 by download, $159.95 on CD-ROM, and $474.95 for a five-user site license. A free thirty-day trial version is available.
- **TimeReporter for Carpe Diem** is designed for use with the desktop timekeeping program Carpe Diem. This version of TimeReporter

downloads clients and project data from your PC and uploads time entries from your handheld at each HotSync. You can enter time using the standard Palm OS time selector or input your time with Graffiti, sort time entries by client or project, and filter time entries by day/week/month, client/project, and status. The program uses configuration settings identical to those on the Carpe Diem Electronic Time Sheet system. For pricing information, call 1-800-477-6763 (**http://www.best-software.com/Products/TimeTracking/index.asp**).

- **TimeReporter for Timeslips** is designed for use with the desktop timekeeping program Timeslips. This version of TimeReporter downloads clients, tasks, and references from your PC and uploads time and expense entries from your handheld at each HotSync. Multiple users can HotSync their handhelds to a common Timeslips database or to different databases. The program costs $119.95 by download, and $129.95 on CD-ROM. See **http://store.yahoo.com/iambicstore/timfortim.html**.

§ 19.4 Suggestions for Using a Timekeeping Program

Here are some suggestions to facilitate the use of any Palm OS timekeeping program:

1. If the program sorts projects alphabetically, and you work on only a handful of projects during any given day, you can force those projects to appear at the head of the list by temporarily adding a punctuation mark in front of the first letter of the name of the project. (The alphabetical sort function places punctuation before letters.) For example:

   .Brown v. Black
   .McCullough v. Maryland
   .Smith v. Jones
   Adams v. Wilson
   Alexander v. Thomas
   Allison v. Ward

   If you want those items to appear in an order other than alphabetical, add numbers. (The alphabetical sort function places numbers after punctuation but before letters.) For example:

   1.Smith v. Jones
   2.McCullough v. Maryland
   3.Brown v. Black
   Adams v. Wilson
   Alexander v. Thomas
   Allison v. Ward

By the way, this hint works on PCs as well, since most files are (or easily can be) sorted alphabetically.

2. Create templates of common descriptions within the timekeeping program if possible, or use Graffiti ShortCuts (see Section 15.5). For example, you can create a Graffiti ShortCut so you need to input only "ℓtw" instead of "Telecon with." Supplement your own Graffiti ShortCuts with PalmLaw Graffiti ShortCuts,[2] a downloadable file containing Graffiti ShortCuts for 120 legal words and phrases.
3. Finally, no matter which timekeeping program you use, make it easy to get to by remapping the button you use least to take you directly to your timekeeping program (see Section 15.2).
4. A simple but effective trick to remind yourself to restart your timer after taking a break from a work session at the office is to leave a stylus on the keyboard of your desktop PC.

Notes

1. To "sort" means to configure a list of items in accordance with a designated principle. For example, sorting by client or project would arrange items in alphabetical order; sorting by date would arrange them in chronological order. Many applications also allow you to toggle between a principle and its inverse, so you can easily view items in reverse chronological order, which is actually very handy in a timekeeping program, since it can be convenient to put the most recent entries first.

2. Available for free download at **www.handango.com**

The Handheld Mobile Office

20

§ 20.1 Overview

One of the many beauties of a Palm Powered™ handheld is that it can greatly reduce the quantity of paper and gadgets necessary to be productive while you are away from your office. Even without any additional software or paraphernalia, your handheld gives you convenient, interactive access to your calendar, contact information, and to-do list when you travel. As discussed in previous chapters, you can install add-on programs that allow you to use your handheld anywhere to read and reply to e-mail, read and edit word-processed memoranda and documents, do legal research, and keep track of your billable time. With the backlight, you can view your handheld comfortably while traveling during the evening hours, without the glare of overhead lights in planes, trains, and automobiles.

So before you go on a business trip, pack your handheld instead of your briefcase. Instead of bringing paper versions of memoranda, e-mail, documents, and legal research, HotSync them to your handheld. Just before you leave, HotSync once more to install the latest information from your AvantGo channels.

This chapter describes ways to use your handheld's built-in capabilities as handy travel companions, and also covers a variety of additional software and hardware that can lighten your load, help you stay organized, and get things done while you are on the road.

§ 20.2 Keeping Track of Travel Information

Even without any add-on programs, your handheld can serve you well as an organizer for your travel information. Date Book is a natural for keeping track of your itinerary: insert flights as events with departure as the start time and arrival as the end time (rounding to the nearest five minutes, as required by the Palm OS Set Time box). Insert the name of your hotel as an event beginning some time after the last real event of the day, and insert trip-specific details such as confirmation numbers in an attached note. Insert the airline's name and telephone number in Address Book, and include your frequent-flier number and any other continuing details in a note attached to the contact record. Insert the hotel in Address Book as well for ease of future reference to its telephone number, address, and driving directions. Create a category in Address Book for Airlines, Hotels, or simply Travel. A handy trick is to set an alarm to go off at the time you need to leave for the airport in time to catch your plane.

If you want a more sophisticated itinerary program, Gulliver has preinstalled information for airlines, airports, hotels, and car rental companies worldwide, so you need only tap a pop-up menu instead of using Graffiti to insert a lot of information. The menus are editable so you can add vendors that are not on the preinstalled list. Other advantages of Gulliver are (1) you can enter exact arrival and departure times, which automatically show up in Date Book; (2) there are predefined fields for all key items of information (such as prices, rates, confirmation numbers, non-smoking preferences) so you can easily remember to consider all of these details; (3) all hotel, airline, and car rental company numbers are in the same place, which facilitates those last-minute confirmation calls; and (4) you can beam your itinerary and all its current details to other handheld owners, which secretaries and significant others will appreciate. Gulliver (**www.northisup.com**) is $19.99.

§ 20.3 Keeping Track of Expenses

There is an expense program called Expense built in to every Palm OS handheld. Once you are familiar with the main applications you will find it easy to learn Expense, since it uses the standard Palm OS elements: categories, the standard edit menu, and a "Details" button yielding a screen with pop-up menus for category, type of expense, form of payment (cash or credit), currency, vendor, and city. You can attach a note to a record—actually, two notes—one of which is headed "Attendees" but accepts any text. Expense has several characteristics unusual for the built-in programs: (1) its Expense Type pop-up menu of twenty-eight types of business trip expenses is not editable; (2) you can insert records for only fifteen different trips (the category function serves as the title for a trip record), and (3) after HotSyncing, you must go to Microsoft Excel to open your expense report.

If you prefer a more sophisticated expense program, try a timekeeping program that also tracks expenses (such as AllTime, Time Logger, and TEAK, which are described in Chapter 19) or one of the many, many expense programs available for the Palm OS, a tiny sampling of which includes ExpensAble (**www.landware.com**, $29.95); ExpensePlus (**www.palmgear.com**, $49.95), ExpenzPro (**www.palmgear.com**, $39.95), and HBExpense (**www.palmblvd.com**, $19.95).

§ 20.4 Outlines and Checklists

While To Do List and Memo Pad are adequate for creating basic lists on your handheld, there are some simple yet powerful programs that allow you to create detailed outlines and checklists. Both outliners and checklists are crucial tools in the practice of law, and having them on your handheld allows you maximum flexibility, since you can add things when and where you think of them. You can use an outliner to clarify your thoughts about a project, organize legal research, write rough drafts of documents, plan case strategy, and manage large projects. You can use checklists to create templates that you can tweak to create customized to-do lists for new projects that are similar to past projects.

With BrainForest (**www.ultrasoft.com**, from $19.95), you can create multilevel outlines in which you can easily move and rerank items, open and close specific branches so you see as much or as little detail as you like, and attach long notes to each item. You have the option of having checkboxes next to each item, so the outline can also serve as a to-do list for the project. BrainForest synchronizes with its full-featured companion desktop program. Another popular outliner program is ThoughtManager (**www.handshigh.com**, $19.95).

With SuperList2 (**www.palmblvd.com**, $12), you can create up to 250 master lists, each of which forms the basis for a working list that you create by tapping individual items in the master list, or by using the "grab all" command. You can remove an item from the working list with two taps. The program is perfect for creating templates for packing lists, attendance lists, shopping lists, and other repeating tasks. An updated version, SuperList3 ($19.99), lets you create multilevel outlines as well as lists.

§ 20.5 Calculators

The basic Palm OS Calculator program is adequate for many needs. In addition to saving you the trouble of bringing along another gadget in addition to your handheld, the benefits of using Calculator are (1) you can copy and paste numbers from and to other programs on your handheld (including the spreadsheet programs discussed in Section 20.6), and (2) you can view your twelve most recent calculations (tap Menu → "Options" → "Recent Calculations" or use the command shortcut /I).

If you prefer a more sophisticated calculator, try Parens Lite, which should be in the Add-on folder on your PC (C:\Palm\Add-on). If it is not, you can get an upgraded shareware version for $11.95 at **www.palmblvd.com**.

If you need a powerful, easily portable financial calculator, get Financial Consultant (**www.landware.com**, $19.95), which has over ninety functions including amortization, discounts, future/past dates, interest rate conversions, internal rate of return, and loan payments. Use it for calculations involving savings, loans, leases, and mortgages (including Canadian mortgages).

§ 20.6 Spreadsheets

You can download, create, and edit Excel spreadsheets on your handheld using any of the following full-featured spreadsheet programs. On the Palm OS, vertical and horizontal scrollbars give you access to the multiple columns and rows common in a spreadsheet document.

Quicksheet (**www.cesinc.com**, $19.95), Quickchart (free with Quicksheet), and Quickword (see Section 18.2), make up the Quickoffice suite of Palm OS programs. Quicksheet allows you to create or HotSync what are effectively Excel documents on your Palm, read and edit them there, and HotSync the edited version back to your PC. Quickchart allows you to create bar, line, and pie charts from data in Quicksheets.

Other popular spreadsheet programs are Iambic Software's TinySheet (**www.handango.com**, $29.95) and Sheet To Go (**www.dataviz.com**, $69.95 as part of the Documents To Go DataViz Office suite, which includes Word To Go [see Section 18.2] and SlideShow To Go [see Section 20.7]).

§ 20.7 Microsoft PowerPoint™

With Slideshow To Go (**www.dataviz.com**, $69.95 as part of Documents to Go), you can install and view PowerPoint files on your handheld. While you cannot create or edit slides on your handheld, you can use this program to rehearse your presentation without using your laptop.

If you have a Visor, you can actually present a PowerPoint program with your handheld, and leave your laptop at home. Presenter-to-Go (**www.margi.com**, $199) includes a Springboard module that lets you connect directly to a digital projector. Like Slideshow To Go, Presenter-to-Go does not allow you to create or edit slides on your handheld; you must HotSync slides from your PC. Nor does Presenter-to-Go support the fancy slide transitions, animation, or audio-video features available on Microsoft PowerPoint, and you must remove these features before HotSyncing the slides to your handheld.

§ 20.8 Vindigo®

Vindigo is a personal navigation program that helps you find restaurants, stores, and entertainment in major cities in the United States and in London. See Section 2.15 for a detailed description of its features.

§ 20.9 Travel Clocks

Even without any add-on programs, your handheld can serve you well as a travel clock. To view the time: either (1) tap Home, (2) in Date Book, tap the date indicator and hold your stylus down (the current time appears for a few seconds, then disappears); or (3) if you have one, go to your timekeeping program. Most of them display the time somewhere in one of their main views. (Later model Palms include a basic clock as one of the built-in programs.) When you travel across time zones, reset your handheld's clock (see Section 15.3), and insert a reminder in Date Book or To Do List to change the time back after your trip.

To use your handheld as an alarm clock, insert any word as an event in Date Book at the time you want to wake up (I use the word "alarm"), and set the alarm to go off zero minutes before the event. For multiday trips, you can move the event to the following day by simply changing the date in the Event Details box (see Section 11.8). To ensure you hear the alarm, be sure the sound is on and set on high (see Section 15.3), and place your handheld face down on a bedside table.

If you want a flexible clock that shows the time, date, and monthly calendar in a customizable view; has two alarms that you can set once to go off at the same time on any or all days of the week; has a view that allows you to see the time in two time zones in addition to your own; and has easy-to-set countdown and stopwatch timers, download the popular freeware program BigClock (**www.gacel.de**).

§ 20.10 Travel Accessories

Your handheld can even replace your laptop on the road. Portable full-size keyboards that fold up to be not much larger than a handheld are available for the various handheld models at numerous Web sites, including **www.expansys.com** (for the Sony Clié), **www.genovation.com**, **www.landware.com**, and **www.palm.com**. Other travel essentials are cords to recharge and HotSync your handheld, so you can leave the cradle behind. You can also get snap-on modems, protective cases, extra styli, screen protectors, and a growing variety of accessories at these Web sites, among others.

Ethics, Privacy, and Security Issues

21

§ 21.1 Introduction

The mobility of handheld PDAs is a double-edged sword when it comes to guarding the privacy and security of information on PDAs. Their small size makes them convenient to carry but also easy to misplace or lose, and they are tempting targets for thieves and others with malicious intent. The security and privacy risks associated with misappropriated PDAs and the confidential information stored on them can be mitigated by the programs and strategies discussed in this chapter. However, an increase in security generally brings with it somewhat of a decrease in convenience. For example, password-protecting your PDA each time you turn it off makes it difficult to use the PDA for driving directions, since it usually requires two hands to insert a password. Every lawyer using a PDA should balance the costs, risks, and benefits to determine the optimal level of security for his or her PDA.

§ 21.2 Ethical Considerations

A lawyer who keeps confidential client information on his or her PDA should show due diligence in taking reasonable and prudent steps to set up and maintain security precautions to prevent disclosure of client confidences stored on the PDA. In order to remain private, the information on a PDA must be secure. The goal should be to attain a reasonable level of security in order to reduce the risk of a breach in security, and therefore the potential for unauthorized disclosure of private information.

§ 21.3 Basic Security Practices

The first step in keeping a PDA secure is to keep it physically with you as much as possible. When you are at your desk, keep it in its HotSync cradle; when you leave your desk, take it with you in your purse or pocket. Treat it with as much caution as you treat your wallet; store it and carry it in a way that precludes access by unauthorized parties. Be especially vigilant in public, in court, at a deposition, or in any situation that puts you in close proximity with opponents. Consider using a lanyard-type arrangement such as **Force.com's** The Bond.[1]

To mitigate the loss of productivity in case of a lost PDA, back up your data by HotSyncing frequently. If your PDA goes missing, you will lose only the information you inserted in your PDA since your last HotSync. You can easily create a replica of your old PDA by performing a "Desktop overrides handheld" HotSync with a new PDA (see Sections 2.3 and 10.2).

To increase the chance that a lost PDA is returned to you, be certain to include your contact information in the Owner section of the Preferences application. This information appears when the device is first turned on if you have locked the device using the password protection of Palm's built-in Security application. If the device is not locked, anyone with a basic knowledge of the Palm operating system knows to go to the Owner screen to find this information. In addition, there are lost-and-found services such as Boomerangit[2] and StuffBak[3] that provide you with a coded identification label to stick on your handheld device. The finder need only call the toll-free number included on the label to arrange for the item to be returned to you (at your expense).

There are two other basic security measures every PDA user can apply immediately. First, take care to avoid a mistake common to neophyte PDA users: do not keep personal information such as your Social Security number, PIN numbers, bank account numbers, and home security system code numbers in a note attached to your own contact record in Address Book. At first glance, this appears to be a logical and convenient place to keep such data, but it is a serious security breach, because this information remains attached to your contact record when you beam it to others. If you identify that contact record as your business card, you share that information with everyone to whom you beam your business card. If you must keep such sensitive information there, at least create two contact records for yourself, and ensure that the one you designate as your business card is the one from which you have removed this information.

The second basic security measure regards beaming. Simply put, whenever you beam sensitive information, ensure that your PDA is aimed only at intended recipients. According to Palm, the beaming range is from four to thirty-nine inches, and within a relatively narrow arc, but experience has shown that these are parameters are somewhat conservative, and that it is possible for multiple PDAs to receive the same beamed information simultaneously. To be on the safe side when beaming sensitive material, ensure that only those you want to receive the beam are within at least six to eight feet from your PDA. For example, avoid beaming confidential information across a conference table if your opponents are sitting near the intended recipient of the beamed information.

§ 21.4 Using the Built-In Palm Security Program

The next level of security after keeping track of the physical location of the device and practicing safe beaming is to use the built-in Security function that comes with every Palm Powered™ PDA. This is a relatively low-level layer of security, but it is free, easy to use, and certainly better than nothing. This program allows you to password-protect individual records in any of the four main applications (Date Book, Address Book, To Do List, and Memo Pad), and to lock the device so that it cannot be turned on without inserting the proper password. You can set the Security program to either mask or hide all private entries. When the records are masked, you see a grey strip in place of the text constituting a record. When the records are hidden, they become invisible until you unselect the "Hide Records" option and insert the correct password. Since the "Hide Records" option requires you to affirmatively recall that the invisible record exists, it seems to be a somewhat risky option to use if you rely on your PDA to recall appointments and other information in the first place.

To lock your device, either go to the Security program and tap the "Turn Off & Lock Device" button, or set the pen swipe feature to the "Turn Off & Lock" option (see Section 15.2). Once this option is set, all you have to do is drag your stylus from the bottom of the Graffiti area to the top of the screen to turn off and lock the device. More recent versions of the Palm Operating System (versions 4.0 and above) have an Auto Lock option that allows you to set your handheld to lock automatically when you turn it off, at a preset time each day, or after your handheld has been inactive for a period of time of up to ninety-nine hours.

If you forget your password, you can always perform a hard reset on the device, which deletes all the information on the handheld, and then perform a "Desktop overwrites Handheld" HotSync to restore all the data.[4]

However, using only the built-in Security program presents several serious vulnerabilities. First, earlier versions of the Security application (versions 3.5.2 and below) have a serious weakness. @stake, Inc., a digital security consulting firm, has pointed out that anyone with reasonable technical skills could easily bypass the password protection of a locked device, by means of a backdoor built into the system in order to allow Palm OS programmers to debug certain files.[5] @stake even described this scary scenario: "Because it is possible to install applications onto the Palm OS device while the 'system lockout' functionality is enabled, an adversary could install a keystroke monitoring program in which any passwords could be recorded and retrieved at a later date. This recorded data could be retrieved though the debug mode, as well. The possibility also exists for such a program to save the contents of memory after cryptographic operations take place, hence retrieving the plaintext of encrypted memos, keys, or other data."[6] This security flaw can be fixed by installing the add-on program ShortFix[7] or upgrading to Palm OS 4.0 or higher.[8]

Second, the built-in Security program is only as good as the password you provide. Avoid short passwords, and those consisting of names or dates. A good password contains at least six to eight characters, with a combination of punctuation marks, numbers, and upper- and lower-case letters.

The third weakness of the built-in Palm security program is that the password is synced to the desktop computer, where it is vulnerable to discovery by hackers and unauthorized users.

The recently released Palm OS 5.0 has more enhanced security capabilities than earlier versions, including features allowing third-party add-on programs to incorporate biometric verification methods such as handwriting, voice recognition, and fingerprints. It also includes built-in encryption software, so that add-on programs need not include their own encryption systems.[9] Because the Security application in Palm OS 5 is so different from previous versions, many of the add-on programs discussed below do not work with Palm OS 5.

§ 21.5 Add-On Security Programs

There are a variety of choices available to current Palm OS PDA users who want a stronger security system than the Security applications of Palm OS 4.1 and below (and who don't want to purchase a new PDA with Palm OS 5 and then wait for third-party developers to write programs that take advantage of its security capabilities). The three main categories of add-on security programs are (1) programs to lock the device, (2) programs that provide a combination of locking and encryption capabilities, and (3) programs to encrypt specific information in the device.

Locking the device is an appropriate first step towards better security. Some popular lock-only programs include EasyLock,[10] Padlock Hack,[11] OnlyMe,[12] and OneTouchPass.[13] They are all variations on the same basic theme. With EasyLock, you unlock your PDA by pressing one, or optionally two, of the hard buttons on the PDA, rather than inserting a password. (This approach relies on the assumption that someone who finds your PDA is not aware that pressing just one or two physical buttons unlocks the device.) Padlock Hack allows you to unlock your PDA by pressing a longer combination of hardware buttons, and has AutoLock and TimeLock functions similar to those in Palm's Security version 4. OnlyMe automatically locks the PDA when you turn it off, and your passcode to unlock it can consist of any combination of writing Graffiti letters or numbers, tapping the program's on-screen keys, and pressing the device's hardware buttons. OneTouchPass has the most exotic variation: instead of writing characters or pressing buttons, you tap on one or more specific points of a photograph you select.

It's a good idea to have redundant security features, such as encryption for sensitive information as well as general password protection for the entire device. There are a variety security programs that allow you to both lock the device and encrypt selected information. In deciding which program is best for you, consider such factors as how easy the program is to use, how convenient it is to use (for example, does it have an automatic lock feature, or do you have to remember to lock the device yourself?), how long it takes to encrypt and decrypt information, whether it avoids the problems of the built-in Palm Security system (does the program store the password on the PDA or transfer it to the desktop during HotSync operation?), and whether the password is masked when inserted (so that the screen reads "********") to prevent an onlooker from learning the password. Finally, how powerful is the encryption key?[14] Encrypted data can be decoded using powerful computers, but is probably safe from most thieves intent on selling your handheld rather than learning your secrets.[15]

Add-on programs that allow you to both lock your device and encrypt information on it include the following:

- MovianCrypt[16] uses 128-bit encryption to encrypt each individual record in the four main Palm applications (Date Book, Address Book, To Do List, and Memo Pad) as it is stored, and to decrypt each record as it is accessed. The PDA is automatically locked when it is turned off or when it turns off automatically. According to its developer, MovianCrypt is compatible with other third-party applications, and transparent to end users.
- PDABomb[17] uses 128-bit encryption to encrypt both built-in Palm OS applications and databases used by third-party programs. PDABomb allows you to password-protect data transfer methods such as Hot-

Sync and beaming via the infrared port. You can allow either an unlimited number of password attempts, or set the "bomb" to activate after three to ten failed attempts at inserting the correct password. When the bomb goes off, PDABomb deletes all the data and applications from the PDA. (If the bomb is accidentally detonated, this information can be retrieved by performing a restorative HotSync operation.)

- PDADefense[18] comes in two versions: Standard and Professional. The Standard version uses 64-bit encryption to protect any designated data on the PDA, has a bomb feature that deletes all databases in the PDA's main memory and disables data transfer methods such as HotSync and beaming, stores only an encrypted form of the password on the locked device, and erases the encryption key from the device after it is locked. Inserting the correct password causes the encryption key to be regenerated. The Professional version adds extra security measures, including 128-bit encryption.
- PDASecure[19] provides a wide array of features, including a choice of six different encryption algorithms for 128-512 key bit encryption, virus protection, timed features for encryption and password protection, password protection for HotSyncing, encryption for private records or all records on built-in and third-party applications, and display of owner information on lockout screen to aid in recovery of the device.
- TealLock[20] provides 128-bit password protection and encryption; activation by power off, time of day, day of week, or elapsed time; password protection for HotSyncing; Data Self-Destruct; and it is compatible with Palm OS 5.

For those needing a more targeted approach to security than the comprehensive programs listed above, there are smaller add-on programs designed to protect only specific information. One category of these programs encrypts data such as passwords, credit-card numbers, and PINs, and includes such programs as eWallet,[21] Keyring,[22] and Strip.[23] Another category includes programs designed to replace the built-in Palm Memo Pad with a secure version that encrypts each memo; examples include Secure Memo Pad,[24] CryptoPad,[25] and ReadThis.[26]

§ 21.6 Security Considerations for Wireless PDAs

There are various security issues to consider in connection with wireless PDAs, or any nonwireless PDA to which you have attached a wireless external modem. First, if the device is used to access a network containing confidential information (such as a law firm's intranet), it is essential that the device itself be protected by a password, and ideally by user authentication as well, to minimize the risk that an unauthorized user can access the network. Second, it is obviously a good idea to encrypt sensitive transmissions. The Palm i705 boasts Palm's MultiMail Deluxe software which, along with its desktop counterpart, automatically encrypts e-mail messages when they are sent and decrypts them when they are received. With other PDAs, use an add-on program such as movianVPN[27] to ensure secure wireless transmissions. Finally, for wireless PDAs capable of accessing a law firm network, a system should be in place in which the firm's information technology department can quickly remove the device's access permissions to the network upon notification of its loss or theft.[28]

§ 21.7 The PDA as Part of a Secure Network

Finally, it is crucial to note that securing data on a PDA does *not* automatically secure the corresponding synchronized data on the desktop computer. Nor does securing data on the desktop or network automatically secure the data on the PDA. Creating a secure desktop or network environment is beyond the scope of this book, but here are some issues that a law firm's information technology specialists should consider when PDAs are added to the computer mix:

- A crucial part of protecting the security of the PDA is to protect the network and desktop. It is possible for a hacker to attack a PDA by putting a malicious program in the Palm Add-on folder of a desktop computer, which would then be installed on the PDA at the next HotSync.
- Set up systems to authenticate both the user and the device for both syncing and wireless access to the network, in order to protect against scenarios such as a malicious intruder with a stolen user name and the same model PDA as the authorized user attempting to obtain the data that is on the authorized PDA by placing an identical PDA in the user's HotSync cradle when the user is away from his or her desk, or a disgruntled employee attempting to sync confidential information onto an unauthorized device.
- Maintain organizational control over who can synchronize what data, and maintain a log of synchronization events.
- Consider creating and maintaining specific security protocols and standards for PDA use within the organization, including the effective use of password protection (including the Turn Off & Lock function), encryption software, and virus protection programs.

§ 21.8 Viruses and the Palm Operating System (Palm OS®)

As of November 2002, there have been only three known viruses[29] designed to attack the Palm operating system: the Palm.Liberty.A Trojan horse discovered in August 2000;[30] and the Palm.Phage.Dropper[31] virus and Palm.Vapor[32] Trojan horse, both discovered in September 2002. None of these produced many infections, and the containment and removal of the malicious code was rated as easy (for the Trojan horses) and moderate (for the virus).[33] However, it is important to be aware of the vulnerabilities of the Palm OS, and to put in place appropriate software for antivirus protection, such as McAfee VirusScan-PDA,[34] F-Secure Anti-Virus for Palm OS,[35] InoculateIT,[36] PC-cillin for Wireless for Palm OS,[37] and Symantec's AntiVirus for Palm OS.[38]

One of the vulnerabilities associated with PDAs is that the PDA may be the agent for introducing a virus into a network. As Palm explains, "[t]he malicious code may execute on the handheld itself or on networked computers once an infected file is transferred onto the network. Infections are generally transmitted through e-mail attachments. A messaging server that inspects attachments before sending them to the handheld can mitigate this risk."[39] However, there are other methods for transmitting viruses as well: "If a user syncs a PDA with the desktop at home and then syncs it at work, the PDA can act as a carrier for a virus and infect the network."[40] In addition, it is technologically possible that an application beamed onto a PDA could also contain viruses designed to attack the PDA or the computer with which it is HotSynced. For maximum security, therefore, it is important to screen for viruses at every step of the transmission process.

Notes

1. There is even a device, the Kensington PDA Saver (**http://www.istidata.com/Product_Kensington_pdasaver.htm**), that you can use to lock your PDA to your desk. Since one of the primary benefits of a PDA is its portability, this would be an example where the decrease in convenience would far outweigh the benefits of increased security.
2. **www.boomerangit.com**
3. **www.stuffbak.com**
4. As discussed in Section 21.7, securing items on the handheld does not automatically secure the synced version of the information on the desktop, which has both advantages and disadvantages.
5. Security Advisory: Palm OS Password Lockout Bypass (March 1, 2001), **www.atstake.com/research/advisories/2001/a030101-1.txt**
6. Ibid.
7. **http://www.freewarepalm.com/utilities/shortfix.shtml**
8. Devices running Palm OS 3.1, 3.3 or 3.5 can be upgraded to Palm OS 4.1 by purchasing and installing the upgrade available from Palm. See **www.palm.com/software/palmosupgrade_4-1**

9. "Palm OS 5 Security Features" (**www.palmsource.com/enterprise/Palm_OS5_security.pdf**); see also "Security" at **http://www.palmsource.com/enterprise/security.html**, and Randi D. Bemiss, "PalmSource Partners with RSA Security," *Law Office Computing* (June/July 2002): 24.

10. **www.dseifert.com/easylock**

11. **http://ourworld.compuserve.com/homepages/mcdan/padlockhack.html**

12. **http://www.tranzoa.com/onlyme/onlyme.htm**

13. **www.onetouchpass.com**

14. To encrypt data is to translate it "into a secret code. Encryption is the most effective way to achieve data security. To read an encrypted file, you must have access to a secret key or password that enables you to decrypt it." From Webopedia, **www.pcwebopedia.com/TERM/e/encryption.html**. "The difficulty of cracking a key goes up exponentially with the size of the key. A small network of Pentium computers that can search a billion keys a second can crack a 40-bit encryption key in 18 minutes. Double the key length to 80 bits and that network would have to gnaw away at it for quite a while longer—about 38 million years. With 128-bit encryption (technology that has been available for more than a decade), it would take a billion of these networks roughly 10 trillion years." Simson Garfinkel, "The Net Effect: The Undefended Airwaves," *Technology Review*, September 2002, **http://www.technologyreview.com/articles/garfinkel0902.asp**.

15. Mike Rohde, "Palm Security," **http://www.palmtipsheet.com/html.texts/tipsht05.html**.

16. **http://www.certicom.com/index.php?action=product,mcrypt**

17. **http://products.asynchrony.com/PDABomb**

18. **http://www.pdadefense.com**

19. **http://www.trustdigital.com**

20. **www.tealpoint.com/softlock.htm**

21. **www.iliumsoft.com/site/ew/ewallet.htm**

22. **http://gnukeyring.sourceforge.net**

23. **www.zetetic.net**

24. **www.geocities.com/freewarepalm/security.html**

25. **www.palmblvd.com/software/pc/CryptoPad-2000-10-12-palm-pc.html**

26. **www.palmblvd.com/software/pc/ReadThis-1999-05-13-palm-pc.html**

27. **http://www.certicom.com/index.php?action=product,mvpn**

28. *White Paper: Handheld Security for the Mobile Enterprise,* Palm, Inc., September 2002, **http://www.palmone.com/us/pdfs/handheld_security.pdf**

29. Technically, there are three different kinds of malicious code: viruses, worms, and Trojan horses. "Viruses are codes that attach themselves to host programs and propagate to other programs [where] they can destroy or alter data. Worms perform pre-programmed attacks on networked computers. Trojan horses are programs that masquerade as a harmless application while performing a hostile action." *White Paper: Handheld Security for the Mobile Enterprise,* Palm, Inc., September 2002, **http://www.palmone.com/us/pdfs/handheld_security.pdf**. For the sake of brevity, I will refer to all of these simply as viruses.

30. **http://securityresponse.symantec.com/avcenter/venc/data/palm.liberty.a.html**

31. **http://securityresponse.symantec.com/avcenter/venc/data/palm.phage.dropper.html**

32. **http://securityresponse.symantec.com/avcenter/venc/data/palm.vapor.html**

33. See the previous three footnotes.

34. **http://us.mcafee.com/root/Package.asp?PkgID=151**

35. **www.f-secure.com/wireless/palm/av4palm**

36. **http://cws.internet.com/virus-inoculate.html**

37. **http://www.trendmicro.com/en/products/desktop/pcc-wireless/evaluate/overview.htm**

38. **http://ses.symantec.com/products/products.cfm?productid=237**

39. *White Paper: Handheld Security for the Mobile Enterprise,* Palm, Inc., September 2002, **http://www.palmone.com/us/pdfs/handheld_security.pdf**

40. Dave Johnson, "The Real Cost of Handhelds," (quoting Doug Neal), *Handheld Computing Mobility* 1.0 (November-December 2002): 27. Available at **http://www.palmdigitalmedia.com/product/detail/7507**

Troubleshooting 22

§ 22.1 The Basics of Troubleshooting a Palm OS Device

The Palm operating system is, by design, quite simple, and there are a fairly limited number of things to do in the event that something goes wrong. Fortunately, the Palm operating system is also relatively stable, so you may find that you rarely have to invoke these solutions.

If the device does not turn on. Once the batteries have been properly charged, the device should turn on once you press the power button or any of the four main hardware buttons. If it doesn't, perform a soft reset: gently press the recessed reset button on the back of the device by inserting a reset tool into reset hole. Metal styli frequently include a reset tool; to access it, twist off the top of the stylus. You can also use the end of an unfolded paper clip or an earring post.

If the screen freezes. First try turning the device off and then back on. If that doesn't work, try a soft reset. If a soft reset doesn't work, try a warm reset, which is just like a soft reset except that before pressing the reset button, press and hold the Scroll Up button on the front of the device. Release the Scroll Up button once the Palm logo appears on the screen. If a warm reset doesn't work, perform a hard reset, which is just like a warm reset except that you (1) press and hold the power button instead of the Scroll Up button while pressing the reset button, and (2) press the Scroll Up button in response to the warning message that you are about to erase all your data. (Pressing any other button at that point transforms the hard reset into a soft reset.) Since a hard reset indeed erases all your data, perform a "Desktop overwrites Handheld" HotSync afterwards to restore the lost data.[1]

If taps don't register properly. If you find that you have to tap anywhere other than directly on an on-screen button in order to activate it, tap Home → "Preferences" → "Digitizer" to recalibrate the screen. This consists of tapping in the center of a series of targets, just as you did when you turned your device on for the first time.

If you can't find an application. Make sure that the upper right corner of the applications launcher screen (which you can get to by tapping the Home button) says "All." If it says anything other than "All," such as "Main," "System," or "Utilities," the screen shows only the applications in that particular category. Tap the word in the upper right corner of the screen to bring up the pop-up menu of all the categories of applications, and tap "All."

If you can't find a record within an application. Make sure that the upper right corner of the screen says "All." If it says anything other than "All," such as "Business," "Personal," or "Unfiled," the screen shows only the records in that particular category. Tap the word in the upper right corner of the screen to bring up the pop-up menu of all the categories in that application, and tap "All."

If you can't receive a beam. Tap Home → "Preferences" → "General," and make sure that the Beam Receive feature is turned on. Align the two devices so that there is a clear path between the two infrared ports, and ensure that the devices are from about four to thirty-nine inches apart.

§ 22.2 Answers to Specific Questions

How do I figure out the name of my device? Go to the HotSync application and look in the upper right corner. This question arises when you want to register or pay for an add-on program, since the developer sends you an unlock code that works only on your device. Be certain that you provide the exact name of your device, with spaces, punctuation, and upper- and lower-case letters clearly indicated.

How do I create a business card? Go to (or create) a contact record for yourself in the Address Book application. In Address View, tap Menu → "Select Business Card" and select "Yes" on the confirmation screen. Once you have created your business card, you can send it in a single step by pressing and holding the Address Book hardware button for a few seconds. You don't even have to turn on the device first, since pressing any hardware button turns the device on.

How do I add owner information? Tap Home → "Preferences" → "Owner" and insert identifying information such as your name, telephone number, and e-mail address. This information appears on the first screen that appears when the device is turned on after being locked.

How do I check the battery level? Go to the Applications Launcher screen. At the top of the screen is a battery icon illustrating how much power remains in the battery.[2]

How do I check the amount of available memory? Tap Home → Menu → "Info." If it is not already selected, tap "Records" to see the percentage of free space remaining in your handheld's memory.

How do I find out what version of the operating system or applications are on my device? Tap Home → Menu → "Info" → "Version." The version of the Palm OS running on your device is displayed at the top of the screen, along with your device's unique ID number. (This ID number should also be printed on the back of the device, but it may have worn off.) The rest of the screen displays a list of the versions of all the applications on your device.

How do I beam a record? Select the record you want to beam, and do one of the following: (a) draw the command stroke and tap the beam icon in the floating command bar, (b) draw the command stroke and write the letter "B" in Graffiti, or (c) tap the menu button, then tap the option to beam the record. (This is "Beam Event" in Date Book, "Beam Address" in Address Book, "Beam Item" in To Do List, and "Beam Memo" in Memo Pad.)

How do I beam a category of records? Select the category you want to beam, then tap Menu → "Beam Category."

How do I beam an entire application? Tap Home → Menu → "Beam" → the name of the application you want to beam → "Beam." Applications with a padlock icon cannot be beamed.

How do I delete an application? Tap Home → Menu → "Delete" → the name of the application you want to delete → "Delete." Remember that when you delete an application, you also delete all the data that you created using that application, plus any data that can be read using that application. For example, deleting a document-reader add-on program may also delete all your memos, since you can usually read memos using a document-reader program. You can reinstall the deleted information with a "Desktop overwrites Handheld" HotSync.

§ 22.3 Solutions to Specific Problems

What should I do if my device keeps turning itself off? The Palm operating system is designed to shut off the device after no more than three minutes of inactivity to prevent unnecessarily depleting the battery. To set the time period to the full three minutes, tap Home → "Prefs" → "General" and select "Auto-off after 3 minutes."

What should I do if my device doesn't show the correct date? Tap Home → "Prefs" → "Set Date" and insert the correct date.

What should I do if the HotSync doesn't work ? Ensure that the device is securely placed in its cradle, and that all plugs connecting the HotSync cradle to the desktop computer are firmly seated in their respective locations. Confirm that the HotSync Manager program is running on the desktop, and that the HotSync cradle is connected to the proper serial port as indicated in the Local tab of the Setup screen of the HotSync Manager.

What should I do if I forget my password? If your device is not locked, first HotSync to back up private entries, then tap Home → "Security," tap within the dotted lines where it says "-Assigned-" → "Lost Password." As the warning screen tells you, "deleting a lost password will remove all records marked Private. Previously synchronized private records will be restored at the next operation." Tap "yes" to proceed. Be sure to HotSync to restore any private records.

If your device is locked, a hard reset is your only option.[3]

What should I do if I have a problem not listed here? The manuals that come with each Palm OS device provide a wealth of detailed information. If you cannot locate your manual, check the manufacturer's Web site; Palm maintains on its Web site PDF versions of the handbooks for all its handhelds, including discontinued models as far back as the Palm III.

If you cannot find the answer in the handbook or on the manufacturer's Web site,[4] consult one of the Palm OS message boards[5] (where Palm users share information) to see if your problem has been discussed, and post a message yourself if it hasn't. Another on-line option is to run a search on an engine such as Google to see if the solution has already been published on the Web. Finally, call the manufacturer's technical support line; depending on the terms of your warranty, this service may be free.

Notes

1. Of course, this will not restore data you inserted on your handheld after your last HotSync.

2. The power level is shown graphically only. If you prefer to see a number indicating the remaining battery level as a percentage, you can install an add-on program such as Battery Meter Hack, **http://www.palmblvd.com/software/pc/Battery-Meter-Hack-1999-10-29-palm-pc.html**

3. However, if your device is running Palm OS 3.5.2 or below, and you have not corrected the security flaw described in Section 21.4, you could take advantage of this weakness by installing "No Security" (**http://www.geocities.com/SiliconValley/Cable/5206/nosecurity.htm**), which allows you to reset your password without performing a hard reset or losing any unsynced private records.

4. Palm's Customer Service and Support page (**http://www.palmone.com/us/support/intl**) contains a lot of information, and is available to all, not just Palm customers.

5. Two such message boards can be found at **www.palmblvd.com/boards/index.html** and **www.pdalife.com**

Appendix A

Palm Powered™ PDAs: A Comparison of Models

Factors to Consider in Choosing a PDA

The relative importance of the following factors depends upon your personal priorities.

1. **Purpose.** The first thing to consider when contemplating the purchase of a PDA is what you want to use it for. If constant wireless e-mail access is your main concern, you might want to investigate the BlackBerry by Research in Motion,[1] which produces a non-Palm PDA that focuses heavily on continuous, real-time wireless e-mail. If e-mail is a lesser concern, your next choice is between the Palm Powered™ family of PDAs, and their rivals, the Pocket PCs.
2. **Operating system.** While both Palm Powered™ PDAs and Pocket PCs have their sometimes vocal proponents, the choice is really one of personal preference; neither operating system is clearly technologically superior to the other. Some users like the Pocket PC despite its relatively higher price because they like seeing a smaller version of Windows on their PDAs. Other users swear by the simplicity and robustness of the Palm operating system. You might want to visit an electronics store, a computer store, or an office supply store, play around with working versions of both a Pocket PC and a Palm Powered™ PDA, and see which alternative feels better to you. Keep in mind that with a Palm Powered™ PDA, you

can customize your PDA to a much greater extent than is possible with a Pocket PC, since there are many more add-on programs available for Palm Powered™ PDAs. The advance of technology and the development of Palm OS add-on programs have diminished the advantages Pocket PCs used to have over Palm Powered™ PDAs. Versions of both are now available in color; versions of both are now available with Word-compatible software already installed; and, thanks to Palm OS add-on programs such as Jot and MyScript, you don't even have to use Graffiti to input data, but can use writing closer to your own natural handwriting.

3. **Internal versus external batteries.** Many PDA users feel that the higher price of a PDA with an internal lithium battery is worth the convenience of having the PDA recharging constantly while it sits in its cradle, or when it is connected to a recharging cord plugged into a standard electrical outlet. Others, however, prefer to maintain a supply of AAA batteries rather than be at the mercy of an electrical outlet. Unless you frequently travel to remote locations where you cannot plug in your HotSync cradle or travel recharging cord, it is probably more convenient to avoid the handhelds requiring AAA batteries.
4. **Expandability.** One of the more exciting developments in PDA technology in recent years in the inclusion of expansion slots, which allow you to temporarily insert more data and memory into your PDA, and add hardware devices that transform your PDA into a cell phone, camera, music player, or a global positioning system (GPS) device. The complication with expansion options is that each of the three main Palm Powered™ PDA brands—Palm, Handspring, and Sony—have different, sometimes proprietary technologies for expansion, and they are not completely interchangeable.[2] In choosing whether to use Palm's Expansion Card, Handspring's various Springboard expansion modules, or Sony's various Memory Stick expansion modules, consider the specific devices and content available for each system, as well as their compatibility with your other computer hardware. (The Web sites have up-to-date information.) Currently, Handspring's built-in Springboard expansion slot is the most versatile, allowing you to transform your Handspring Visor temporarily into a digital camera, mobile phone, MP3 player, or GPS device. However, a variety of peripherals compatible with other brands is available as well, and the number of options will increase over time.
5. **Built-in wireless.** If you plan to use your handheld for wireless connections the bulk of the time, consider a Palm i705, one of the Handspring communicators, or the Samsung Palm Powered Phone. While all of these (except the Palm i705) are also cell phones, they can be used as well to access e-mail and surf the Internet. If your wireless

use will be infrequent, a good choice may be to get a PDA without built-in wireless capacity, since you can always get a snap-on modem to use when you prefer to have wireless capability.[3]

6. **Memory.** This is much less of an issue than it was even a year ago, when PDAs with only 2 MB of memory were more readily available than they are now. (Bargain seekers take note: older, refurbished PDAs may still have only 2 MB of memory, which may seem like a lot, but fill up quickly once you start adding programs.) Most of the PDAs currently in production have 8 MB or 16 MB of internal memory, in addition to memory you can add by inserting an Expansion Card (up to 32 MB capacity) to your Palm PDA, a Springboard (up to 16 MB capacity) to your Handspring Visor, or a Memory Stick (up to 128 MB capacity) to your Sony Clié. When it comes to memory, more is always better.
7. **Color screen.** The only disadvantages to PDAs with color screens are: (1) they cost a bit more, and (2) they are occasionally hard to read when viewed in bright sunlight. The advantages are that they are much easier to read most of the time, and they are much nicer to look at.
8. **Screen resolution.** In the Palm Powered™ family of PDAs, your basic choice is between the standard 160 x 160 pixel display of most devices produced by Palm and Handspring, and the 320 x 320 pixel display of the Sony Clié.[4] The latter costs more, but the difference in screen resolution may be worth it to you. This factor must be seen in person, so if you think screen resolution may be important to you, take the time to compare and contrast the screens of actual working models at a electronics, computer, or office supply store.
9. **Convergence.** This is the term used to describe the joining of two distinct functions in one PDA, primarily the convergence of the PDA and the cell phone. There are now a variety of such devices available, and the prices are higher than for straightforward PDAs, even before the cost of the wireless plan by a provider such as Sprint. If you normally carry a cell phone, you should consider whether you want to carry just one device, rather than both a PDA and a cell phone.[5]
10. **Appearance.** Some people love the high-tech, professional look of the sleekly designed Palm m500 series. Others prefer the slightly more utilitarian look of the Handspring organizers. The amazing new Handspring communicators will surely develop their own devotees as well.
11. **Compatibility with colleagues.** This is a factor to consider if you want to have the option of beaming documents or software from PDA to PDA. While colleagues with both Palm Powered™ PDAs and Pocket PCs should be able to synchronize with a firm's computer system, choosing one operating system for the entire firm reduces the risk of incompatibility problems, as well as simplifying matters for the information technology department.

12. **Price.** As you will note in the charts below, there is a wide range of prices of Palm Powered™ PDAs, with the more desirable features (a higher definition or color screen, 16 MB of memory, an integrated cell phone) commanding the expected premiums. Nonetheless, you can sometimes find good deals on a company's next-to-most-recent model, or on models that are about to go out of production. The past few years have shown that even after a particular model is discontinued, you can still obtain hardware accessories to fit that model, often at greatly reduced prices. Compatibility of add-on software is not really an issue unless you get a very old model, such as one of the original PalmPilots, which cannot easily be upgraded to the latest version of the Palm operating system. Check around for falling prices and special deals. Especially if you are uncertain whether a PDA is for you, consider starting with a used or refurbished PDA,[6] available on many Web sites including the online outlet stores at Palm[7] and Handspring,[8] **www.used-palms.com**, and **www.ebay.com**. You can always trade up to a better model, so save all packaging, inserts, CDs, and accessories so you can get a good price when you trade it in.

Palm™ Brand PDAs

The following chart compares the main characteristics of Palm brand PDAs produced by and available from Palm at the time this Appendix was written.

	Palm m105	Palm m125	Palm m130	Palm m500	Palm m515	Palm i705
Size	4.66" × 3.12" × .72"	4.82" × 3.1" × .87"	4.8" × 3.1" × 0.9"	4.5" × 3.1" × 0.4"	4.5" × 3.1" × 0.5"	4.7" × 3.1" × 0.6"
Weight	4.4 oz.	5.3 oz.	5.4 oz.	4.0 oz.	4.9 oz.	5.9 oz.
Memory	8 MB	8 MB	8 MB	8 MB	16 MB	8 MB
Battery	AAA batteries	AAA batteries	internal rechargeable lithium battery	internal rechargeable lithium battery	internal rechargeable lithium battery	internal rechargeable lithium battery
Color screen	no	no	yes	no	yes	no
Built-in wireless Internet access	no	no	no	no	no	yes
Expansion slot	no	Yes: MultiMediaCards[10] (MMC) or Secure Digital (SD) cards[11]				
Price	$99	$169	$249	$199	$399	$399

As always, be sure to check the manufacturer's Web site for information about more recent models.[9]

Handspring™ Brand PDAs

Handspring produces two distinct categories of Palm Powered™ PDAs: straightforward PDAs (which Handspring calls organizers), and PDAs bundled with a cell phone (which Handspring calls communicators). Oddly, the organizers consist of three versions of the Visor and one version of the Treo, while all the rest of the communicators are Treos.

There are several key distinctions between the Handspring family of PDAs and their Palm-brand cousins:

1. All Handspring organizers (but not the communicators) have some form of an expansion slot, primarily for Handspring's proprietary Springboard expansion module. A list following the charts below illustrates the variety of Springboard modules currently available.
2. Handspring PDAs tend to have 16 MB of memory rather than 8 MB; the reverse is true for Palm brand PDAs.
3. Half of the Handspring PDAs (the Treo 90, the Treo 180, the Treo 270 and the Treo 300) come with a built-in QWERTY thumb-keyboard instead of an on-screen Graffiti area.[12]
4. An extremely anecdotal, subjective distinction is that Handspring organizers tend to look just slightly less "professional" and more "techie" than some of the Palm brand PDAs, especially the sleekly designed Palm m500 and Palm m515.

The following charts compares the main characteristics of the Palm Powered™ PDAs (both organizers and communicators) produced by and avail-

Handspring Organizers

	Visor Neo	Visor Platinum	Visor Pro	Treo 90
Size	4.8" × 3.0" × 0.7"	4.8" × 3.0" × 0.7"	4.8" × 3.0" × 0.7"	4.2" × 2.8" × 0.65"
Weight	5.4 oz.	5.4 oz.	5.7 oz.	4.0 oz.
Memory	8 MB	16 MB	16 MB	16 MB
Battery	AAA batteries	AAA batteries	internal rechargeable lithium battery	internal rechargeable lithium battery
Color screen	no	no	no	yes

	Visor Neo	Visor Platinum	Visor Pro	Treo 90
Built-in wireless Internet access	no	no	no	no
Expansion slot	Springboard	Springboard	Springboard	MultiMediaCards (MMC) or Secure Digital (SD) cards
Data input	Graffiti	Graffiti	Graffiti	built-in QWERTY thumb-keyboard
Price	$149	$149	$199	$299

Handspring Communicators

	Treo 180	Treo 180g	Treo 270	Treo 300
Size	4.2" × 2.8" × .82"		4.2" × 2.8" × .82"	4.4" × 2.8" × .82"
Weight	5.2 oz.		5.4	5.7
Memory	16 MB		16 MB	16 MB
Battery	internal rechargeable lithium battery		internal rechargeable lithium battery	internal rechargeable lithium battery
Color screen	no		yes	yes
Built-in wireless Internet access	yes		yes	yes
Expansion slot	no		no	no
Data input	built-in QWERTY thumb-keyboard	Graffiti	built-in QWERTY thumb-keyboard	built-in QWERTY thumb-keyboard
Service providers	Cingular Wireless, VoiceStream Wireless, and other providers using the Global System for Mobile Communications (GSM) system			Sprint
Coverage	worldwide		worldwide	United States
Price	$399 with service activation $599 without service		$499 with service activation $699 without service	$499

able from Handspring; as always, check the Web site for the most up-to-date information.[13]

Examples of Springboard Modules available for the Handspring Visor[14]

- Magellan's GPS Companion turns a Visor into a global positioning system device, allowing you to determine your exact location and access detailed street-level maps nationwide, with directions to any specific destination. It also includes a speedometer and compass.
- An electronic version of the New Merriam-Webster Dictionary allows a Visor to access over 100,000 words, and 300,000 definitions, synonyms, antonyms, and other related words.
- PowerOne Finance Calculator turns a Visor into a multifunctional financial calculator with capabilities such as those available on traditional business calculators made by Texas Instruments and Hewlett Packard. You can export the results of financial calculations to your Visor's Memo Pad, then HotSync, and transfer the data to any of your primary computer's other programs.
- Presenter-to-Go allows you to connect your Visor to a digital projector, so you can give (although not create) PowerPoint presentations using your Visor instead of a laptop. An IR remote control is also included, so you can direct the presentation from anywhere in the room.
- ProRecord Digital Voice Recorder allows you to record audio files directly into your Visor, so you can link voice messages to items in your Date Book, To-Do List, and Memo Pad. After HotSyncing, you can even send the voice files as attachments to e-mail. This module provides 8.5 hours of recording time, which can be spread among up to 1,024 individual messages. Note that this module does not convert voice messages to text.

Sony Clié®

At the top of the line is the Sony Clié, which has the highest resolution display of all the Palm Powered™ PDAs. The 320 x 320 pixel displays are significantly clearer than the standard 160 x 160 pixel display on Palms and Handsprings. Like Handsprings, Cliés come with an expansion slot (for Sony's Memory Stick accessories) and some models have a built-in QWERTY thumb-keyboard. The higher-end Cliés are particularly fancy, with a swivel screen, built-in camera (in the PEG-NR70V), and MP3 player.

The following chart compares the main characteristics of the Palm Powered™ PDAs produced by and available from Sony; check the Web site for up-to-date information.[15]

	Sony Clié PEG-NR70V	Sony Clié PEG-NR70	Sony Clié PEG-T665C
Size	5.5" × 2.9" × 0.7"	5.5" × 2.9" × 0.7"	4.75" × 2.9" × 0.5"
Weight	7.0 oz.	7.0 oz.	4.9 oz.
Memory	16 MB	16 MB	16 MB
Battery	internal rechargeable lithium battery	internal rechargeable lithium battery	internal rechargeable lithium battery
Color screen	no	no	yes
Built-in wireless Internet access	no	no	no
Expansion slot	memory stick	memory stick	memory stick
Data input	Graffiti or keyboard[16]	Graffiti or keyboard	Graffiti
Built-in camera	yes	no	no
Built-in MP3 player	yes	yes	yes
Built-in QWERTY thumb-keyboard	yes	yes	no
Price	$599.99	$499.99	$399.99

	Sony Clié PEG-T615C	Sony Clié PEG-SJ20	Sony Clié PEG-SL10
Size	4.8" × 2.9" × 0.5"	4.1" × 2.9" × 0.7"	4.1" × 2.8" × 0.7"
Weight	4.9 oz.	4.9 oz.	3.6 oz. (w/o batteries)
Memory	16 MB	16 MB	8 MB
Battery	internal rechargeable lithium battery	internal rechargeable lithium battery	AAA batteries
Color screen	yes	no	no
Built-in wireless Internet access	no	no	no
Expansion slot	memory stick	memory stick	memory stick
Data input	Graffiti	Graffiti	Graffiti
Built-in camera	no	no	no
Built-in MP3 player	no	no	no
Built-in QWERTY thumb-keyboard	no	no	no
Price	$299.99	$199.99	$149.99

Samsung

The following chart describes the main characteristics of the only PDA produced by and available from Samsung Electronics Co., Ltd; check the Web site for current information.[17]

	Samsung SPH-I300 Palm Powered Phone
Size	4.9" × 2.28" × 0.82"
Weight	6 oz.
Memory	8 MB
Battery	internal rechargeable lithium battery

Notes

1. **www.blackberry.net**

2. A recent set of additions to the Handspring Springboard modules are a series of Springboards called MemPlugs, which are adaptors allowing you to use other kinds of expansion cards on your Handspring Visor. These include the MemPlug SD/MMC adaptor for MultiMediaCards and Secure Digital cards, the MemPlug Memory Stick adaptor, and the MemPlug SmartMedia Memory Card adaptor.

3. These modems, as well as certain other add-on hardware such as portable keyboards, fit onto the serial connector found at the bottom of every PDA. This is the connector used to fit the PDA on its HotSync cradle, and is distinct from the various other expansion slots found on particular PDA models.

4. Pixel is derived from the phrase "picture element," and is the term for a single point in a graphic image. The more pixels in a given display area, the sharper and clearer the image tends to be.

5. If you get a combination PDA and cell phone, you will also want to get a small headset so you can speak on the phone and write in the PDA simultaneously.

6. Many popular Palm Powered™ PDAs are no longer in production. These include all four versions of the original PalmPilot (the PalmPilot 1000, the PalmPilot 5000, the PalmPilot Personal, and the PalmPilot Professional), all five versions of the Palm III (the Palm III, IIIe, IIIx, IIIxe, and IIIc), both versions of the Palm V (the Palm V and the Palm Vx), both versions of the Palm VII (the Palm VII and the Palm VIIx), the Palm m100, and the Palm m505. Full descriptions of these models are still available at Palm's Handheld Hall of Fame at **http://www.palmone.com/us/products/handhelds/other/**. Also no longer in production are the Handspring Visor Prism and the Handspring Visor Edge, although they are still described in full on Handspring's Web site at **http://www.handspring.com/products/outlet/index.jhtml**. IBM no longer makes its Workpads c500 and c505, which were clones of the Palm m500 and m505, respectively. The Kyocera QCP 6035 SmartPhone is also no longer being made.

7. **http://store.palm.com/outlet/main.asp**

8. **http://www.handspring.com/products/outlet/index.jhtml**

9. **http://www.palmone.com/us/products/handhelds**

10. A MultiMediaCard (MMC) is about the size of a postage stamp, around 2 millimeters thick, weighs about 2 grams, and can hold up to 64 MB of information or memory capacity.

11. A Secure Digital (DC) memory card is approximately the same size, thickness, and weight as a MultiMediaCard, but uses more recent technology that incorporates a higher level of security for the data on the card.

12. You can still use Graffiti with these models, if you install the add-on program Jot, which allows you to write Graffiti directly on the display screen.

13. **www.handspring.com/products**

14. A complete list of all Springboard modules available is at **http://www.handspring.com/products/sbmodules/index.jhtml?_requestid=260208**

15. **www.sonystyle.com**

16. These models have both a built-in QWERTY thumb-keyboard and a dedicated, on-screen Graffiti area, in contrast to the Handspring Treos, in which no portion of the screen is specifically designed for Graffiti input. As noted, you can still use Graffiti with Treos if you install an add-on program such as Jot. With these Cliés, however, you can use either the keyboard or Graffiti right out of the box.

17. **www.samsungusa.com**

Appendix

B

How to Find Add-On Software for Palm Powered™ Handhelds

There are many thousands of add-on programs available for download onto Palm Powered™ PDAs. Many of these programs are law-related, and many, many more could be of great use to lawyers in their professional and personal lives. Rather than undertake the Sisyphean task of listing all of these programs and the Web sites on which they are available, this appendix describes various ways to locate Palm OS add-on software on the Internet for yourself.

The easiest way to locate the many add-on software programs mentioned in this book is to go to the specific Web site cited in the text as part of the discussion of the program. While all of these URLs were correct when this book was written, the Internet is constantly changing, so a particular Web site may no longer exist, or may no longer include a particular software program, or the program itself may no longer be available from any source.

If you cannot locate the program you want at the cited Web site, and if the program is still available elsewhere, you can usually locate it fairly quickly by using an Internet search engine (such as Google) and conducting a search using the exact name of the program (in quotation marks) and the word "Palm." (In fact, searching on the Internet was precisely how I located almost all of the programs I discuss in this book.) The same program is often available from multiple Web sites.

If the program is no longer available, or if you'd like to research alternatives to that particular program, an Internet search for "Palm" and a descriptive term or two usually yields fruitful results. For example, a Google search for "timekeeping" and "Palm" just turned up 4,890 entries, of which the first twenty included twelve different add-on timekeeping programs for Palm Powered™ PDAs.

Another way to search for add-on software is to see what's available on the many Web sites that contain a wide variety of Palm OS add-on software. Foremost is the Web site of palmOne (the new company formed by the merger of Palm and Handspring in late October 2003), **www.palmOne.com**, which at the time of writing had over 3,088 add-on programs in its Business and Professional category, including 163 programs in its Law subcategory.

Another excellent set of resources is the information, add-on software, and downloadable documents available on the Web sites listed in "Bob Ambrogi's Top Ten Law-Related Web Sites" in Part 3 of this book, "Other Voices," which covers the handful of lawyer-specific Web sites currently in existence.

Finally, each of the following Web sites contain a huge variety of add-on programs. All of these sites are searchable, so searches for such terms as "law," "legal," "business," "professional," and "timekeeping" should lead you to appropriate kinds of programs. In addition, programs are categorized within each site, so check out programs in categories such as law, business, professional, and personal productivity.

- **http://mobile.yahoo.com** (click on "PDA Downloads," then on "Palm OS")
- **www.Download.com** (click on "Palm OS" under the Mobile heading)
- **www.EuroCool.com**
- **www.FreewarePalm.com**
- **www.Handango.com**
- **www.PalmGear.com**
- **www.PalmOpenSource.com**
- **www.PalmPilotArchives.com**
- **www.the-Gadgeteer.com**
- **www.Tucows.com (click on "Palm OS")**

Appendix

C

Alternative Graffiti® Characters

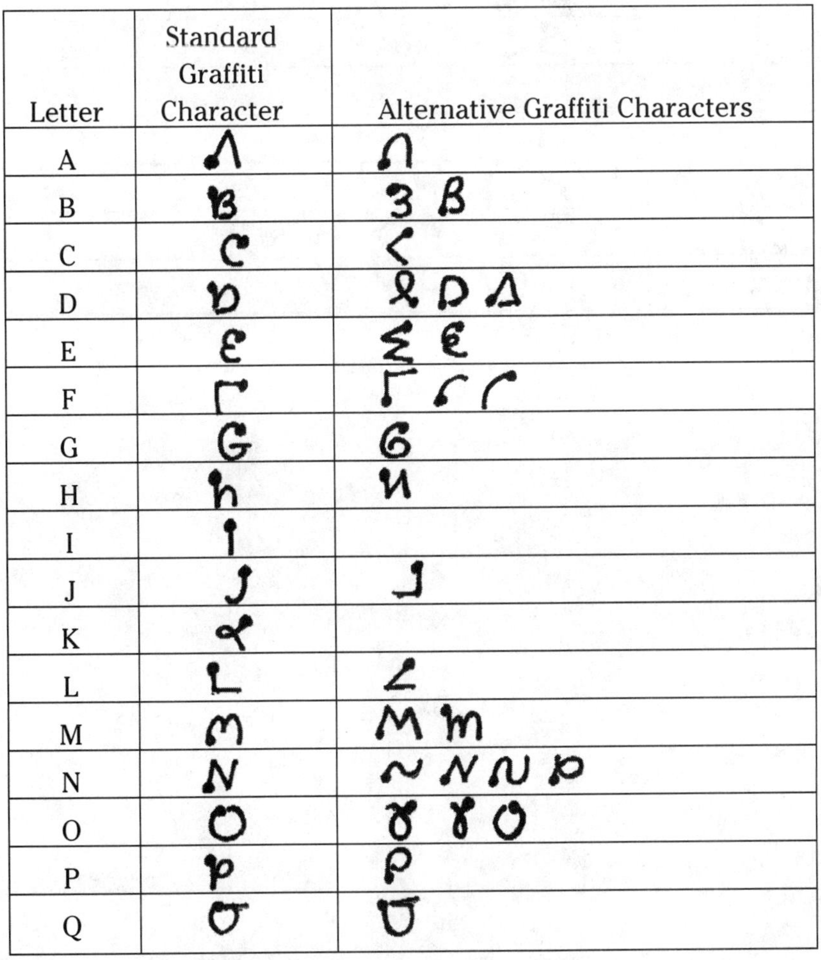

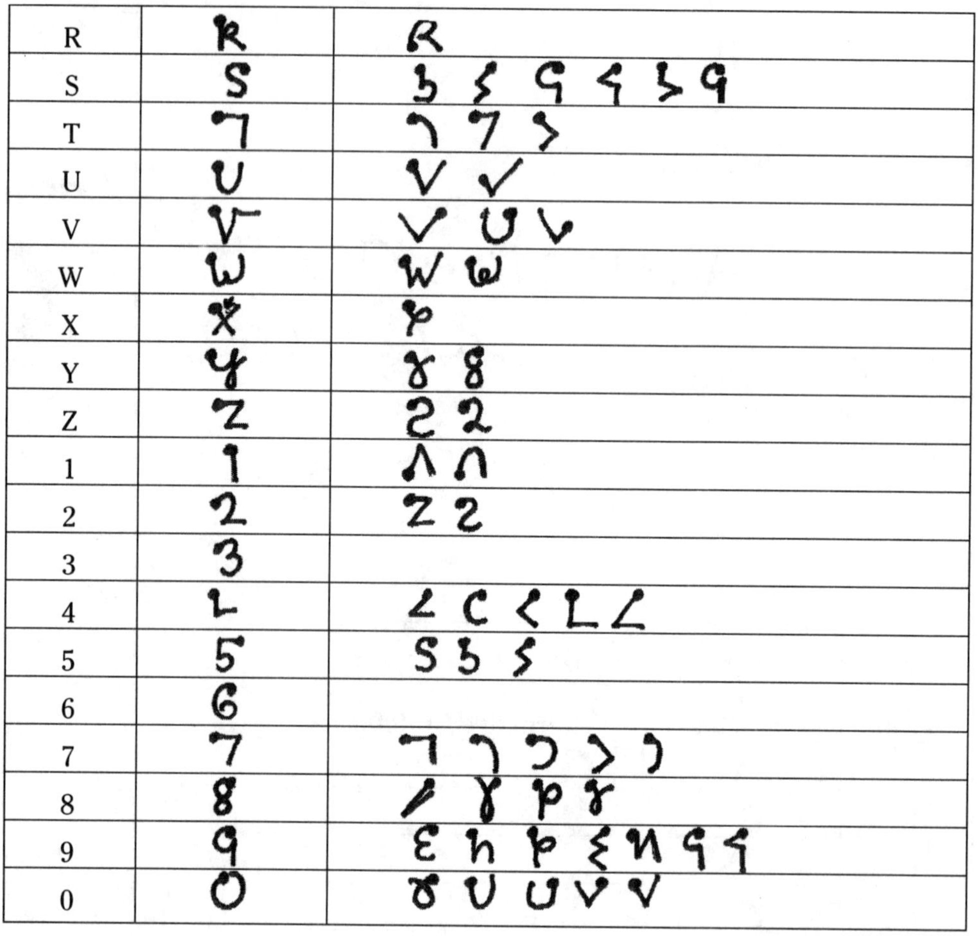
R
S
T
U
V
W
X
Y
Z
1
2
3
4
5
6
7
8
9
0

Bibliography

Barich, Tom with Mariva H. Aviram. *Palm Computing for Dummies: Quick Reference.* Foster City, CA: IDG Books Worldwide, 2000.

Butter, Andrea and David Pogue. *Piloting Palm: The Inside Story of Palm, Handspring, and the Birth of the Billion-Dollar Handheld Industry*. New York: John Wiley & Sons, 2002.

Carlson, Jeff. *Palm Organizers*. Berkeley, CA: Peachpit Press, 2000.

Collins, Corbin. *The Little Palm Book*. Berkeley, CA: Peachpit Press, 1999.

Dyzsel, Bill. *Palm for Dummies*. Foster City, CA: IDG Books Worldwide, 2001.

Ehrenman, Gayle and Michael Zulich. *Mastering Palm Organizers*. San Francisco: Sybex, 2000.

Johnson, Dave and Rick Broida. *How to Do Everything with Your Palm Handheld.* Berkeley, CA: Osborne/McGraw-Hill, 2000.

Pogue, David. *PalmPilot: The Ultimate Guide,* 2d ed. Sebastopol, CA: O'Reilly & Associates, Inc., 1999.

Salkind, Neil J. *PalmPilot and Palm Organizers!: I Didn't Know You Could Do That. . . .* San Francisco: Sybex, 2000.

Index

How to Start and Build a Law Practice, Fourth Edition. Jay Foonberg's classic guide has been completely updated and expanded! Features 128 chapters, including 30 new ones, that reveal secrets to successful planning, marketing, billing, client relations, and much more. Chock-full of forms, sample letters, and checklists, including a sample business plan, "The Foonberg Law Office Management Checklist," and more.

Law Office Policy and Procedures Manual, 4th Ed. A model for law office policies and procedures (includes diskette). Covers law office organization, management, personnel policies, financial management, technology, and communications systems.

Law Office Procedures Manual for Solos and Small Firms, Second Edition. Use this manual as is or customize it using the book's diskette. Includes general office policies on confidentiality, employee compensation, sick leave, sexual harassment, billing, and more.

The Lawyer's Guide to Extranets: Breaking Down Walls, Building Client Connections. Well-run extranets can result in significant expansion in clientele and profitability for a law firm. This book takes you step-by-step through the issues of implementing an extranet.

The Lawyer's Guide to Marketing on the Internet, Second Edition. This book provides you with countless Internet marketing possibilities and shows you how to effectively and efficiently market your law practice on the Internet.

Legal Career Guide: From Law Student to Lawyer, Fourth Edition is a step-by-step guide for planning a law career, preparing and executing a job search, and moving into the market. This book is perfect for students currently choosing a career path, or simply deciding if law school is right for them.

Making Partner: A Guide for Law Firm Associates, Second Edition. If you are serious about making partner, this book will help you formulate your step-by-step plan and be your guide for years to come for your decisions and actions within your firm.

Managing Partner 101: A Guide to Successful Law Firm Leadership, Second Edition is designed to help managing partners, lawyers, and other legal professionals understand the role and responsibilities of a law firm's managing partner.

Persuasive Computer Presentations: The Essential Guide for Lawyers explains the advantages of computer presentation resources, how to use them, what they can do, and the legal issues involved in their use. It covers how to use computer presentations in the courtroom and during meetings, pretrial, and seminars.

Running a Law Practice on a Shoestring. Offers a crash course in successful entrepreneurship. Features money-saving tips on office space, computer equipment, travel, furniture, staffing, and more.

Successful Client Newsletters. Written for lawyers, editors, writers, and marketers, this book can help you to start a newsletter from scratch, redesign an existing one, or improve your current practices in design, production, and marketing.

Telecommuting for Lawyers. Discover methods for implementing a successful telecommuting program that can lead to increased productivity, improved work product, higher revenues, lower overhead costs, and better communications. Addressing both law firms and telecommuters, this guide covers start-up, budgeting, setting policies, selecting participants, training, and technology.

Through the Client's Eyes, Second Edition. Includes an overview of client relations and sample letters, surveys, and self-assessment questions to gauge your client relations acumen.

Wills, Trusts, and Technology. Reveals why you should automate your estates practice; identifies what should be automated; explains how to select the right software; and helps you get up and running with the software you select.

Winning Alternatives to the Billable Hour: Strategies that Work, Second Edition. This book explains how it is possible to change from hourly based billing to a system that recognizes your legal expertise, as well as your efficiency, and delivery winning billing solutions—for you and your client.

Women Rainmakers' Best Marketing Tips, Second Edition. This book contains well over a hundred tips you can put to use right away that will have a positive effect on your marketing strategy. Anyone involved in marketing a firm can benefit from the down-to-earth advice in this book.

Order Form

Qty	Title	LPM Price	Reg Price	Total
______	ABA Guide to Lawyer Trust Accounts (5110374)	69.95	79.95	$________
______	ABA Guide to Prof. Managers in the Law Office (5110373)	69.95	79.95	$________
______	Anatomy of a Law Firm Merger, Second Edition (5110434)	74.95	89.95	$________
______	Changing Jobs, 3rd Ed.(511-0425)	39.95	49.95	________
______	Compensation Plans for Lawyers, 3rd Ed. (5110452)	84.95	99.95	$________
______	Complete Guide to Marketing Your Law Practice (5110428)	74.95	89.95	$________
______	Complete Internet Handbook for Lawyers (5110413)	39.95	49.95	$________
______	Computerized Case Management Systems (5110409)	39.95	49.95	$________
______	Connecting with Your Client (5110378)	54.95	64.95	$________
______	Do-It-Yourself Public Relations (5110352)	69.95	79.95	$________
______	Easy Self Audits for the Busy Law Firm (511-0420P)	99.95	84.95	$________
______	Essential Formbook, Vols. I and II	*Please call for information*		
______	Flying Solo, Third Edition (511-0463)	79.95	89.95	$________
______	Handling Personnel Issues in the Law Office (5110381)	59.95	69.95	$________
______	HotDocs in One Hour for Lawyers, Second Edition (5110464)	29.95	34.95	$________
______	How to Build & Manage an Employment Law Practice (5110389)	44.95	54.95	$________
______	How to Build & Manage a Personal Injury Practice (5110386)	44.95	54.95	$________
______	How to Start & Build a Law Practice, Fourth Edition (5110415)	57.95	69.95	$________
______	Law Firm Partnership Guide: Getting Started (5110363)	64.95	74.95	$________
______	Law Firm Partnership Guide: Strengthening Your Firm (5110391)	64.95	74.95	$________
______	Law Office Policy & Procedures Manual, 4th Ed. (5110441)	109.95	129.95	$________
______	Law Office Staff Manual for Solos & Small Firms (5110445)	59.95	69.95	$________
______	Lawyer's Guide to Marketing on the Internet, 2nd Ed. (5110484)	69.95	79.95	$________
______	Living with the Law (5110379)	59.95	69.95	$________
______	Making Partner, Second Edition (511-0482)	39.95	49.95	$________
______	Managing Partner 101, Second Edition (5110451)	44.95	49.95	$________
______	Persuasive Computer Presentations (511-0462)	69.95	79.95	$________
______	Practicing Law Without Clients (5110376)	49.95	59.95	$________
______	Running a Law Practice on a Shoestring (5110387)	39.95	49.95	$________
______	Successful Client Newsletters (5110396)	39.95	44.95	$________
______	Telecommuting for Lawyers (5110401)	39.95	49.95	$________
______	Through the Client's Eyes, Second Ed. (5110480)	69.95	79.95	$________
______	Wills, Trusts, and Technology (5430377)	74.95	84.95	$________
______	Winning Alternatives to the Billable Hour, Second Ed (5110483)	129.95	149.95	$________

***Handling**
$10.00-$24.99 .... $3.95
$25.00-$49.99 .... $4.95
$50.00+ $5.95

****Tax**
DC residents add 5.75%
IL residents add 8.75%
MD residents add 5%

Subtotal
***Handling $________**
****Tax $________**
TOTAL $________

PAYMENT

☐**Check enclosed (to the ABA)** ~☐**Bill Me**
☐Visa ☐MasterCard ☐American Express

____

Account Number Exp. Date Signature

Name Firm
Address
City State Zip
Phone Number E-mail address

Mail: ABA Publication Orders, P.O. Box 10892, Chicago, Illinois 60610-0892
♦ Phone: (800) 285-2221 ♦ FAX: (312) 988-5568
E-Mail: service@abanet.org ♦ Internet: http://www.abanet.org/lpm/catalog

Source Code: 22AEND499

CUSTOMER COMMENT FORM

Title of Book: ______________________________

We've tried to make this publication as useful, accurate, and readable as possible. Please take 5 minutes to tell us if we succeeded. Your comments and suggestions will help us improve our publications. Thank you!

1. How did you acquire this publication:

- ☐ by mail order
- ☐ by phone order
- ☐ at a meeting/convention
- ☐ at a bookstore
- ☐ as a gift
- ☐ don't know
- ☐ other: (describe) ______________________________

Please rate this publication as follows:

	Excellent	Good	Fair	Poor	Not Applicable
Readability: Was the book easy to read and understand?	☐	☐	☐	☐	☐
Examples/Cases: Were they helpful, practical? Were there enough?	☐	☐	☐	☐	☐
Content: Did the book meet your expectations? Did it cover the subject adequately?	☐	☐	☐	☐	☐
Organization and clarity: Was the sequence of text logical? Was it easy to find what you wanted to know?	☐	☐	☐	☐	☐
Illustrations/forms/checklists: Were they clear and useful? Were there enough?	☐	☐	☐	☐	☐
Physical attractiveness: What did you think of the appearance of the publication (typesetting, printing, etc.)?	☐	☐	☐	☐	☐

Would you recommend this book to another attorney/administrator? ☐ Yes ☐ No

How could this publication be improved? What else would you like to see in it?

____

____

____

Do you have other comments or suggestions? ______________________________

____

____

Name ______________________________

Firm/Company ______________________________

Address ______________________________

City/State/Zip ______________________________

Phone ______________________________

Firm Size: ______________ Area of specialization: ______________

We appreciate your time and help.

Fold

NO POSTAGE
NECESSARY
IF MAILED
IN THE
UNITED STATES

BUSINESS REPLY MAIL

FIRST CLASS PERMIT NO. 16471 CHICAGO, ILLINOIS

POSTAGE WILL BE PAID BY ADDRESSEE

AMERICAN BAR ASSOCIATION
PPM, 8th FLOOR
750 N. LAKE SHORE DRIVE
CHICAGO, ILLINOIS 60611-9851

Fold